ANGLO PORTUGUESE NEGOTIATIONS

ANGLO PORTUGUESE NEGOTIATIONS RELATING TO BOMBAY 1660-1677.

SHAFAAT AHMAD KHAN, LITT. D., F. R. HIST. S.

GYAN

Published by

Gyan Publishing House
5, Ansari Road
Daryaganj, New Delhi-110002
Phone: 011-47034999, 9811692060
E-mail: books@gyanbooks.com

Distribution Network
gyanbooks.com
India, USA, Canada, UK, Australia, France

ISBN : 978-81-212-9570-3 (PB)
First Published, 1922

2nd Impression 2023

Printed at: Gyan Press, Delhi.

ANGLO PORTUGUESE NEGOTIATIONS
Author: SHAFAAT AHMAD KHAN

ALLAHABAD UNIVERSITY STUDIES IN HISTORY.

PUBLISHED UNDER THE SUPERVISION OF

SHAFAAT AHMAD KHAN, LITT. D.
University Professor of History, Allahabad.

ANGLO PORTUGUESE NEGOTIATIONS RELATING TO BOMBAY 1660-1677.

BY

SHAFAAT AHMAD KHAN, LITT. D., F. R. HIST. S.

University Professor of History

Allahabad

PREFACE

" This is reprinted from an article in the Journal of Indian History, Series No. 3, September, 1922. I hope the second edition will enable me to incorporate further researches into the subject, and to remove a few typographical mistakes."

SHAFAAT AHMAD KHAN.

The University,
Allahabad, India.
27th November, 1922.

CONTENTS.

The Anglo-Portuguese Negotiations Relating to Bombay, 1660—1677.

By

DR. SHAFAAT AHMAD KHAN.

BOMBAY possesses a singular power of arousing the interests of its citizens in its chequered annals, and a band of distinguished historians has carried on the pious task of recording its phenomenal growth in a series of luminous monographs and comprehensive gazetteers. Campbell has compiled an admirable collection of representative data in the *Bombay Gazetteer Materials*, Vol. XXVI ; Edwardes has given a masterly sketch of the rise of Bombay ; Douglas has traced its history in his *Bombay and Western India*; Dr. Da Cunha has written a brilliant sketch, supplying a rare collection of tränscripts from the Portuguese records; Mainwaring's *Crown and Company*, and Malabari's *Bombay in the Making*, throw further light on some of the most important aspects of the history of Bombay. Cobbe's *Bombay Church*, 1766; Bruce's *Annals*, 1810 ; Danvers' *Portugese in India*, 1894 ; Forrest's *Selections from the State Papers, Home Series*, 1887 ; Birdwood's *Report on the Old Records of the India Office*, 1890 ; W. Foster's *English Factories in India* and *Court Minutes of the East India Company*; Hedge's *Diary* and Kaye's *Administration of the East India Company* contain very useful information on the early settlers. The list of travellers who visited Bombay is by no means small. Mannuci, Fryer, Ovington, and a host of others, whose accounts are preserved in the British Museum, furnish many a picturesque detail, and we still derive invaluable information on some obscure points of its history from the accounts of these pioneers.

These are our principal authorities for the study of the history of Bombay; and it would be difficult to find a better collection of essential data. There is, however, one aspect of the history of Bombay which seems to me to have been ignored by its historians. They have neglected to emphasize the importance of the Anglo-Portuguese negotiations, and have contented themselves hitherto with a brief account of the unfortunate squabbles between the Portuguese Viceroy and the English Commanders. A deeper study of the data reveals the existence of a continuous chain of negotiations exhibiting constant action and reaction, and mirroring the leading stages in the intercourse of England with Portugal, during the years 1660–77. For Portugal, it will be remembered, ceded Bombay at a time when her political existence was at stake, and when the Peace of Pyrenees had revived the danger of Spanish invasion. She was, moreover, at war with the Dutch, and her devastating wars with Spain and the United Netherlands had brought her to the verge of bankruptcy. It was at this critical moment of her history that Charles came to her rescue, and supplied her with disciplined troops that ultimately won her independence. Bombay and Tangier were a totally inadequate return for these services, and the documents reproduced below show clearly that the Portuguese were not willing to part even with Bombay. For only three years after the signing of the Treaty we find the Portuguese King ordering his Viceroy at Goa to collect large sums for the purchase of Bombay from Charles. That the purchase was not effected was due solely to the inability of the latter to collect the necessary amount. Charles, at any rate, would have been only too glad to sell it, as he was in considerable financial difficulties at the time, and found it impossible to prosecute the Dutch War with vigour.

Another important feature of these negotiations is their wealth of information on the commercial usages of the period. For it was not merely a question of petty dues and vexatious tolls; it was the vital problem of the security of the Company's trade, and the safety of its subjects.

There was another important aspect of this quarrel. The elaborate reports of the Council, the active support of the King, and the numerous representations to the Portuguese Government, show the intimate connection between the foreign and the economic policy of England; while the keen and sustained interest manifested by Charles II in the varied colonial and commercial activities of the times vindicate that monarch from the reckless charges hurled by his opponents.

My attention was first directed to the importance of these negotiations in 1917, when I was engaged on researches into the history of the "*East India Trade in the XVIIth Century.*"* Further searches in the Public Record Office, the British Museum, and the India Office, revealed the existence of a large amount of data. Very few of the documents reproduced below have been printed *in extenso*; and the lack of a suitable

* The book is bring printed by the Clarendon Press, Oxford, who hope to be able to bring it out in October, this year.

monograph on this important subject has long been felt. Dr. Da Cunha and Sir George Forrest have published only a few important letters, and the large collection in the Public Record Office has not been tapped at all. I have already given extracts from the pamphlets in the British Museum on the "Company's War with Aurangzebe" in Number I, Volume I, of the *Journal of Indian History*. All of them deal directly or indirectly with Bombay. Alexander Hamilton's pamphlet has been deliberately left out, as I think we have placed too much reliance on his statements. He is obviously prejudiced, and I have found it difficult to verify his statements.

The majority of the documents reproduced below have been transcribed from the C. O. 77, in the Public Record Office, Chancery Lane, London; a few, specially the *Court Minutes*, have been copied from the magnificent collection in the India Office Record Department, while the remainder were taken from the documents in the British Museum. The Department of MSS., British Museum, contains a series of records of the highest value to the student of seventeenth century British India. A short account of these documents was published in Number I, Volume I, of the *Journal of Indian History*. It was not, however, exhaustive, and I hope to be able to give a complete bibliography of MSS. relating to seventeenth century British India in the next number of the *Journal*.

The first English visit to Bombay was paid under very unpropitious circumstances. The Anglo-Dutch fleet proposed to attack Botelho's squadron, which was supposed to have returned to Bombay, and a strong fleet, consisting of six Dutch and six English ships, sailed on October 8, 1626. The following account of the first English visit to Bombay will be found of interest.*

"1626. October 8. The Dutch and English fleets sailed from Swally." October 10. "Met two Dutch ships, the *Zierikzee* and *Wapen* [*Van Zeeland*] from Batavia." October 12. "Anckored five miles off Bumbay, we thinkinge our enimye the Portingall had bene there, but he was not there with anie shipps." October 13. "We and the whole fleet, both of English and Dutch, went into Bumbay and came to an anckor in 9 fatham; one pointe beareing WNW, per compasse, the other SSW; the one three mile off, the other 3 leagus off. This was in the entringe of the harbor." October 14. "This daie we went with the whole fleete in farther, neare a smalle towne or village, where there were Portingalls. We

* (Compare Marine Records, Volume 43; William Foster, *English Factories in India*, pp. 142-3.)

anckored, and rode a mile of in 6 faddam, one point per compasse bearinge WSW, 5 mile of, the other S and by W, some 5 leagus of. We came soe neere the towne with two of our shipps that wee drove them all awaye with our great ordnance, viz., the *Morrice* of the English, and the *Mauritius* of the Dutch. In saftie we landed our men on shore, whoe pillaadged the towne and set their houses all on fire, with their fort neer the water side. Yea, we staide there the 15th daye, doeing all the spoyle that possiblie we could; but we got nothing to speak of but vittull. Soe when wee had done all the harme we could, the 15th daye in the evening wee got our men aboord, leaveinge the towne on fire. And the 16 daye in the morneinge, when the wind cam of shore, wee wayed anckor and went off to sea againe."

The allied fleet did not apparently inflict serious damage on the Portuguese shipping, for Bombay was only a small village at that time. Mr. William Foster has published a most interesting map of Bombay by David Davis, the master's mate on board the *Discovery*, in the *English Factories in India*, while Sir Henry Morland and Sir James Campbell have written an interesting note on this sketch, in their *Bombay and Western India*, Vol. I.

David Davis supplements the above account.

"1626. October 12. We waied and sayled in neere the going into the baye, to see if the Portingalls weare ther. And the Commanders sent their shallupps to chase fisher boats that were in the offing, whereof they took two, the one loaden with salt, which came out of the baye, the other a fisher boate." October 13. "We went into the baye and roade without the stakes." October 14. "The *Moris* and two Dutch shipps went in neere the greate howse to batter agaynst it; in which batterie two of the *Moris* ordnance spilt. The same daie we landed 300 men, English and Dutch, and burnt all their kitjonns howses (houses thatched with the leaves of the coco palm) and tooke the greate howse with two basses of brass and one faker of iron." October 15. "All our men embarqued aboorde the shipps, beinge Sonday in the evening, and lefte the greate howse, which was both a warehouse, a frierry, and a forte, all afire burning with many other good howses, together with two nywe frigetts not zett frome the stockes nor fully ended; but they had carried away all their treasur and all things of any value, for all were runde away before our men landed." October 16. "In the morning we wayed and sayled out of Bumbaye."

The last account of this adventurous visit supplies further details. "October 12. Anchored four leagues from "Bumbaye"."

October 15. "In the morning strode in and ankered, and landed of the *Eingles* and the *Duche* sum 400 meane at the leaste, and took the forte and casell and the towne, and sett fire of it and all the towne and all the howses in thereaboutes, the pepell being all run away that night and ded carray away all the best cometieies [commodities] levein nothein but trashe." October 16. "In the morningen we sete sayle and came out to seae."

President Kerridge's summary of this exploit is interesting enough. The joint fleet entered "all togeather into the port of Bombaye ; where finding little or noe resistance, they landed some people and sett fire on all that could bee burned in a small fort and monastery adjoyning, where was found only two or three little peeces ordinances of meane vallewe, the inhabitants fledd with what was portable. This exploit acted, the limitted tyme expired, and noe other shipps appearing, they joynctlie returned towards Swalley." (President Kerridge and Messrs. Wylde, Burt and Page at Surat to the Company, November 29, 1626.)

The Company at this period was maturing its projects for the acquisition of a convenient harbour on the western coast of India. This was due partly to the comparative insecurity of their position at Surat, and partly to the extension of their trade in the East. As regards the first, the Moghul Emperors had guaranteed them a succession of privileges in a series of farmans, and a comparison of these privileges with the narrow "mercantilism" of Colbert and the narrower "bullionism" of the Restoration. Parliament brings out clearly enough the immense superiority of the Moghul Government, so far, of course, as freedom of commercial intercourse is concerned. The amount of customs duties levied by the Governors at Surat was ridiculously small, and European travellers were greatly struck by the active encouragement of trade, the comparatively liberal policy of the Moghuls, and the beneficent religious freedom enjoyed by their subjects. The English Company in India enjoyed commercial privileges at a time when trade monopolies, tariff wars, vexatious customs duties, and narrow bullionism throttled European commerce; and though they were sometimes subjected to fines and even imprisonment, it was due partly to the piratical tendencies and roving propensities of their own countrymen. The Governor could hardly be expected to note the innumerable shades of the European trader, for the licensed trader and the respectable interloper merged imperceptibly into the pirate.

These advantages were, however, outweighed by positive disadvantages. The Company's factors found it difficult to protect its commerce from the ravages of the pirates, the attacks of tyrannical or greedy Governors, and the undisguised hostility, first of the Portuguese, and then of the Dutch. The combination of Dutch power, prestige, and ingenuity with the absolute rule and despotical ways of the Surat Governors was fraught with serious evils; and the consummation of this alliance showed the calculating and shrewd servants of the English Company the absolute necessity of a sound, secure harbour for their growing shipping and expanding commerce. The policy of fortified towns, which Sir Josiah Child advocated, and which has been exaggerated by Sir William Hunter and a host of lesser luminaries into a policy of conquest, took its rise at this period. The English merchants had already tried it at Lagundy and Armagon; while the disturbances in the Moghul Empire, in 1626, the ceaseless attacks of the Portuguese, and the growing ill-feeling between the Dutch and the English contributed to the growth of a consistent theory, aiming at the protection of commerce by fortified towns, convenient and commodious harbours, and disciplined troops. The Dutch had carried it out with conspicuous success, and the comparative freedom of their colonies from invasion, the unusual expansion of their commerce, and the remarkable successes they had achieved in diplomacy no less than on the battlefield were due partly to their active support and employment of capable men, but mainly to their energetic pursuit of the principle of fortified towns. The Company had already embarked on this policy in two notable cases; its factors now urged it to carry it still further, and to occupy Bombay. The English Company was the first to notice the importance of that harbour, and as early as 1628 proposals were formulated for its occupation.

The following extract from a Despatch of James Slade, Master of the *Blessing*, at Swally, to the Company is interesting. (See Foster, *op. cit.*, pp. 216-7.) Slade refers to the "conferrence in consultation about a place of fortification," and adds that "as yett nothing (has been) don nor resolved on where or when it may be don." "*London's Hope*", or *Khor Jarama* had been suggested as a suitable place, but its "barrenness" deterred the Company, and Bombay seemed to have been the next best choice. Slade's account of the landing of British soldiery at Bombay is interesting. "Here, after wee had bin before it 24 howers, the Commanders being aboard of us resolved to goe with all our bardges and boats to view the place, to see if wee might land without danger. After there departure from aboard of us, it was Mr. Wills his fortune and myne to come after them our shalloop, and after our departure from our ships wee espied a boat . . . coming (near) the forte, it shott divers times at us, and som small shott plaied at us out of the corner of the wood where the boats lay. Notwithstanding, wee went aboard of her, which wee found to be one ground, and the people fledd; whereupon wee landed and, being seconded by two or three boats of men that followed us, wee martch up to the forte, which was left voyde unto us. Som of our men fired a house, by which accident the Commanders perceiving the *SUCCESSE* cam ashore unto us; where wee continued till night and till next day in the evening, at which time, the whole towne and forte being burnt to the ground by the Dutch and us, wee departed. This towne yealded noe benefitt to us nor the Dutch, there being nothing left in it that was worth carradge, except it were salt fish and rice, which was consumed with fier. The rest of there goods, in regard of our long being before wee had landed, they had conveyed away." Slade decided against the occupation of Bombay, it being "no good place to winter in, it being open to the westerly [wind?] and no sucker for them from the winter. What other place there is in this sound, which is deepe and undiscovered by any of us, to winter in, is un(known) to us then that were there present." Other places were suggested for the purpose. The Company had already advised their President at Surat to secure a suitable harbour, and Kerridge himself was in favour of Bombay. *Kerridge assured them as regards the climate of Bombay. "Bombay", he stated, "is noe ill ayre, but a pleasant, fruitfull soile and excellent harbor, as experience of our own people doth testifie." He, however, found it difficult to secure it, "as the Portingall, whose country it is, will with their uttmost force prevent its commerce and bee perpetuall disturbers of the prosecution." The Dutch, too, were suspicious of these designs and refused to co-operate with the English Company in its attack on Bombay. Kerridge's proposals to the Dutch "principalls in the behaulfe of both Companies unto a friendlie conjunction in the attempt, and equall division of the successe, whereby we intended a double fortification" were viewed with suspicion, and they rejected the project as "incommodious", and absolutely refused "conjoying".

The next Despatch of Kerridge, dealing with Bombay, is dated January 4, 1628.† The Company, it is clear, was determined upon carrying out their policy of fortified towns, and Bombay was too tempting a bait to be ignored by the Directors. The President was able to satisfy their curiosity, for "one Richard

* (Despatch to the Company, November 29, 1626.)
† (O.C. 1264; compare Public Record Office, East Indies, Vol., IV., No. 7.)

Tuck, an English sayler," who had long served the Portuguese and frequented the place, supplied him with valuable information. This is by far the earliest account of Bombay by the English, and it deserves reproduction here.

" The iland called Bumbaiee in some places thereof is within muskett shott off the maine of Decan, divided by a small creeke from another iland called Salsett; both which seeme one land and make butt two channells or entrances, one to the southwards of the sayd ilands and thother to the northwards, which last is neare unto the iland of Bassein, and from the sea twixt itt, and Bassein maketh a navigable river, called the river of Bassein, howbeitt within, near unto Salsett, the passage twixt the maine and itt is very shoale and narrow; butt the entrance to the southwards is a large channell, where shipps of greatest burthen may boldly enter laden and ride lanlockt within a bay, free from all winds and weather, being the same where your people demolished a fort or chappell of the Portugalls last year, within which some 3 leagues they have another village and small fort, to keep the Mallabar frigates from rounding the iland, where is so little water that every ebbe the people of the maine, being the subjects of Nizam Shaw, king of that part Decan, may wade over. The inhabitants both of Bumbaiee and Salsett are poore fishermen and other labourers, subject to the Portugall; whither as well the Portugalls as the Moore's cattle come from the iland of Bassein and from the maine to feed. It is in length twixt 6 and 7 leagues, lying N and S, but in breadth little more than an English mile. It is not unlikely that the Portugalls have made choice of the fittest place to fortefy, being the same already mencioned."

Kerridge concludes by pointing out the necessity of fortifications, and suggesting suitable places for that purpose.

The project, however, was laid aside, for the present, as the Company was in serious financial difficulties, and the institution of Courtens' Association, combined with the vacillating policy of Charles I, rendered it impossible for its factors to expand its commerce. The Portuguese, the Dutch, and the pirates were a source of constant anxiety, and the Directors could not attract sufficiently large funds from the public to be able to prosecute that lucrative trade with success. England enjoyed an ominous quiet of ten years, and the people saw with growing indignation the gradual disappearance of a number of is most hallowed institutions. The parliament had ceased; the city of London lay at the feet of the conqueror, and the thriving citizen was naturally shy of risking his money in a venture of whose utility he was by no means certain, and whose prospects could not be compared with those of the rival Company. The ten years of calm were succeeded by another ten years of disorder. Commerce declined; trade languished; commercial enterprise was killed, and the merchant watched and—prayed.

During the interval, the Company's servants continued to visit Bombay and to pay a fearful toll for their intemperance. President Methwold describes the results of their sojourn in Bombay during the latter part of 1635. "Wee were not present to observe our people's misdemeanours; but wee have heard enough to believe that the Portugalls' desires to gratify them with all convenient freedome, and that liberty too much abused in excessive drinking of toddy and arracke, shortened the lives of many which expired there, and so weakened the rest that wee are persuaded a more infirme company of men never (was) brought unto this port." Toddy and arrack shops in Bombay, it must be observed, exacted a monstrous due throughout the seventeenth century, and not even the stringent regulations of Aungier and Oxinden could reduce its high death-rate, or reform the morals of the motley crew who resided in Bombay.

It seems to have produced a peculiar kind of terror among the Company's servants, and there are numerous references to its unhealthy climate in the Company's early records. The Rev. Mr. Ovington (*Ovington's Voyage*) declared "Bombay was nought but a charnel-house, in which two monsoons were the age of the man"; while Dr. Fryer enumerated the diseases from which people suffered with the zeal of a physician. According to him, the chief diseases were "fluxes, dropsy, scurvy, barbiers or loss of the use of hands and feet, gout, stone, malignant and putrid fevers," and a disease named "*Mordisheen*", or "Chinese death". Between 1686 and 1696, there was, moreover, a severe outbreak of plague in Western India, which wrought havoc in Bassein, Thana, and Chaul, and nearly emptied Bombay of its inhabitants. About the end of 1691, Bombay contained only about eighty Englishmen, many of whom were ill; the five civil servants in 1691 had dwindled to three in the following year, and by October, 1696, only twenty-seven Englishmen were alive. Ten years later, we find the same tale of depopulation and disease. Poor Waite wrote mournfully in 1706: "We are only eight covenant servants, including the Council, and but two that write, besides two raw youths taken ashore out of ships, and most of us sick in this, unhealthful, depopulated and ruined island." His next letter referred again to the virulence of disease. "We are six including your Council, and some of us often sick. It is morally impossible without an overruling Providence to continue longer from going underground, if we have not a large assistance." His final appeal for help in 1707 showed the helplessness of the Company and its factors. "My continued indisposition and want of assistance in this unvery-healthful (*sic*) island has been laid before the managers and your Court. Yet I esteem myself bound in gratitude, and I will briefly inform what material occurs till I leave this place or the world." *

It was partly the unhealthy climate of Bombay that prevented the Company from occupying Bombay, but the main cause was the disturbed state of the country, and its paucity of resources. The establishment of the Protectorate, and the vigorous foreign policy of Cromwell restored confidence among the merchants, and enabled them to prosecute their trade with vigour. This revival of commercial enterprise and colonial development found a characteristic expression in the proposal of the East India Company to acquire a "safe and commodious harbour" in India. The original project was again considered, and President Blackman adduced forcible arguments in favour of that plan. "Wee were never soe sencible of the want of a port in these parts (as that wee might call our owne) as wee are at present, and are like to bee if these wars continue. Doubtless a faire opportunity may now present by a treaty with Portugall, who hath enow to spare, and wee believe willing to spare on easy terms. What the Dutch hold in Zelon (Ceylon) wee believe the Portugalls would bee willing wee should enjoy, if by our assistance they could bee driven out ; which were noe hard matter to doe, if the Parliament would please to engage therein. . . . If this could bee effected, the honour of our nation in these parts would much bee advanced, our priviledges in all places increased (which are now much impaired), your customes of Gombaroone not onely established but much augmented, and you enjoy as great a royalty of the seas in these parts as formerly the Portugalls did, and the Dutch, wee believe, will do, if not prevented."

A similar suggestion was made by John Spiller in April, 1654. He showed that the acquisition of a convenient "castle" or towne "about Suratt or on the coast of India," would be a

* Compare, *Selections from State Papers : Home Service.* Despatch to Directors, June 1, 1696 ; do., October 27, 1691 ; do. October 15, 1696.

means of increasing " their strength, force, and honour in the(se) Orientall parts."

The proposals were viewed with favour by the Company, and representations were actually made to the Protector for " the settlement of a nationall interest in India." Oliver Cromwell's attitude towards the East India Company has been strangely misrepresented by Sir William Hunter. There is no evidence to believe that he took a keen interest in the East India Company. The data are too scanty to enable us to decide on this point with certainty. He himself told the Company that he was too busy with " Publiqe affaires " to be bothered by the private bickerings of the two Companies ; and the few references to his policy in the Company's Minutes are too vague to be of any help to the student.

That he was a friend of Maurice Thomson is clear from the data at our disposal * ; that he sympathised with some princi-pals of the Thomson party is no less clear from the references to the proposals of the Assada Adventurers. The latter wanted to " procure a nationall interest in some towne in India to make the scale of trade for those parts." They aimed, moreover, at establishing settlements in Assada and Pulo Run, absorbing the Guinea trade, and securing liberty for the Assada settlers to trade freely in the East. It is possible that Cromwell did not know the real position of the Company in the East, and probable that he desired to replace the Joint-Stock system by a modified form of the Regulated system. This is borne out by an interesting letter in Thurloe's *State Papers*,† dated early in January 1655, stating that "the merchants of Amsterdam were greatly disturbed by news from London that it was Cromwell's intention to dissolve the present East India Company and declare the trade free and open."‡

Cromwell's perception of the difficulties involved in the consistent application of Thomson's theories led to a modification of his original views. He probably knew the dangers surrounding the early traders to the East; he had possibly heard of the early exploits of the Dutch and the Portuguese in the East ; he was certainly aware of the importance of security to English traders and its necessary corollary, the acquisition of a port on the western coast of India. The formulation of various proposals for the attainment of this salutary project is in itself an

* Compare, C. M. Andrews, *British Committees, etc., of Trade.*
† Volume III, page 80.
‡ Compare also, Firth, C. H. *The Last Years of the Protectorate.*

indication of the greater security and increasing confidence which the masterful rule of the Protector had conferred on the country. But their importance consists chiefly in their influence on the subsequent history of the Company's policy in the East. As pointed out above, the Company had considered favourably enough some of the suggestions of their factors as regards Bombay, but it could not carry it out, owing to the causes enumerated above.

Under Cromwell, the original plans underwent modification, and the initiative in this movement was taken by some of the most enterprising men of the period. The following petition of the East India Company brings out the effect of this policy. "Having with all respect and thankfulness considered His Highnesses' intention to endeavour the settlement of a "nationall interest in India", they propose as places most convenient, the town of Bassein, with the port "Bone Bay", thereto belonging, on the coast of India, and the town and coast of Mazambique, on the coast of Melinde, with the several fortifications, privileges, trade and other benefits belonging to them."*

Four years later the Company reiterated its desire to secure a stronghold on the western coast of India. "Wee doe hereby give you power to treate for the obteyning of the said port of Danda Rajapore, Basseene, Bombay, or Carapatam, or such other healthfull place upon the coast of Mallabar as you shall upon certaine knowledge or information know to be fitt for securing of our shipping, and that hath a good inlett into the countrie and trade, and such other conveniences and accommodations as are necessary for a settlement."† The following year the request was repeated, and a desire expressed to secure Danda Rajapore, owing to its central position. The Directors returned to the subject in 1660, and informed their President that they had "some conference with the ambassadors of Portugall for the resigning of one of their holds in India unto us, but have found them very high and exceeding unwilling to part with anythinge whilst there is the least hope or probabilitie to keep it to themselves."

The Company was, however, aware of the difficulty of fortifying Bombay, and their repeated requests may have been due partly to the influence of some of the members of the Thomson party. Their financial condition prevented them from embarking on an enterprise of whose magnitude they had been frequently

* *Petition of the East India Company to the Lord Protector*, C. O. 77, Vol. VII, No. 92, 1654.

† Dated April 9, 1658.

informed, and this hypothesis finds some support in the fact that they refused to co-operate with Charles II in the settlement of Bombay. A certain amount of help was rendered, but that was dictated solely by the fear that the intervention of a third party may ultimately lead to the abolition of their privileges, and the opening of the East India Trade to outsiders.

Of the various proposals submitted to the Protector, the most original is that of Richard Wylde. His *Remonstrance to Cromwell* contains many striking suggestions; and his practical experience, thorough knowledge of India, and wide outlook, render the pamphlet exceedingly useful. The *Remonstrance* is exceedingly rare, and I have discovered only one copy in the British Museum. Wylde's is the boldest of all the proposals relating to the East India Trade, and his conception of that trade as a " national trade ", no less than his enunciation of a vigorous commercial policy, are marked by originality and insight. Numerous references to Wyld will be found in Foster's *Court Minutes* and *English Factories in India.*

WYLDE, OF THE EAST INDIA TRADE (BRITISH MUSEUM, *SLOANE MSS.*, 3271).

To his Highnes the Lord Protector of this Commonwealth of England, Scottland and Irelande, etc.

The humble remonstrance of
Richard Wylde Marchant.

Representing the true, and reall state, as to trade into the East Indies, And Meanes for setling the same in its right Course; And regaining the lost honour, and repute of the Nation, in those remote parts of the worlde etts.

HUMBLY SHEYING

That, notwithstanding those most rich trades of India, Persia, etts have had the unhapines, to fall into the hands of an evill affected people, that have manadged the same to this day; slighted and neglected, in a time, when we had both meanes of stocke, and shiping suffitient to have obteined the Soveraigntie of those seas; As had the Portingall for above 200 years; to whom they apeared in their true worth, and vallue; bringing hoame every yeare (no ship Miscarying) Rich goods, to the vallue of two Millions, and a halfe upon Register, besides Pearles, Diamonds, Rubies, etts: Preatious stones, ambergrirse, Musk, and other rich Drugges unregistred, of very great vallue. And of late years in some Measure, have the Dutch partaken thereof, as by the yearly retourns in spices, and other goods, to the vallue of 11: or 12: hundred thousand pounds, besides their many plantations of great Consequence. By the inconsiderate weaknes of our State, that gave way to some evill affected members of our Companie, to assist the Dutch, in beating the Portingalls quite out of all those Spice Ilands, and settling themselves in other places; which don, in most ingratefull manner, Murtherd our people in Amboyna; and in the ende thrust us also out of all; Not soe much as affording us any trade into their spice plantations, to the great shame, and dishonor of our nation, in those remote parts of the worlde.

In soe much, as those soe rich trades seeme, at this time, unto many men to be of little or no vallue; and all hopes of Planting ourselves in anie porte utterlye lost, in the opinion of some men, that affect not plantations, as nott willing the state should have any interest therin; or insight into their willfull Miscaried actions, as I have enlarged in my Remonstrance latelye delivered unto your Highnes.

Yett, are nott these trades the worse, because neglected, and slighted (like Pearles before Swine) by those that were intrusted therwith. Neither are all hopes of gaining some safe harbor, altogeather lost; Though the Portingalls have long since seased on, and still hould most of the best ports betweene Cambaya; and Cape Commorin, on the coast of India, three onlye excepted, to say Danda Rajapore, Rajapore, and Dabull; all good harbors, but in possession of the Natives, a stout, and warlike people, Nott to be attempted without aparent danger, and lost laboure. Experiment the Dutch, who nottwithstanding all their great force by sea; by which they have beaten the Portingalls from all trade, between port, and port in India, (which is the Cow that gives the milke of profitt) by shiping, have not gotten any Considerable port from them; other then Open Roades, upon the Spice Ilands; (that of Malaca excepted: rather a Charge, then benifitt unto them) except in hindring others from passage through that streight, unto China, and Japon; Nor is Jacatra, on Java Major, their prime Rendevous for all shiping and trade, other then an open roade, where their ships ride out of the Comand of their owne Ordnance, subject enough to ruine, by a stronger force, as by your Highnes' favor I shall enlarg in itts proper place hereafter.

Here I did intend with your Highnes favor and patience, to have gon on, in ralating the true, and reall worth, of every particular trade, beyond the Cape of good Hope, As the Gould coast, Sofala, Mosambeeke, Bombas, Melinde, upon the coast of Africa, The Red Sea and Bussora, in Arabia; Persia, India within and without Ganges; The Ilands of Zeilan, Sumatra, Java Major, Borneo, Molluca, Banda, Macassar, and Mannillas, etts; China, and Japon; But finding my worke to growe larger then I intended, I have thought good to leave them, for an other occasion; And with your Highnes leave, will proced unto the Meanes, wherby we may best gaine some Convenient harbor for our ships and people to winter in, which I finde May and wilbe don, better by fair Meanes then by force, As hertofore in anno 1628: when I was Presidente in Surratt, and we att Mortall warre with the Portingall; I being in treaty with the Great Mogull; Emporer of India; about aiding him by sea, in the takeing in of the Iland, Cittie, and Fort of Diu, and Daman; within his Dominions, and neer unto Cambaya, and Suratt; which the Portingalls have held above 200 yeares: the Conditions on our part, were as Commodious, and advantagious as we desired.

Being thus engaged, our deseigne became discovered to the inhabitants of Diu; (the place we Cheiflie aymed att, as being a very good harbor for our retreit) who foreseing that they were not able to defend themselves against both our forces both by land and sea; sent one of their prime Men of their Cittie to perswade me to desist from the intended warre. Butt when he saw that I was engaged soe farre, as I could nott fall of[f] with honour, he then opened his Minde unto me in plaine termes, shewing me his Commission, to treat with me about surrender of the said towne, and Castle of Diu, as Choosing rather to putt themselves into the hands of Christians, though enimies, and of different opinion, then to Cast themselves on the Mercy of Moores, and Infidells.

The Cheife Conditions required by them from us, were enjoyment of their Religion, and estates, freedom of trade on our ships into all ports of India, etts: and into England also, if they would, as free denisens, and Protection against other Portingalls, and their deadly enimies the Dutch; unto all butt this latter we had easily Condescended; Butt they being to[o] strong for us by sea, and noe Comission from the King or Company, we excused to treat any more therin; as we had don the like with the Great Mogull, untill we had Commission from hence to Confirme and warrant our proceedings. Herof I gave the then Governour of our Company notice, by a privat letter perswading him therunto, by many sound reasons; Butt however, relished by him etts., here at home, I never heard more of itt, other then that (by their next letter) I was Called home, as a privat trader only; and I coming thence in 1630, both that, and the other with the Mogull failed, and came to nothing; To say the truth, our Comp[a]. never really desired any plantation in India, for the reasons already deliverd.

This fair oportunitie neglected, Another was ofred, by the said Mogull, for aiding him in the gaining of Danda Rajapore, Rajapore, and Dabull, all very good harbors, he intending to Make a Conquest of Decam* and Vissapore, in whose Dominions, those ports lay, and in or about 1640 Moved the same to Mr. Fremlen, then President; butt he seeing the Companie did slight the first offer from the Portingalls, and noe after Commission from them, he durst nott entertaine itt; though extreamlye Convenient for the Companie and Nation. Yett did this produce good effects, for the Portingalls hearinge herof, and having fower, or five ports, between those of Danda Rajapore and Dabull, were fearfull that the Mogull had no good intention to themward, did therefore the yeare following, send to the English in Suratt, to treat of a Cessation of Armes, untill a peace were Concluded in Europe, which they did earnestlie desire; the Vice Kinge of Goa, ofring to deliver up the said towne of Diu into our hands, with free accesse, and trade into all their Portes, soe as we would joine with them in a warre offensive and defensive against the Dutch; this being refused, a Cessation of Armes onlye with free trade into all parts, was Concluded, and hath Continued ever since, without any just Cause of breach on either side.

* [*sic*]

All which fair offers, though then unhapilie lost, may yett give hopes of gaining one or more of those portes, by one meanes or other for itt may be Conceaved the King of Portingall will upon the before mentioned Conditions, deliver up the said Port of Diu, or other, upon very reasonable termes; or had your Highnes an Agent, or Consull there with Comission to treate with those people, who are now growen poore, and Necessitated, as beaten from all trade and Comerce, betweene port and port in India by shipinge, may be more willing to putt themselves under your Highnes Protection, then heretofore, by how much they know you better able to protect them, then were the Companie, and this without any breach, or offence to the Dutch; so also May the Great Mogull, willinglie embrace an ofer of aiding him by sea, in his warre against the Decamees*; which he hath long desired, upon what termes soever, we shall demand, the Castles, and fortes of each place excepted. All which being left unto your Highnes better Judgment and Consideration, whether of those three waies may be most advantagious to the Commonwealth, and most honorable to the Nation; That of the voluntary surrender of the towne of Diu, by the inhabitants therof, in my Judgment seemes to promise least of Charge and expence, and most of freedom and saftie; and may be expected upon more reasonable termes then the other; for the greater part of the inhabitants are Moores, Banians, heathen; the second greater part are Mestiso or mixt Portingalls, naturall borne Indians, of long descent from Portingall men and Indian women; the third and lesser part, that are Naturall born Portingalls, are the garison souldiers, Priests, and friers; both th'one and th'other much necessitated by the decay of trade, and wilbe willing to putt themselves under any goverment that will give them libertie of Conscience, their estates, freedom of trade, and protection from their enymies; which as things now stand in India, they can expect from no Prince butt from your Highnes, which may be a strong Motive both to them, and others to a revolt, when they shall see them thrive, by an open and free trade, without desturbance from their own nation, who will nott dare to make any breach for feare of farther mischeife; Nor from the Dutch, that have no Cause to be ofended; Neither yett from the Mogull, who hath divers times attempted the taking therof; butt wanting forces by sea, hath bin forced to a dishonorable retreat with losse.

* [sic]

Nor is itt altogeather unlikelie, that some of the Dutch garison, of the Moluca, and Banda Islands, may take example from the other, their present Condition being little better then slaves, out of hopes of ever seeing their owne Country, except by meanes of some spetiall friends; Nor doe they enjoy any trade, except in triviall things, more then for provision of vitualls and cloathing then for encrease of stocke; these discontents may soe worke upon their slavish spiritts as to putt them upon a revolte, upon assurance of freedom, and libertie of trade, and Protection, etts.

But this, and all the rest failing, (which I am Confident will nott) or not to be putt in practise upon any sudden intention of gaining the soveraigntie of those seas, and with them the whole trade of India, etts, to this Comonwealth, without which we cannott well enjoy any without many Jarrings and diferences between us and the Dutch, whom to out of all those trades, wilbe but (Lex tallionis), what they have long laboured, and had even now effected itt, with us; had not your Highnes beaten them into better manners here att home; to effect which two waies are ofred to your Highnes having first a large Nationall, or state stocke wherewith to worke, and Cary on soe honorable, and profitable dessigne, and v[i]ndicating the Many Injuries, and loste honnor and reputation of the Nation in those parts.

The first is, that a Continued faire and freindly corespondencie be helde with them, for some years, to take of[f] feares and Jealiousie, and secure them, yett for three or fower yeares to send out 10 or 12 good ships every yeare the greater part for trade between port and port in India itt self, for increase of stocke, and some of the bigger ships to be sent home with goods, in suply of those trades in Europe and elswhere, yett soe as they may be retourned thither in due time; that having there 30 or 40 ships, with 20 of your Highnes frigatts of warre, to be sent thither under pretence of some other dessigne, in the West Indies or Brasill; and all to meete att a certaine Randavous, those ships in India to be furnished with all sorts of needfull provisions, of vittualls and cloathing for both fleetes for two years, if itt be thought fitt. And from thence to proceed, soe as they may arrive at Jacatra at the end of May, or beginning of June, when all their best ships are gon disperst to the Eastward in way of trade, some few ould ships only left, as serving more for warehouses then for defence, these being easily seased on, the town beseeged by sea, and by land also by the Matran or Emperor of Java, to whom they maybe threatned to deliver itt up in case they shall refuse to yeald upon fair termes; in the Mean time, from their first entring the road, there must be spetiall care had soe to blocke up the river, as that noe boates may goe out to cary Newes of our ships being there, and soe divert their Coming home that yeare, which els they will come in as Ignorant of what passeth; and after the blocking up of the towne, the better part of the fleete, to retourne to the streights of Sunda, to intercept the fleete from Holland, if nott don in our Channell att their going out, advise whereof would be sent by an expresse to our fleet; That being don heer, and the Suratt and Goe fleets beinge surprised, they may send severall squadrons to the Moluca, and Banda Ilands, and take their ships in the roads, about the time of their being laden, and ready to come thence and by the way backe, to ly in waite for the China and Japon ships, and intercept them: all which being surprised the towne will have little stomacke to hould out, if nott releived by the Javaes by land.

Butt, in case this shall not please your Highnes, a second way is to sende out in one yeare (provision being made before hand in India, as is said before) 40 frigatts of warre about the End of December, that May arrive there about the beginning of June in one full bodie, to Meete the trading ships with provisions, in the Road of Bantam, or elswhere apointed. Soe may the worke be don in one yeare, for Jacatra being surrendred, all the rest must follow, as wanting provisions or starve. And this don, there wilbe little to be don with the Portingall, as being inconsiderable by sea; whereof we must endeavor to Make ourselves Masters before we can enjoy all those rich trades to ourselves alone.

Having thus laid open the richnes of those trades of India, etts. togeather with the manner of gaining some, or all the Ports the Portingalls hould, and the whole soveraigntie of those seas, and therwith the whole trade therin, I shall now with your Highnes favor and leave, propose a way of raising a state or Nationall stocke.

The Nationall stocke to be thus raised.

1 : H. 100 thousand pounds, in Bristoll, and all Wales, in 3 yeares.

2 : H. 100 thousand p°. in Plimouth, for Devonsheir, and Cornwall, and Counties adjacent.

3 : H. 100 thousand p°. in Portchmouth ; for the Ile of Wighte, Hamsheir, Dorset and Counties about itt.

4 : H. 100 thousand p°. in Dover for Kent, Sussex, Suries [Surrey], etts. Counties.

5 : H. 100 thousand p°. in Harwich, for Essex, Suffolke, Norfolke, etts.

6 : H. 100 thousand p°. in Newcastle, for Yorksheir, Lincolnsheir, etts.

7 : 8 : 9 : H. 300 thousand p°. in the Cittie of London, and Liberties therof.

10 : H. 100 thousand p°. in Westminster, Innes of Court, Law[y]ers and gentlemen, Custom and Excise Men ; and all other oficers of state, and Comon wealthe.

Or 1000 : thousand p°. thus raised upon landed men, and such as have 1,000*li*. Personall estate, and upwards, to be paid in three years, by equall proportions.

He that hath 100*li*. lands a yeare, to putt into stocke 30*li*. in 3 years, and he that hath 200*li*. to pay in 50*li*. and soe rising 20*li*. upon every 100*li*. land increase ; and he that hath 1,000*li*. personall estate, to putt in 30*li*. and he that hath 2000*li*. to putt in 60*li*. and soe rising, under which sommes noe man to be prest to adventure, unles willinge therunto, and such to have libertie to putt in what sommes they please.

That every such proportion of 100 thousand pounds, pay 25 thousand pounds a year, into stocke for 3 years, and doe build every yeare a ship of 7 or 800 tons or two ships of 3 or 400 tons apeece, as shalbe allotted to their division and these to beare the names of the Ports, and Counties laid to itt.

That every such port, after the first 3 years, have one shippes lading of goods every year out of India Consigned unto itt, to be ther disposed of, either for the Counties use, or transportation, that soe that trade may be disperst into all parts of the Land, as well as in this Cittie.

The stocke for a state action to be thus raised oz. That, ther be borrowed, of the Cittie of London, and Westminster the somme of ten hundred thousand pounds, for 7 years, To be paid into stocke in 3 years, that is 333 thousand 333 pounds, and a noble every yeare in this manner oz.

H. 600 thousand p°. of the first twelve Companies.

H. 200 thousand p°. of the twelve inferior Companies.

H. 100 thousand p°. of Westminster, Innes of Court, Lawers, and gentlemen, oficers of state, Custom house, and excise men; etts.

H. 100 thousand p°. of gentlemen, tradesmen, seamen; such as are no freemen butt live in Southwarke and subarbes, within the lines of Comunication.

H. 2,000 thousand p°. to be paid in 3 years; whereof 270 thousand p°. to be sent out the first yeare, as quicke stocke, in goods and Monies and stores upon 16 ships, and the two last years, 250 thousand p° a yeare in goods and monies, with 16 ships a yeare for trade in India, soe may 10 of the first ships be expected home, att the end of two years, or 27 Months att most, and soe every yeare, 10 ships may goe out, and 10 com hoame; and 10 remayning in the Cuntry, with 5 ships more added to them for trading ships of 400 tons apeece, to be built of the 30 thousand p°. remayning: which will encrease the trading ships to 15 to staye there in the Cuntry, untill a greater nomber be added to them by increase of stocke; soe as, the first 10 ships may well bring hoame, 9 or 10 hundred thousand pounds in goods (God sending all safe hoame) upon the first Adventure. And if itt shall please your Highnes, to joine the trade of Guynny to this of India, that will suplye this with a great parte of stocke in treasure and Ellophants teeth; soe May Many sorts of goods fitting Guinny, be provided in India; and a ship or two of 3 or 400 tons May be sent directly out of India with goods for Guinny, wher having landed such goods for that place, may proceed with others, and slaves for the Barbados, and other plantations wher Callicoes, and divers sorts of stuffes made in India, are very proper for those hott Cuntries, which after some experience and use, may grow into request, and add increase of trade, within our selves, without need of any of our neighbours linen cloath; which by heavy Impositions laid thereon, may in time beat out of use, and being Callicoes etts. Indian Comodities in use, as also in Virginia, and New england, etts.

All which being humbly presented unto your Highnes most serious Consideration, as the richest Jewell of trade, in the whole world, with the soveraigntie of those seas, once reduced into your sole possession (wherunto this discourse doth only ayme) will render your Highnes name most renowned, and famous, in the foremoste parte of the world; by vindicating the Nations lost honnor, and reputation, and recovering those soe rich trades, to this Commonwealth; of long time obstructed and kept from us, by our fals freinds, wherby they thought to make themselves absolute Masters of those seas; which they had effected, had nott your Honors greate wisdome, providence and power overawed them, and beaten them into better behaviour here at hoame, and Laid them under hattches; In which Condition itt wilbe wisdom, according to the true interest of state, to keep them, above all the Nations in the world (as most able to doe mischeife) all whom they would have commanded by sea, had they bin Masters of your Highnes forces, and Consequentlye of our Narrow seas; If there be anything either in the whole or in part, or else, wherin your Highnes shall desire farther satisfaction, I shall in all humble manner attend your Highnes pleasure, whensoever you shall please to Comand me, and apointe a meanes wherby I may have accesse unto your Highnes which I have endeavord for Many monthes togeather in all which I could obteine butt one admittance only, and that soe short, as gave nott leave to move these and other matters of high Concernement as to those soe rich trades of India etts. In which reguard I have thought it fitt nott onlye to present the same unto your Highnes by this, and other severall Remonstrances; butt also most humbly to offer my person, with my best endeavors, in the reall effecting of what I have propounded; soe please your Highnes to Countenance my proceedings with the Agency, or Consullship of Surratt; that I may have meanes, wherwith to maintaine your Highnes honor, and the Nations Esteeme in those parts: where I dare assure your Highnes no Englishman wilbe better wellcom; nor was either before or since in greater favor with the Great Mogull, then my self; as all the Nation that have bin in those partes, both can and will Justifie, if required therunto.

Lastlie, I make bould to putt your Highnes in Minde of the Pearl fishing, which hath bin these two Monthes obstructed, and is like to be neglected for this year, by the sinister working of some enimies, with those that had begun to subscribe a stocke for trade, and disharting others from subscribing, that had promised, in soe much as those that had subscribed fall of, by which meanes all is at a stand, and the time soe far spent as little hopes are left for a preparation thereunto; unlesse itt shall please your Highnes to grant me the Agencie, or Consulship of Surratt, for 3 years; or untill the trade be settled, by a state, or Nationall stocke, the best way, for Honor, Profitt, and safetie, in which time I doe not doubt, butt soe to worke with those people of Diu, or some others, as to gaine a safe and Commodious Harbor wherin to settle, without which itt wilbe dificult to gaine the soveraigntie of those seas, and benifitt of those soe rich trades, which neither the Company nor those that presse for an open trade desire should fall into your Highnes and states hands; ayming more at their owne privat interest, then the generall good; for which cause, and for that I have acquainted your Highnes with their miscaried actions, they are all become my enimies; seeking by all meanes to possesse your Highnes that all my informations, as to those trades, and their Neglects, are not reall; though nothing more of truth, which I shalbe able to Maintaine, at a fair hearing before your Highnes to whom I much desire to give full satisfaction, to every particular, which they shall not, cannott disprove. Lett not therefore (I humbly beseech you) my weake, though true relations finde in your Highnes lesse of credit, then the thing itt self meritts upon due examination; because I am not in that flourishing Condition, as they are, that have long since sought my ruine, for no other cause then seeking the generall good, in prevention of their sinister ends. My owne ayming at nothing more, then a little subsistence, as encoragment to my honest and faithfull endeavors, if made instrumentall therin.

Charles II's restoration solved many of the most perplexing problems which had taxed the resources and exhausted the patience of the Directors. The position of the Company had to be defined anew, if it was to take its place by the side of the well-known institutions of England; while clear and definite rules had to be laid down for the conduct of its servants towards the Indians and the Free Traders. The question of fortified places, the future policy of the Government as regards the export of bullion, the grant of a new Charter—these were some of the problems that awaited solution, and upon a patient and tactful handling of these questions depended ultimately the safety of the Company's servants in the East.

I have already discussed the relation of the Company to Charles II in Chapter II of my work on "The East India Trade." The Anglo-Portuguese negotiations relating to Bombay supply, however, the best illustration of the salutary policy of the Government as they are the clearest indication of the essentially "commercial" considerations that dictated the foreign policy of Charles.

The East India Company had mooted the project of the acquisition of Bombay in February, 1660, to the Portuguese Ambassador, but had received a discouraging reply. (*See supra.*) The suggestion was, however, conveyed to the Portuguese King, and in the summer of the same year Francisco de Mello, the Portuguese Ambassador, proposed a match between Charles and Infanta Catharine, daughter of John IV, and sister of the reigning king, Alfonso VI. He offered the cession of Tangier and Bombay, commercial privileges and complete liberty of conscience for English merchants, and a dowry of two million *crusados*. Albemarle and Sandwich seem to have strongly favoured the match; Ormond and Clarendon approved of it; Bristol alone opposed the project. The Treaty was signed on June 23, 1661, and the marriage followed on May 21, 1662. Charles became pledged to assist Portugal with 2,000 foot, 1,000 horse, and 10 ships of war until her independence was attained. English help was greatly needed at the time, for the pacification of Catalonia and the Peace of Pyrenees had enabled the Spanish King to send a large number of troops to reconquer Portugal. That there was a possibility of the Portuguese being reconquered by their hereditary enemies is clear from the events of 1662-3, when Don Juan overran Alamtejo; it is no less clear that it was the English auxiliaries under Schomberg and, later, the French contingents, that won Portugal her independence, on February 13th, 1668.

Closer examination of the Treaty of 1661 shows clearly enough that it was a one-sided bargain, and its execution revealed at once the hollow foundations upon which that imposing fabric was reared. Tangier proved weak, barren, and expensive; Catharine was dull, plain, and sickly; the payment of the money specified in the Treaty was irregular, and Charles found it difficult to extract a satisfactory sum from the impecunious, elderly hidalgoes, "sitting up in bed, like poor Tasso's father, at five o'clock in the morning, darning a single pair of worsted stockings"; while the old Cromwellian soldiers, and the desperate Irish Catholics who had been skilfully manœuvred into Portugal, and fought at Amegial (June 8, 1663,) and Montes Carlos (June 17, 1665,) added another element of anxiety. It was, however, the provision relating to Bombay that proved a source of constant trouble to Portugal and England. It involved the Company in endless negotiations, fruitless despatches, ceaseless complaints, and constant worry. Many of the difficulties from which the Company suffered so severely would have been avoided, if the representatives of the East India Company had been requested to advise the Crown on the drafting of the Treaty. Their practical experience, mercantile shrewdness, and thorough knowledge of the coast would have been invaluable to the Government. There is reason to believe that they were consulted on the subject; they probably knew that the fortification of the place would be attended by an expense which their depleted treasury could hardly bear; and they wisely refused to send out men and shipping to Bombay at their charge. The following extract from their *Minutes** shows clearly enough the trend of their policy: "The Lord Chancellor having made an offer to the Company to consider whether it would be to their advantage to despatch men and shipping at their own charge 'to possesse, maintaine, and fortify Bone Bay,' or to undertake part of that charge jointly with the King, or leave it wholly to His Majesty, after serious consideration they came to the conclusion that it would be no advantage to them to act in the matter, and they desired the Governor with some of the Committee to wait upon His Lordship, thank him for his offer and for telling them about it, and inform him that the Company cannot see that any advantage would accrue to them, and therefore they humbly leave it to the King's good-will and pleasure." The only help afforded by them consisted in finding money necessary for manning and victualling the four ships sent out by the King and in lading them back again.

* *Court Book*, Vol. 24, p. 412.

The King's difficulties had thus begun at the very outset of this enterprise, and his troubles multiplied with the lapse of time. The main causes of this disastrous policy was the gross, nay, culpable ignorance of Clarendon. Article XI of the Treaty declared that the " King of Portugal, with the assent and advice of his Council gives, transfers, and by these presents grants and confirms unto the King of Great Britain, his heirs and successors for ever, the Port and Island of Bombay in the East Indies with all its rights, profits, territories and appurtenances whatsoever thereunto belonging, and together with all income and revenue, as also the direct and absolute Dominion and Sovereignty of the said Port and Island of Bombay, and premises, with all their royalties, freely, fully, and absolutely." Of the geographical position of Bombay, Clarendon wrote: " And for ever annex to the Crown of England the island of Bombay, with the towns and castles therein, which are within a very little distance of Brazil."* Such a misty notion of the elementary facts of geography seems to imply crass stupidity on the part of Clarendon, and the British Government had itself to thank for the troubles in which it was subsequently involved.

The Portuguese were not slow to take advantage of these uncertainties, and their Governor indulged in the congenial task of raising trivial technical objections, and delaying the cession of Bombay on various pretexts. It is amusing to read the tedious, frivolous, and wearisome correspondence between the Portuguese Governor and the English Resident, the English King and the Portuguese monarch. The negotiations are of great importance to the student, for they reveal to us in a flash the essentially economic character of the Governments of the period. The quarrels over commerce and plantation in the eighteenth century have diverted the mind of the student from the study of the last half of the seventeenth century. A deeper study of the institutions and constitutions of the States of this period reveals a mass of tendencies converging upon a central point that is remarkable. Commercial, industrial, and colonial considerations dictate here, as elsewhere, the policy of the State, and Charles' Government advocates the cause of the Company with a vigour, energy, persistence and decision that recall the direct, forcible methods of the Protectorate. The frequent "gratuities", " gratifications ", "loans" and " gifts " recorded in the Company's *Minutes* may, no doubt, have influenced the direction of the King's policy. But the principles underlying his colonial and commercial administration had been enunciated immediately on his return in 1660, and his

* Clayton's *Personal Memoirs*, Vol. II, p. 189.

attitude towards the Company was based ultimately on his perception of the absolute necessity of safeguarding the East India Trade by the Joint-Stock system. The following letter is, I believe, the earliest account of the proceedings at Bombay. Charles' instructions were the subject of keen dispute between the two kings, and "as they were the subject of lengthy negotiations and tedious correspondence," they are printed along with the minutes of the Council (*see below*).

Browne thought that "Bombay extended itself from the south point of the said Island to the Northward as far as the Bay of Bassein, and so in towards the main to meet again with the south point intirely one Island to containe the wintering harbour of Trombay." The English commanders must have been greatly perturbed by the appearance of the little hamlet without the "castles and towns" which Clarendon's fertile imagination had conjured up.

Public Record Office. C. O. 77, Vol. VIII, No. 141,

EXTRACTS FROM CAPTAIN ARNOLD BROWNES JOURNALL OF SOME TRANSACTIONS IN INDIA CONCERNING THE ISLAND OF BOMBAIM, &C.

Upon the Earle of Marlborough's arrivall at Bombaim, he did declare to the Vice Roy of Goa that his Commission led him to receive the Island for the use of his Majesty of England by his soldiers, before he could proceede to go to Goa, and so requested the Vice Roy's speedy answer thereto—the Vice Roy demanded whether the Earle had a special power from his Majesty of England to empower Collonel Hungerford to receive the Island, and give a sufficient Discharge to which he answered that he had no such power, but that the Collonel was Sir Abraham Shipman's successor and therefore thought him a fit person to receive the Island and give a Discharge for it. So in 3 or 4 dayes the Vice Roy answered positively that he would not deliver the Island to any man whatever that had not his Majesty of England's speciall procuration to that purpose. Which we had not.

In this Juncture of affaires arrives Sir Abraham Shipman, who we expected to have gott an effectuall Procuration from his Majesty. But when Sir Abraham came ashoare and delivered the Kings Majesties Letter to the Vice Roy, and though he received it with reverence, yet was not satisfied therewith, but demanded if he had nothing els to which Sir Abraham answered Nothing but his Patent. Then the Vice Roy made an objection that the Kings Majesties Letter had not the Kings hand to it, and that it was not a Procuration, but a private Letter from his Majesty to him and then shewed Sir Abraham the King of Portugal's instructions to him Not to deliver the said Island to any, except they brought the King of England's special Procuration.

And to the same purpose the Vice Roy wrot a Letter to his Majesty of England.

After this denyall Sir Abraham proceeded to Goa, and there it was the sence of the Governor and most of the Gentry that the Island of Bombay Should be delivered to Sir Abraham and wrot to the Vice Roy but upon Sir Abraham's delivery thereof to the Vice Roy, he received answer from his Excellency that he would not deliver it, the word Procuration being nominated in his Orders from his Majesty of Portugall.

Public Record Office, C. O. 77, Vol. VIII, No. 141.

And whereas we supposed, by the Platt the Pylott gave in, and the opinions of the antientest Commanders, that Bombay extended itself from the South point of the said Island to the Northward as farr as the Bay of Basseen, and so in towards the Main to meet again with the South point intirely one Island to conteine the Wintering harbour of Trombay. We find the sayd Compass to conteine three intire Islands, two of them to say Tanna which is the Northermost, and butts to the barr of Basseene and Salsett which is Southward of Tanna (on which is the Wintring harbour of Trombay) are places of good Consideration much better then the Island of Bombay which is next Southerly to Salsett and divided from it by a Navigable Channell.

December 10*th* 1662.

SWALLY HOLE.

[*Endorsed.*]

10*th December* 1662.

Extract out of Capt. Brownes Journall when he Returned from Bombaim with the Earl of Marlbrough. Received from the East India Company at the Comittee 11th January 1676/7 from Mr. Hublon.

Entred B. 156.

The following letters from the Portuguese Governor throw further light on the proceedings of the two parties. Castro, it must be noted, deliberately omits a reference to the terrible hardships which Marlborough and his men suffered. These were due mainly to his dilatory policy and disingenuous devices. It is not surprising that enforced inactivity, and fearful ravages of disease should have made some of the men desperate ; but we have no reason to believe that the Portuguese Governor was subjected to personal abuse. His statement that they used him " worse then if they were Hollanders, and with less sivilitye then if I were a blackey Moore," must be accepted *cum grano salo.*

THE GOVERNOR OF BOMBAY'S LETTER TO THE QUEEN.

(*Copye.*)

Public Record Office, C. O. 77, Vol. VIII, folio 271, No. 138.

SENORA

Because its certaine that Generall Malbrugh and the English of his Company (to excuse themselves in the ill usage they did mee in this voyage) will tell in Englande more then they ought, or what hath happen'd, I am necessitated to give your Majestie an account of thier excesses, and my owne suffrings, (for they could not use myselfe and the rest of the Portugueses worst) which they did with such scorne to our nation, that your Majestie is obliged to Cause that the publikenese of thier punishment may serve for an example hereafter, and since your Majestie knows mee you may beleeve that I shall say nothing

Public Record Office, C. O. 77, Vol. VIII, folio 271, No. 138.

in this paper, but what I will bee able to shew Authentiquely, and of which your Majestie may bee informed by the persons of the Shipp wherein I came, for though they bee of another beleefe than ours yett they will speake truth, if they are not hinder'd by thier feare of Malbrugh, who did not onely aprove of the robberys, and affronts of Captain Richard Meynars, but alsoe increased the cause of my Complaynt, useing mee worst then if they were Hollanders and with lesse sivilitye then if I were a blackey Moore like those they tye by the leggs in the Indies, I boare my life with feares not being onely treaten'd by the Common insolencye but alsoe by the power of Generall Malbrugh; Captain Richard Meynors assureing mee that they would Cutt of my head for having made the protests, and requests, which was convenient to the service of the king my Master, and they denyed mee the Succour that the most Serene King of Englande obliged himselfe by the Capitulations of Peace to give us, which I have along with mee, for in the Islande of St. Laurence, the Blackeymoores, in that of Anjuame the Moores, and in Cochim, the Hollanders, were more friendely with Generall Malbrugh and the English Captains then the Portugueses of said Islands; I being sutt* in the Indie, and surounded, the saide Generall would give me no favour, or helpe at all; This his unreasonablenese, and the not bringing with him, a procuration from the King of Englande, (like one that Came upon the buisnese of Persia, and not upon the Ingagements of Portugall,) was the reason wherefore the Islande of Bombaim had not been delliver'd him; I hope that your Majestie (as so good a Catholique and a Portuguesa) will bee pleased to see my protests and letters, which side Generall Malbrugh caryes with him, and I assure myselfe that your Majestie will Judge I have Complyed with my obligation, and alsoe because I am now ready to delliver up sayd Islande (as the King my master Comands me) unto what person soever shews mee the most Serene King of England's Comission to recieve the same, and satisfye the Conditions of the agreement.

* [*sic*]

The master of the Shipp Leopard who cary'd mee from Portugall to the Indie, is the onely man amongst all, that helped us, wherefore I ought to desire your Majestie in the name of the king my Master to honnor and favour him, and I shall receeve it, as a greate one, if in the first navy that setts out, your Majestie would make him a Captain of a Shipp, and that your Majestie would bee pleased to Comand mee (in these parts) in your Royal service, which I shall observe with that love, respect, and zeale, whereunto I am obliged, our Lord preserve your Majestie &c.

ATTO. DE MELLO DE CASTRO.

BACAIM *Decembre 3rd* 1662.

[*Endorsed.*]

BACAIM.

The Governor of Bumbaim Antto. de Mello de Castro's letter to the Queene.

Decembre 3rd, 62.

Complayneing of the Earl of Marlburgh's hard usage of him, and of Capt. Mynor's for robbing him.

THE LATE GOVERNOR OF BOMBAIM'S LETTER TO THE KING.

Public Record Office, C. O. 77, Vol. VIII, 275, folio No. 140.

(*Copye translated out of Portugues.*)

SENOR

I am necessitat'd to make my Complainte unto your Majestie upon the late proceedings of Captain Richard Meynor, and afterwards of Generall Malbrough's towards mee, which rays'd to soe greate an Excesse, that all respect was lost, and our lives indanger'd ; By two papers that both Carrye Signed by mee, your Majestie will see my Sufferings, and true meaneing, they (I trust) will tell your Majestie yett more then I say, and seeing I came imbarqu'd under your Majesties protection, and Royal worde, the wronge that was done mee runns upon your account, wherefore it is but Justice I should expect of Royal Greatnesse the Satisfaction thereof ; and seeing I did not delliver up the Islande of Bombain, for want of a procuration from your Majestie, and Likewayse because they would never succour mee (it beeing an obligation by the agreement) and the necessitye being soe great, I beleeved that your Majestie (as soe Just a Prince) would have layed the punishment upon the offender, and have thought I had done my obligation (beeing pleased to consider) how much a subject of honnor ought to Contribute to his Kings Service.

The Master of the Shippe Leopard, who Came in my Company, hath been the onely person that used us well, for which reason I finde myselfe obliged to give your Majestie this account, as I will, to the king my Master desireing his Majestie to doe the said Captain honnor and favour, and I should recieve a greate one, if in the Fleete that your Majestie sends next towards Bombaim, I might see him a Captain of a shippe. And though not concearning myselfe for all the subjects your Majestie hath, yett it shall appeare how much Inclined I am unto your Majesties Service, having been one of your Majesties soldiers (when even your owne Subjects were in Rebbellion against you) in Company of Prince Robert, of whome your Majestie may Informe your selfe with how much love (at that time) I served your Majestie, which this day is much increas'd, with what I owe unto the most Serene Queene, our Infanta, in whose Companye our Lorde preserve your Majestie Many happye yeares.

ANTO. DE MELLO DE CASTRO.

From BACAIM *the 3rd of Decembre* 1662.

[*Endorsed.*]

BACAIM.

A Copye of Ant°. de Mello de Castro late Governor of Bombaim's letter to the King. *December 3rd* 1662.
Read Novembre 25, 1663.

Co[m]plaineing of Capt. Maynors.

The following letter from Charles II traces the progress of the King's disillusionment regarding Bombay. His castles, gold mines, and Golconda diamonds disappeared, and in their place remained only a poor, little hamlet, bleak, barren and unhealthy, adding not a little to the financial difficulties of the period. The difficulties, it must be noted, were confined hitherto to the possession of the island. The greater difficulty of deciding the geographical position of Bombay had not arisen yet.

Public Record Office, C. O. 77, Vol. IX, folio 26, No. 17.

LETTER TO SIR ABRAHAM SHIPMAN WITH ORDERS TO THE VICE ROY OF GOA, TO SURRENDER BOMBAIM.

WHITEHALL *October* 31*st* 1663.

Sr,

Att My Lord Marleborough's returne his Majesty heard from his Lordshipp how unworthily the Vice king of Bombaim Dom Antonio de Mello de Castro had proceeded, denying the surrender of that Place and Island to his Majesty, according to the Article inserted in the Treaty with the King of Portugall, and his supposed Instructions to that effect. And besides the affront done to himselfe therein, his Majesty did with much trouble of mind, reflect upon the sufferings you and the Troops under your command, would undergoe by this disappointment ; of which he hath caused those Complaints to be made in the Court of Portugall, which such a proceeding deserves. In which he is promised all due satisfaction, the first earnest of which is the sending New Letters to the Vice king, commanding him immediately to surrender the Place into the hands of those the King Our Master shall appoint to receive it. Which Letters together with a Copy of them, goe here inclosed, in Portugais and English if you should chance not to understand that language. Which said Originall Letters, it is his Majestys Pleasure, that you cause to be delivered to the said Vice king, demanding the execution of the Contents of it, according to which you are to take possession of what they will deliver into your hands, directing yourselfe therein by those Instructions My Lord of Marleborough hath already, or may with this send to you, in case his Indisposition in the Country will permitt him to write by this occasion. And if in the Surrender any thing be deteyned from you that you thinke the Article in the Treaty (of which you will also herewith receive an Authenticke Copy) entitles his Majesty to, you are to take what is given, and protest against the detention of the rest.

This is sent to you by the way of Aleppo at randome, suspecting much the certainty of its arrivall ; the other (for there are two Letters of the same kind sent from the Court of Portugall) shall be sent you by Sea, with more particular directions and succours for yourselfe and your men, as soone as his Majesty can dispatch a Shipp into those parts. In the meane time, Sir George Oxenden hath it very particularly recommended to him by the East Indy Company to supply you to the utmost of their power, with all things you or your men shall stand in need of; which is promised with the conveyance of these letters to you. Public Record Office, C. O. 77, Vol. IX, folio 26, No. 17.

[*Endorsed.*]

Whitehall, 31*st October* 1663.
To Sir Abraham Shipman, by the way of Aleppo with Order to the Vice Roy of Goa to surrender Bombair [*sic*]
The Duplicat with succours, to be sent by sea.

The following letter from Sir Abraham Shipman shows the fearful havoc wrought by disease, disappointment and delay, and Shipman informs Marlborough that, "of the 400 and odd men that were brought out of the Downes of officers and soldiers, we have not left above 140"; at times, indeed, "they had not twenty men to stand to their armes to doe their dewtie." The condition of the miserable expedition was pitiable in the extreme, and Shipman himself fell a victim to disease.

ANGEDIVA. LETTER FROM SIR ABRAHAM SHIPMAN TO MARLBOROUGH, GIVING AN ACCOUNT TO THE EARL OF THE MEN WITH HIM. Public Record Office, C. O. 77, Vol. IX, Folio 33, No. 21.

MY VERY GOOD LORDE

I understand by Captain Nicholas Millett that your Lordship gott salfe to the Island of Santa Ellena which I was extreame Glad of soe that I hope his Majestie is thoroughly Informed of our Conditiones here yet my lord sence your departuere wee have binn in much worse Condition then you lefte Us, haveing had a Verry Greate Mortalety Amoungeste Us, for of 400 and ode men that wee brought out of the Downes of officers and souldiers wee have not left Above 140 besides at one time wee had not twenty sound men to stand to their armes to doe there dewtie and daiely being threatned by the Kinge of Decann that hee would expell Us hence, if it bee our Elle fourtunes to stay Another Winter I doe not know what will beecome of Us Unless it please God to Give helth to our peopell for if any more dies wee shall be in a Verry sad Condition. I doubt not but your Lordship hath donn your utmoste to pres them to it.

My Lord this is the seconde sicknes I have had sence I came uppon this Island and am now soe fainte that am not Abell to Right more God sendinge me helth I shall more in large by the shipes and there fore Crave your Lordeshipes pardon who is my Lorde your most humble sarvant at Command

ABRAHAM SHIPMAN.

ANGEDIVA *the* 18*th November* 1663.

[*Endorsed.*]

* Angediva *November* 18*th* 1663. [*sic*]*

Sir Abraham Shipman to My Lord of Marleborough Giving Account of the Men with him.

The following letters from Henry Gary will be found interesting. They are written in the peculiar nonsensical vein characteristic of that eccentric individual, and supply a vivid account of Shivaji's raid. Gary asserts that "he made a greate destruction of Houses by fir uppwards of 3,000, and carryed a vast treasure away with him, it is credibly reported neere unto tenn millions of rupees." Dr. Fryer describes Gary as a "Person of a Mercurial Brain, a better merchant than a soldier."* He seems to have been proficient in the principal European languages, and is said to have "written a Piece in Arabick, which he dedicates to the Viceroy of Goa." After many vicissitudes, he fell into the responsible position of Governor of Bombay, but his "unadvised vaine glorious boastings", as Sir George Oxenden put it, disgusted every one and he handed over his charge to a more capable man. Yule, Strachey, Foster and others have thrown further light on the mysterious activities of this inexplicable phenomenon. These letters are his couched in the familiar style and reveal several lineaments in the character of this *condottieri* which created more friends than enemies.

Public Record Office, C. O. 77, Vol. IX, folio 38a, No. 24, 2nd letter.

RIGHT HONOBLE

The preceding is transcript of my last furdered to your Lordshipps reception by way of Persia and Aleppo; recommended to Consull Lanog for its mission thince for Christendom, which I hope hee will doe carefully, as I understand hee did my formers, which came safe to his hands though many letters and pacquets that accompanyed them from Bussora miscaried, by the messengers being robbed by the wild Arabs in the desarts. My Lord, I send not now the Copie of Sir Abrahams letter mentioned in my said transcript, because I am confident hee himselfe hath advized his Majesty to what a small number his soldiers are reduced; a mortality (as I was lately emformed) continuing styll among them. God deliver them from that insalubrious clime, or rather make them more temperat, for I am perswaided that the major part dyes of surfeits (were due to their intemperance?) every one heere longingly expects your Lordshipps retourne and the Brahmens are so comfident of it, that many Banians have laid wagers, that your arrivall heere will bee before this month bee quite out; lett me bee bloted quite out of your Lordshipps remembrance if I should not heartyly rejoyce to see that happy howre, and much much * more, to see Ant°. de Mello de Castro sent home laden with machos though they should be of prata; his guiltie contience makes him tremble at every Englishman that arrives at Goa. I shall not ommit to acquaint your Lordshipp what lately happened to this place; Savagee the grand rebell to the King of Decan came heere the 6th of this instant with a considerable Army Horse and foote entring the Towne before the Governor scarce had any notice of his aproache, hee made a greate

* [sic]

* *Travels*, II, p. 30.

destruction of Houses by fire uppwards of 3000, and caryed a vast treasure away with him. It is credibly reported neere unto tenn millions of rupees. Hee sumoned us to compound with him for our lives (as hee did the Dutch) but Sir George retourned the messenger, with an answere that, hee scorned him and that if hee sent him any more messengers, they should never retourne againe; Boath the Companys house and my owne (which adjoynes unto it) were well furnished with mariners, well armed, who divers times salied out uppon his people that came to sett fire to our neighbours houses and killed divers of them, by which meanes, our owne houses were not only preserved from the fiends furie, butt likewise all the part of the Towne round about us; which hath gott us much Honour divers of the greate ones having advized the King Oranzeeb thereof, as on the contrary they have complained of the Governor, who so soone as hee had brought him the news of this rebells aproach, shamfully runn and hyd himselfe in the Castle; the Dutch never salied out though kept theyr house stoutly; This villaine had the plundoring of this place for fower whole days, from Wednesday morning untyll Saturday at fower in the afternoone, in which Intrime hee committed many cruleties, by cutting off of mens hands that could not give him so much mony as hee demaunded, six and twenty did one of our Principall Factors (that was then his Prisoner, butt escaped miracolously Mr. Anthony Smith) see cutt off in a morning besides many heads:

Public Record Office, C. O. 77, Vol. IX. folio 38a, No. 24.

From Achine wee have Intelligence that the Hollanders are not only gone away from that place by stealth, but like wise from all the ports and places where they had factories in that Queenes Dominions, whince it is infered they intend to make a new warr with hir and if possibly make a conquest of hir golden mountaines whince is colected as good gold, as is the Chequine; I cannot record ought else in mind worthy your Lordshipps notice and therefore shall close theis with the wounted subscription of

My Lord
Your Honours
most humble servant

SURAT *the 25th January* 1663/4. H. GARY.

[*Postscript.*]

MY LORD

The inclosed is Copy of Sir Abrahams letter to the vice King, which was sent me by the latter to translate in regard hee could finde noe body else to doe it for him, the English Jesuit being then absent; in reducing it into Portugueze I tooke the freedom uppon me to make it as much in the nature of a Protest as I could and now I thought it very requisit to remitt it unto you for your Lordshipps perusall.

(Sd.) H. G.

MY LORD

Please your Honour to take furder notice that I have likewise beine advised from the Southward that *Coxen* the *Chinches* who tooke Ilha Formoza from the Hollanders is gone against theyr Molluco

Public Record Office, C. O. 77, Vol. IX, folio 38a No. 24.

Islands with 400 saile of Vessailes and the Dutch with 35 ffrigats are gone to see yf they cann regaine theyr Beutifull Island.

(Sd.) H. G.

[*Endorsed.*]

Surat, 25 *January*, 63.
Mr. Gary.

[*Addressed.*]

These
For the Right Honoble, James
Earle of Marlebourgh.

Public Record Office, C. O. 77, Vol. IX, 40, folio No. 25.

RIGHT HONOBLE

Have allready in due obedience to your Lordshipps Commaunds written unto you two severall times by way of Aleppo, which have bein all the opportunities, that happned for conveyance of letters for Europe since your departure; At the foote of my first letter I advized your Lordshipp of the report which then was in Goa, that the Vize rey and Councill had concluded the delivery of Bombaim unto Sir Abraham Shipman, and that it was comfirmed unto me by Father John Gregory the English Jesuit. But my second contradicted it; though it was certenly concluded on and voted by three severall Councills whiles my aboad In Goa that Bombaim should bee delivered unto Sir Abraham Shipman for his Majestys use, the Vize rey telling me so himselfe; and also that hee would suddenly despeede a person towards Sir Abraham with the Order. But my Lord, he never performed that promisse; Hee minding nothing more than to robb the poore people over whom hee is sett to governe; But I hope hee will bee made sensible ere long of the greate abuse hee hath done to our King and Nation.

No longer since than yesterday, I received a letter from Sir Abraham, whose Coppie (conceiving your Lordshipp very anxious to knowe of him and the rest of his Majestys subjects) I have heere inclosed sent you by this conveyance. I shall use the utmost of my endeavors to serve him, in all hee desires. Butt to levy any soldiers heere to recrute him, is all togeather impossible, as your Lordshipp well knowes, in other matters I shall readyly serve him, which shall bee to manifest howe much I am

My Lord,
Your Lordshipps
most humble servant
H. GARY.

SURAT *the 23rd November* 1663.

MY LORD

I had all most forgott to acquaint you that his Majestys Pynk went to Bantam in Aprill last by Sir Abrahams order; but as yett, heere is noe news of hir.

(Sd.) H. G.

[*Addressed.*]

These
For the Right Honoble James
Earle of Marlebourgh
In London.

Public Record Office, C. O. 77, Vol. IX, folio 40, No. 25.

Per via Aleppo.
Recommendata al Consul
della natione Inglese.

[*Endorsed.*]

23rd November 1663.
Mr. Gary's letter to the Earl of Marlborough touching the delay of the delivery of Bombaim by the Portuguese.

The following petition of the inhabitants of Bombay recites the wrongs of the various communities, and prays for the abolition of Foreiros Mayores, or Chief Farmers, whom they denounce as "powerfull, arrogant, and exorbitant violators, Ecclesiastiques as well as Civil." It is the earliest expression of the general sentiments of Bombay citizens, and throws considerable light on the administration of Bombay by the Portuguese. It need hardly be pointed out that the picture is not a faithful reproduction of reality, and the strong denunciation of the Portuguese rule should not prevent us from doing homage to the sterling worth of the early Portuguese. The generation that succeeded them was, however, distinctly inferior in moral no less than intellectual qualities, and the following petition brings out some of the unlovely features of the administration of their Asiatic dependencies in the latter half of the seventeenth century. Mr. Henry Gary had a good deal to do with this outburst of intense loyalty among 123 Christians, 84 "Gentuies" and 18 "Moors".

The Humble Petition and Manifesto which the Inhabitants in General of the Island of Bombaim make to his Sacred Majesty Charles the Second, by the Grace of God, King of Great Brittaine, France and Ireland; Defendor of the Faith, etca.

Public Record Office, C. O. 77, Vol. IX, folio 64, No. 38.

MOST HIGH, MOST EXCELLENT, AND MOST PUISSANT KING, OUR LORD AND PRINCE.

The Inhabitants as well Catholiques as Mahometans and Gentiles Incorporated together, doe manifest unto your Majesty like Loyall Subjects; That, whereas this Island being formerly belonging to the Crowne of Portugall, there were in each Division thereof Foreiros Mayores, or Cheife Farmers; men powerfull, arrogant, and Exorbitant violators, Ecclesiastiques as well as Civil; whose manner of Government was absolute, bringing the inferior sort of us so much under, and

Public Record Office, C. O. 77, Vol. IX, folio 64 No. 38.

made so small accompt of them, as comparatively wee may say the Elephant doeth of the Ant; murdering whome they pleased arbitrarily, as if their will had been a sufficient reason, to satisfie their owne cruel lust against all Right whatsoever; they likewise robbed without the least consideration or feare of the Deity; not suffering the Kings Ministers to take any cognisance of the outrages they daily committed upon us; presumeing much upon their owne Greatnesse (being Fidalgos) and Riches, they had sucked from the vein's of the People, laying what impositions they of their meere wills pleased; which the Magistrates consented unto by the mediation of Bribes, which caused them in lieu of hearkning to our Complaints; rather to prejudice us by favouring, and conforming themselves to the practices of the Exorbitants. None could with liberty exercise their Religion, but the Roman Catholique; which is wonderfull confining with rigorous precepts. They tooke Orphan Children from whomsoever they pleased; and per force made them Christians; stopping the eare to the cryes of the mothers; and kinreds just Complaints of their discontents; Besides infinite other Tyrannies which are so many that tis impossible to sett them all downe in writeing, in so much that this Island was brought to so bad an Estate, so much consumed, so much desolated, and so very misserable; that it moved pity to behold it.

Haveing thus suffered for many yeares; it pleased God of his infinite Mercy to send us the Government of your Sacred Majesty (as a souveraigne medecine for our (otherise incureable) malady which through the malice of the said Exorbitants (who had bribed the Viz Rey Antonio de Mello de Castro) was delayed for a long time, we most anxiously wishing for; and impatiently expecting the good houre of the alteration; which not long since wee were blessed with. From the begining of which to this present, especially under the Government of Henry Gary Esq., wee have found very great tranquillity; every one enjoyeing his owne, with a great deale of liberty; and in Generall the free exersise of their Religion; experimenting universal justice, both small and Great, Rich, and Poore; And that which wee have most reason to celebrate this present Governour for, is, the expedient administration of justice; his continual assisting us with dispatches, the brevity which he uses in concluding our pleas, and his patience in heareing even the least of them; his kindnesse in voiding our expences; so just, disinteressed, pious and pacifique; that wee beseech God to affoord us still the like Government; And, because we have notice given us by what the said exorbitants publish, that they with great summes of money; and by intercession of the King of Portugall endeavour to reduce this Island to his Obedience (as formerly) and Confident hereupon, they thunder out their menaces; that they will have satisfaction for the obedience that wee have to this houre duly paid to your Majesty; Hereof wee doe not in the least doubt; but that they would Tyrannise over us, and shew us Hell in this World, from which Good Lord etca.

Wherefore, wee humbly beseech your Majesty for the love of God and for the wounds of Jesus Christ, to take pity and compassion of us by not consenting to alienate us from your Government, and the Obedience thereof upon any Consideration or agreement whatsoever;

neither to permitt any more Foreiros Mayores in this Island ; because every one was a justiciary in his owne house ; Sithence with the protection of your Sacred Majestys Name, and the Great faith all people had therein ; many came to inhabitt in this Island from other parts, and live subject to its Government ; employing their Stocks in building of Houses ; and buying of possessions for their livelyhood ; which would bee unjust now to bee consumed with the old hatred. For if wee had not experimented the clemency of your Majestys Government, wee should not have had so many quarrills and disputes with the Exorbitants, nor yet have laid out our moneys ; But the hopes affoorded us of your Majestys Paternal care, greatest reputation and piety, give us to believe ; that we shall receive your acceptance of this our Petition and Manifesto, and that your Majesty will graunt our desires herein, upon confidence hereof wee shall enjoy rest and quietnesse, by your Majestys mercy and Clemency.

Public Record Office, C. O. 77, Vol. IX, folio 64, No. 38.

The Originall of this Petition in Portuguez, which remains here in this Garrison of Bombaim upon Record, is signed by 225 of the principalest Inhabitants of this Island, vizt.

123 : Christians
84 : Gentuies
18 : Moores

225 persons in all.

[*Endorsed.*]

To His Sacred Majesty of great Britain.
The Humble Petition of the
Povo* of the Island of
Bombaim.
Its Copie in English.

* [*Note.*—A duplicate copy of the above is endorsed :]

" The Humble Petition of the Inhabitants of
the Island of Bombain.
To his Sacred Majesty,
Translated out of Portuguez."

[*In pencil.*] " Early part of Chas. II."

The following letters give us a glimpse into the tortuous course of the negotiations conducted by the Portuguese Viceroy with regard to Bombay. His policy is best summed up in the following extract from his letter dated December 28, 1662. " As a remedy for all the aforesaid there is only one thing, and that is for Your Majesty to buy this island from the King of England." He had originally suggested 200,000 to 300,000 *crusados* as a reasonable price ; he is now willing to pay double that amount. At the same time that he penned this Despatch, he expressed to the English Commander his readiness to deliver

Bombay provided all the formalities were duly observed. It is difficult to resist the conclusion that the defects in the Letters Patent were regarded as a convenient excuse for delaying the transfer, and this impression is changed to certainty by the perusal of his letter, quoted above. He saw "in the island of Bombay, so many Christian souls which some day will be forced to change their religion by the English," and he feared that the occupation of Bombay will ultimately result in the Portuguese losing "all to the north, as they will take away all your Majesty's trade." It is not surprising, then, to find him wrangling over the delivery of the island, and spinning out time, in the hope, I suppose, of receiving an order from the Portuguese King, reversing his decision. But these hopes were not likely to be realised, for the English Government had already made a representation to the Portuguese Government on the subject. Full account of the early stages of this controversy will be found in *The Report of the Historical MSS. Commission on the Heathcote MSS.* Here it is only necessary to bring out the leading stages of this quarrel. Sir Henry Bennett wrote the following Despatch to the English Ambassador in Portugal (May 14, 1663). "The dishonour and disappointment of such a thing, and the expense His Majesty hath been at to send for it, hath left him in the last resentments against this usage that can be imagined, and I am bid to tell Your Lordship that less than the Viceroy's head, and satisfaction for all the damages and expense His Majesty is exposed to by this disappointment, will not suffice to pay His Majesty for this affront; it being expected that what be done of this kind, and the possessing us of the aforesaid island—*which, by the way, is found to be far inferior to what it was represented*—come from Portugal itself, without the concurrence of any demands or diligences on our side." Two days later Lord Clarendon himself wrote to Fanshaw, the English Ambassador, stating that "if some sudden satisfaction be not given there will soon be an end of our alliance with Portugal." These were strong words, but they were not stronger than those employed by Shipman and others at the time. The Portuguese alliance seems, in fact, to have been thoroughly unpopular, and there was a concensus of opinion that the English Government had been tricked. Mr. Pepys opined that the "Portugese have choused us in the island of Bombay in the East Indys," and Mr. Pepys merely voiced the general feeling on the subject. Fanshaw's representation to the Portuguese Government seems to have had some effect, for the latter assured him that fresh instructions for the surrender of Bombay were being despatched. Fanshaw had added a suggestion that Bassein should be ceded in addition to Bombay. This demand seems to have surprised the Portuguese Court, and they failed to understand the reason for the addition of Bassein to their original demand. On July 25, the Portuguese Ambassador was informed that Charles insisted upon (1) the punishment of the Viceroy, (2) reparation for the expenses incurred, and (3) the cession of the whole of the territory " exhibited formerly to His Majesty in the map, containing not only Bombain, but Salzede (Salsette) and Taan (Thana)."

The King of Portugal, finally, sent an order to the Viceroy, on the 10th of August, 1663, and the energetic action of Charles proved eminently successful. The Portuguese King, however, never ceased to regret the loss of that jewel, and two years later we find him recurring to the proposal of the Viceroy, embodied in his Despatch of 28th December, 1662 (*see above*), ordering him to collect a large amount for the purchase of Bombay from Charles. The latter, it is clear, was prepared to restore it to the Portuguese, provided a substantial amount was paid. This, however, was impossible at the time, and Bombay remained in the hands of the English Government.

In pursuance of this treaty, the King of Portugal had already issued, on the 9th of April, 1662, the following orders to Antonio de Mello de Castro, two days before the issue of the alvara of his nomination as Governor of India, which ran thus :—

" I, King, send you greeting. By the article of the contract which has been agreed on with the King of England, my good brother and cousin, concerning the dowry portion of the Queen, his wife, my most beloved and esteemed sister, which you will receive with this letter, you will understand why and how the port and country of Bombay relates to him, and the obligation I am under for directing the same to be delivered to him. Immediately as you arrive at the states of India you will ask for the credentials from the King by which you will know the person to whom the possession should be given and the delivery made. You will accordingly cause the same to be made in the manner and form of that capitulation observing the same yourself and causing the whole and every part thereof to be duly observed, and direct that the whole may be committed to writing very clearly and distinctly so as at all time to appear the wole that may pass in this affair. You will further send the same to me by different conveyances in order to settle and adjust the acquittance of the dowry promised to the King, and by the other articles of that treaty it will be present to you, the union we celebrated, and the obligation the King has to afford me succour in all my urgencies and necessity I may have. In any necessity you may find it convenient to apply to the English you will do so, at the same time you will assist them in the same way. KING. Written at Lisbon the 9th April 1662."

In justification of his refusal to obey His Majesty's commands, he wrote to the King on the 28th of December, 1662, the following letter :—

" Sir,—It is a more on account of the duty of the post than from any need with the English, who will themselves make them known. For there were many who reproved the excesses of Captain Richard Minors in whose company I came to this State. And General Marlborough continued them with greater harshness even in the Port of Bombay.

"From the report sent with this letter your Majesty will be able to learn that not a day was passed without molestation, and I was sometimes warned that they wanted to kill all the Portuguese. Their senseless provocations might have well led us to use arms in revenge ; but I contented myself with keeping them ready for defence. With more attention to your Majesty's service than to my life, I bore the risk and slights, expecting to send to your Majesty my complaints. I hope the world will see that my patience has not injured my reputation, but on the contrary has increased it for being in the service of your Majesty, who knows to greatly appreciate it, as all my sufferings tend to your Majesty's service.

" It did not appear convenient to hand over the Island of Bombay, as the British refused me assistance every time I asked for it, and Marlborough went so far as to undeceive me not only by words, stating that the capitulations were formal (*modo geral*) and involved no obligation, but also, by actions, handing over wickedly to the Moors of Anjaianne 42 of your Majesty's vassals, among whom there were 27 Christians, whom I had with me in the vessel. They did this in so barbarous a manner and such indecency, that they took from my arms a little child which I had sheltered with the mother in my cabin, because three days before I have stood its god-father at the baptism.

" The reason for not surrendering the island was the same order which I had received from your Majesty, and which I must obey ; and as neither I nor the councillors understand it, it is necessary to report the very words written by your Majesty on this matter, reminding that in case of doubt it was my duty to seek the sense most convenient for your service. The letter says :—"As soon as you arrive at the State of India you shall demand the King's warrant, and thereby you will know the person to whom the possession should be given and the delivery made."

" Abraham Shipman gave me, instead of the warrant, which I asked for, a sealed letter written in Latin, and Letters Patent in English. The letter had defects, as mentioned in the statement I ordered to be written, and the Letters Patent had not the signature of the King of England. I doubted the validity of the one and the other, as all the Letters Patent I have ever seen had the Royal Signature ; and there could be no more reason for the omission in this case than in my letter which was signed. Is it the practice in England for the King to sign or not ? If it is, how is it that the Letters Patent were not signed ; if it is not, how was then the letter signed ? Besides

I thought that there was a difference between the warrant and the missive letter. The letter is for one to whom it is addressed, the warrant is for the public. If Royal Persons do not write warrants as we do, they write instead Letters Patent, which are public and not private or missive letters. If I doubted, Sire, the letter which they call a warrant, how could I hand them over the place, as the conditions under which your Majesty's instructions were given were wanting?

"The same letter from your Majesty to me says that you will know the person to whom the possession should be given and the delivery made. You will accordingly cause the same to be made in the manner and form of that capitulation observing the same yourself and causing the whole and every part thereof to be duly observed.

"The secret chapter which your Majesty sent me says, that the King of England agrees to arrange peace between your Majesty and the Dutch on honourable, advantageous, and safe terms for your Majesty, and, in the event of the Dutch not agreeing to the terms, he will send such a fleet as will defend and protect the Portuguese possessions in India, and that his fleet shall be sent at the same time as the instructions for the handing over of Bombay are given.

"If your Majesty orders me to hand over Bombay, in accordance with the terms of the capitulations, it follows that I cannot hand it over in another form. The terms of the capitulations require that the King of England shall first arrange the treaty of peace; that the Dutch should first either agree to the terms or not and continue the war, and that a sufficient fleet sent to help us in the latter case. Allow me, your Majesty, to copy here the same words from the Latin, which are more powerful than in Portuguese. *Qui, si hujusmodi conditiones concedere recusaverint, tunc dictus Magnæ Britaniæ Rex, cum classem suam ad capiendam possessionem portus, et Insulae Bombaym miserit, tales ac tantas copias simul mittet, instructas tam viribus, quam mandatis, ut possint defendere, ac potegere omnes Lusitanorum possessiones in Indiis Oriantatibus.* So that the King of England, cannot take possession of Bombay, untill after the treaty of peace is made or refused and (*tunc*) then, which is the word exclusive of any other time, if peace is not made he shall take possession, and at the same time send the said fleet with the power and orders to defend us. If your Majesty orders me to surrender in the mode and form of these capitulations, and in no other manner, as said above, when the treaty of peace is neither accepted nor refused, and no fleet has arrived, except three ships, without neither force nor orders to help us, how can I account to your Majesty for delivering the island of Bombay?

"Moreover, I see the best port your Majesty possesses in India with which that of Lisbon is not to be compared, treated as of little value by the Portuguese themselves, I see in the island of Bombay so many Christian souls which some day will be forced to change their religion by the English. How will they allow Catholics to reside in their territories when they hand our Catholics in the island of Anjuame to the Moors? I considered also that your Majesty has no other place to receive and shelter your Majesty's ships and the gallions of your fleet when that bar is closed. The English once there, and the island fortified, your Majesty will lose all to the north, as they will take away all your Majesty's trade. They bring the same articles as we do, and of better quality; they will compel all vessels to be put into that harbour and lay duties as we did formerly, we shall have to receive from them what England sought from us; even the provisions of our land which supply all our fortress, we shall have to buy from them because giving one or two xerafins more for each mura of rice they will gather all and sell afterwards for its weight in gold. Do not believe, your Majesty, that it will be possible to prevent it, for no dilligence will be enough, and that was the manner in which the Moghals have destroyed those lands, through which cause many persons have died from famine. It is yet possible to prevent them from taking away the provisions, for which I have left in those parts necessary instruction. But it is impossible in Bombay, because it is separated from Salsette by only a cannon shot, and it would have to spend more in keeping watch than it would yeild in revenue. Lastly the criminals will find a shelter, and if with the neighbourhood of the Moors they commit so many crimes, how daring will they be with that security?

"That English are at peace with us now, but what would it be in case of war? How can those islands which are the graneries of India, once wedged in between the British and the Mogores (Moghuls) be defended? Who can prevent the natives from passing over; what drugs and merchandise will traders go to Goa in search of?

"I have shown how I have obeyed your Majesty's orders by preserving the reputation of your Majesty's arms, and prevented the total loss and destruction of your Majesty's teritarries by not handing over Bombay.

"Now let your Majesty command the consideration of this subject, remembering that seeing is different from hearing; and as you are my King and Lord, I do my duty in giving this information, that your Majesty may order what is convenient. If it is not liked, I shall be sorry, but it suffices that no blame be attached to me at any time.

"As a remedy for all the aforesaid there is only one thing, and that is for your Majesty to buy this island from the King of England. In another letter to your Majesty I say that your Majesty can give from 200 to 300,000 *crusados* (£25,000 to £37,500) in three years, now I say your Majesty can give 500,000, 600,000. May I undertake to say that all in this state, who would be pleased to be free from such a yoke, would assist in carrying out the arrangement? This purchase will further help to make peace firmer with the English, because such a neighbourhood will occasion every day discontent and strife ending in war. It is necessary to be careful and cautious in this affair, in order that English may know that your Majesty's only motive is the resistance from this State and your desire to remove the discontent from your vassals, because if they understand otherwise everything else will be of little moment to them.

"Forgive your Majesty the fault that may be found in this letter, because the zeal and love with which I writ well deserve it. God preserve the most high and powerful person of your Majesty, as your vassals have need. *Goa 28th December*, 1662."

ANTONIO DE MELLO DE CASTRO.

The King of Portugal had sent to the Viceroy, on the 16th of August, 1663, the following order :—

"I, King, send you greeting. By the way of England, intelligence reached me that in the State of India doubts arose with respect to the delivery of the town of Bombay to the order of the King of Great Britain, my good brother and cousin, in conformity of mine which you carried with you. At this I was greatly surprised and am very sorry, because, besides the reasons of convenience of this Crown, and more especially of the State of India, which made it necessary for me to take that resolution, I wish much to give the King of England, my brother, every satisfaction. For these and other considerations of the same identity, as well as because the King, my brother, must have sent fresh orders, removing every doubt there might have originated from those he sent first, I therefore direct and order that you do, in compliance with those orders of mine which you carried with you, cause to execute the said delivery with every punctually and without the least consideration, as the matter does not admit of any, and the delay is very prejudicial. By complying therewith, as I expect from you, I will consider myself well served by you. If you meet with any impediment from any person, you will order to proceed against him publicly as the case may require. *Written at Lisbon, the* 16*th of August* 1663. KING. THE COUNT OF CASTELLO MELHOR."

The next letter of the King is dated February 8, 1664, and is as follows :—

"By your letter which has been brought to us overland by Manuel Godinho, a Religious of the Company of Jesus, I saw with great pain the difficulties which have been arisen with regard to the delivery of Bombay to the King of Britain, my brother and cousin, according to the capitulations, and the orders I gave you when you left. Whatever is stipulated in the capitulations and reasons for giving contentment to the King, my brother, admits of no doubt; and I trust that with your prudence you have now arranged matters so far that you will carry out my instructions without further delay. Should any fresh difficulties present themselves, I order you to overcome them in a manner that I may feel grateful to you. To the inhabitants of the island you must say that they have misunderstood the Article of Capitulation shown them, as their estates (*fazendas*) will not be confiscated but they will be allowed to remain in possession of them as hetherfore. The only difference will be that they will live under the dominion of the King of Great Britain, my brother, who will rule them with justice and in the freedom of the Roman Catholic religion as it is the practice in Europe among many peoples and cities with similar treaties, and with his power he will defend them and secure them in their trade, that they may attain to the opulence they desire. The King of England also undertakes to protect the places I have in that State, and this was one of the reasons for my giving him that island. The inhabitants of the island are so closely allied by nationality, parentage, and convenience to the best of the Portuguese all over India that I consider the arrangement will be for their common good. You must use all the means in your power to hand over the place soon, as this affair will admit of no delay. Immediately the delivery has taken place you will advise me, as it is of the utmost importance that it should be known here. *Written at Lisbon in Salvaterra de Magos (sic) 8th of February,* 1664. KING. THE COUNT OF CASTELLO MELHOR. For Antonio de Mello de Castro."

The following letter addressed by the Viceroy to the Supreme Court at Goa throws further light on the question :—

Goa :—"I have received a letter from His Majesty, whom God preserve, ordering me to deliver Bombay, but I do not know to whom to deliver it, as Abraham Shipman, in whose behalf the King of England had issued the commission, is dead, and it is not transferable to any other person. And as this order is identical with the one I brought with me, directing that I should demand the credentials from the King to the person to whom the possession of the island shall be given and the delivery made, commiting the whole to writing in order to avoid any uncertainty for all time, in virtue of the capitulations, I thought the matter to belong rather to law and sent the letter and the warrant to the court, requesting them to decide in the mode judicial for the delivery of the Island, thus satisfying both the King of England with what has been promised him, and the King our Lord, by obeying strictly his orders, writing a statement of all the circumstances, as the letter requires and the right demands. I request the magistrate (*desembargadores*) that after reading the papers, and weighing the words, they send me their opinions in writing, to be discussed in the Council of the State, and to settle all other points relating to this affair, and all to be done as quickly as possible. *Panelim, 3rd of November* 1664. ANTONIO DE MELLO DE CASTRO."

The last letter of the Viceroy refers to the same subject.

"Sire :—By the way of England has reached me this year a letter from your Majesty on the surrender of Bombay. Although the warrant that was shown to me was more doubtful than the first, being addressed to a man who was dead, and had no successor ; but, understanding that it was your Majesty's pleasure, and the whole council having decided that possession should be given without further delay, and the Supreme Court of Judicature being of opinion that the warrant, notwithstanding its form, was sufficient, I ordered the Vedor da Fazenda and the Chancellor of the State to proceed to the north for this purpose, and gave them directions (*regimento*) a copy of which I send herewith. I confess at the feet of your Majesty that only the obedience I owe your Majesty, as a *vassal,* could have forced me to this deed, because I forsee the great troubles that from this neighbourhood will result to the Portuguse ; and that India will be lost the same day in which the English nation is settled in Bombay. I have faithfully responded to the trust your Majesty has reposed in me, appointing me to this post and to the honour I have inherited from my ancestors. I have been actuated by these feelings during all the time I have been informing your Majesty of the inconvenience of this resolution, giving my reasons for not surrendering the island. I hope from the greatness of your Majesty that after seeing my papers, you will commend the judgement of my acts, and that they will be found to be in accordance with my duty. Your Majesty being well served of my zeal is the only reward I aspire to. God preserve the Catholic and Royal Person of your Majesty as Christendom and vassals have need. *Goa, 5th of January,* 1665. ANTONIO DE MELLO DE CASTRO."

The following letter from the Portuguese monarch is addressed to the Viceroy, Antonio de Mello de Castro, and runs thus:—

"I, King, send you greeting. On account of the difficulties raised for the delevery of Bombay, I despatched to England Francisco Ferreira Rebello charged with this affair alone, to try to compose this matter, and the Marquis of Sande, my Ambassador Extraordinary, who was in that Court, made all diligence, and finally the King, my good brother, by the goodwill he has for my things, allowed the consideration of an indemnity in money; but he wants such large sums that they reach to millions. Thus it is necessary to make great efforts and to use all means to collect them. As it is not possible to settle this affair without giving at first a considerable sum and as this kingdom with the wars with Castile is found to be in want of means which is well known, it is necessary to draw as great a part of this amount from the State of India, as according to what you wrote me upon the subject it may be possible to obtain. For this reason I order and much recommend that, in the manner that you may deem convenient, you try to collect without deley a contribution, and remit by the first ship all that you can, in order that in case any settlement be arrived at, whatsoever sum is necessary may be ready. And in case it fails the sum collected would remain as a contribution of peace with Holland. This matter being so important to all people, I trust they will contribute with the goodwill that the matter demands, and you will be doing me a particular service in preparing every thing that there is need of. *Written at Lisbon, 15th of April* 1663. KING. THE COUNT OF CASTELLO MELHOR."

The following letters from Cooke trace the progress of the occupation of Bombay by the King's officers, and record the difficulties encountered by him in arriving at a satisfactory arrangement of this dispute. Shipman, it is clear from Cooke's letter of August 26, 1664, died on April 6 of the same year and not in October, as has been alleged by several historians. Cooke's long letter of March 6, 1664, will be found interesting, as in it we can perceive the beginnings of that friction between the King's and the Company's officers which led later on to the cession of Bombay to the Company. It was clear to Charles, and no less evident to the Company, that the existence of two independent authorities within the same sphere would engender ceaseless strife and continual bickering. This was illustrated in the governorship of Cooke. The island was handed over to Cooke in February, and the quaint ceremony is described thus. Cooke, we are informed, "took himself personally the possession and delivery of the said port and town of Bombay, walking thereupon, taking in his hand earth and stones, entering and walking upon its bastions, putting his hands to the walls thereof, and making all other like acts which in right were necessary without any impediment or contradiction." Cooke's account of Bombay will be read with interest by its citizens to-day. "In this Island," he informed the Government, " was neither Government nor Justice, but all cases of Law was (were) carried to Tanny and Bassein." Bombay yielded " nothing but a greate quantity of Coco Nuts and Rice with other necessary provisions."

Cooke's administration of the island pleased neither the King nor the English Company, and they were, on the whole, justified in repudiating his Treaty with the Portuguese. A copy of this Treaty is given below. Careful perusal of this convention shows clearly that the Portuguese were justified in exercising some of the vexatious rights which became a source of constant trouble, as they had been expressly guaranteed by Cooke's Treaty. This was due partly to the apathy of the English Government, who did not repudiate it until after twelve years. Had the " unjust capitulation " to which Charles refers in his letter, printed herewith, been denounced in 1665, the long and tedious correspondence and vexatious retaliatory measures would have been avoided. Both Cooke's Treaty and Charles' letter repudiating it are given below.

Public Record Office, C. O. 77, Vol. IX, folio 91.

HONOURABLE SIR,

The 6th of Aprill 1664 it pleased Almightie God to Calle the Hon'ble Sir Abraham Shipman our Govarnour out of this world, who was pleased to nominate mee Lt: Govarnour to take Care and Charge of his Majesties forces and Affaires in these parts of India, while further orders Comes from England, the which I have excepted Rather then all should goe to Ruine, here not Remaining any person fitt to mannaige the same. By accidente I Remained here my selfe, I shall now doe my dewty and bee Redey at all tymes to bee accountabell when Ever his Majestie please to Command; wee are daylie expecting orders from his Majestie for our Removeing to Bombaim, to bee Cleared of this Unhouldsum Island wheare wee have loste upwards of 250 menn and at presant but one Commision Officer, An Ensigne, alive of all that came out of England, there hath not binn any maide, because to make his Majesties monnys hould out which I hope hee will please to Consider; Sir Abraham Shipman was lickwise pleased to make mee overseear of what Estate hee hath in these parts, the which I cannot Justly advise his executours whilest his Majesties Account bee adjusted, In case there should bee any obgection therein. I hope his Majestie will bee pleased to Consider my willingnes to searve hime haveing Lost my other occationes to Live here in this Remote, Malancolly, Sickly Island to doe him Searvis, besides the extriordinary Charges I am at as Govarnour in housekeeping and Servants which

Cannott bee Avoyded for our nations honnour, the Caire I have of his Majesties Affaires here wanting soe manny Officers and of his Actions &ca. for all which I hope shall desarve the same pay our deasceced Govarnour had which is 40*s*. per day.

Public Record Office, C. O. 77, Vol. IX, folio 91.

I moste humblie pettition for your Honnours favor to Communicate this to his Majestie and when hee pleasseth to Grant mee the said for my Searvisses with a Commision for one yeare or two to sarve as Govarnour in Bombaim I shall as my dewty is except thereof but other waies would bee as willingly Cleared, the Charges being soe great that none cann live in India as a Govarnour ought honnorabley Under the said pay at leaste. I shall esteeme of ann order that I may pass it to his Majesties Account for the tyme I have searved and other waies to Searve if it be his Majesties pleassure I Continuew.

I hope hee bee fully satisfied of my Loyallty and fidelity seeing Sir Abraham Shipman hath binn pleassed to Impose soe Great a truste to mee, which God willing shall all punctually bee parformed. I shall nott further Troubell your Honnour these goeing ovar land by our Shiping shall more Inlarge.

I Remaine Evar
Your Honnours most Humble
and Obedient Sarvant
HUMFREY COOKE.

ANGEDIVA ISLAND IN EASTE INDIA,
the 26th *Auguste* 1664.

[*Endorsed.*]
Anchediva No. 1 : 26 *August* 64.

Mr. H. Cooke
The Govarnours Letter to the
princepall Secretary of State
1664/5.

[The following is inserted as a title at the beginning of the document.]

Mr. Cooks Letter to the Secretary of State upon the Death of Sir Abraham Shipman and his Succeeding in the Government.

The Worshippfull Humphrey Cooke Comander in chiefe of his Majesties Forces in East India Governour of Bombay and Ange Deevar, &c^a^.

Public Record Office, C. O. 77, Vol. IX, folio 98.

Captain James Barker, Captain Robert Bowen and Mr. Charles Higgenson, Comanders and Officers of the Shipps *Royall Charles*, *London* and *America* at Anchor in the Roade of Carwarr. Wheras I have received severall Orders from the Kings Majestie of England and the King of Portugall to the Vice Roy and Councell of Goa, Concerning the surrendring of the Island of Bombay; It is agreed and concluded by the said Vice Roy and Councell that they are ready to deliver upp the said Island according to the Articles between the two Crownes; and hath given mee notice thereof to Embarque my

Public Record Office, C. O. 77, Vol. IX, folio 98.

selfe, all other Officers and Soldjers, to take possession of the aforesaid Island of Bombay in our Kings Majesties behalfe: And to take in our way, a person at Goa to effect the said delivery. Wee having not Shipping here at present sufficient to Transport us, and not knowing what may happen herafter, concerning the above said premisses by delay.

I doe by these require you, the said Captain James Barker, Captain Robert Bowen and Mr. Charles Higgenson Officers &c. in the Kings Majesties name, as you will answer the contrary at your perrill, your assistance herin with your Shipps and men to Transporte my self and said Soldjery, with our Lumber to the said Island of Bombay, which is in your way to Surratt, and you shall have what satisfaction the President Sir George Oxinden shall thinck fitt for the said Transportation. In complyance herin you will doe good service to the King's Majestie, and on the contrary will bee prejudiciall both to the Crowne and Nation.

I desire answer to give Account to his Majestie of my obedience to his Comands. *Dated on Ange Deeva the 26th day of November* 1664.

HUMFREY COOK.

[*Endorsed.*]

Angediva No. 3 : *November* 26, 1664.

Mr. H. Cooke.

A coppy of a Protest made on Ange Deeva for the transporting my selfe and Soldjery for the Island of Bombay in November 26th 1664. To Captain Robert Bowen, Captain James Barker and Mr. Charles Higgenson, Commanders of the East India Companies Shipps.

Public Record Office, C. O. 77, Vol. IX, folio 221.

HON'BLE.

I writt your Honor overland of the 26th August 1664 therin advised of the death of the Hon'ble Sir Abraham Shipman our Governor, of which here inclosed send a Coppy. The *Chesnut Pinck* arrived at Ange Deeva from Persia the 25th October 1664, who brought a Pacquet from his Majestie via Aleppo Dated 26th November 1663, with a Letter inclosed to the Vice Roy of Goa, Don Antonio de Milo de Castro, from the King of Portugall, and second Orders from our Kings Majestie for our receiving the Island of Bombaim, att which, on their receipt, I ordered the *Chesnut Pinck* to saile for Goa, and sent one with the aforesaid Letters and other papers necessary from my selfe to the Vice Roy, demanding in the King's Majestie my Masters name the possession of the said Island of Bombaim and all else as was agreed on by the Articles of peace between the two Crownes: hee received the King of Portugalls Letter with much Ceremony, and answered hee would Comply in the surrender according to the King his Masters Order, withall said hee must have two or three daies time to advise with his Councell: after which the said Vice Roy demands the Orders Sir Abraham Shipman had from our Kings Majestie to Constitute a Lieutenant Governor and my Commission from him: I sent him Coppies of both the said Sir Abrahams Commission under the greate Seale of England and my owne, having them authentickly Confirmed by witnesses, and ordered them to bee Translated into Portuguees, and then to present them (with another Letter I writt him) to the same effect of my first, since which, by the Companies Shipp *London*, I received one from his Majestie to Sir Abraham Shipman deceased, Dated 14th and 17th of March 1663* with a Duplicate of the King of Portugalls Letter to his Vice Roy, the which was sent him and delivered. After a Months debate, both hee and the Councell at Goa concluded a surrender must bee made, and ordered papers to bee drawne upp to that effect, all of them signing for the said surrender. The Vice Roy imediately writt mee to Ange Deeva that it was Concluded to make a rendition to us soe desires that I provide myselfe and Soldjery to receive the Island of Bombaim in our Kings Majesties name and that I should goe to Goa for Orders, and that at my arrivall hee would nominate two persons to goe with mee to deliver us possession. Wee having noe shipps to Transporte our men and Lumber, I dispatched the *Chesnut Pinck* to Surrat to Sir George Oxinden, and sent him a Coppie of the Agreement of the Vice Roy and Councell to Surrender us Bombaim, and that now wee onely wanted Shipping to Transporte us upp.

Public Record Office, C. O. 77, Vol. IX folio 221.

*1663/4.

Therefore I desired him in our Kings Majesties name to order us Shipping for our Transporting, and that when that could not bee donne at Surrat, hee would please to send his Orders to the Commanders of the Compaines Shipps then being at Carwarr lading Pepper, that they might take the Soldjery and Lumber in and Land us at Bombaim, which was in their way to Surrat, and would not have bin 15 daies hindrance to them; herin I send you a Coppie of the said Sir George Oxindens answer to mine, by which you will perceive that hee neither Orders us Shipping, nor writes the Commanders of the Compaines Shipps to effect it, which if hee had, t'would have bin imediately donne, but on the contrary quite discourages us for the taking possession of Bombaim on sleight pretences: which when I received imediately made a protest or demand in his Majesties name to all the Commanders of the Compaines Shipps to Transporte us, their answer (with the Protest) goeth here inclosed, which please to peruse, by which you will find what little service the Compaine or Sir George Oxinden doth here for his Majesties affaires.

I finding our Nation soe backward, and that nothing would prevaile for our Transporting, this bussines being of soe greate importance, both for his Majestie and Nation, and not to let slipp the proffer of the Vice Roy and Councell of Goa, for feare of other resolutions herafter, although it hath bin much to the discredit of our Nation our owne Shipps not Transporting us: I hired fower Barkes at Goa to effect it with our *Pinck* and *Sloope*, which carried all our Soldjery and Lumber; the danger and ill accomodation hath bin much, but rather then to remaine at Ange-Deeva the men were willing to anything. At our arrivall at Goa, before I could get the dispatches for the two persons to bee nominated to goe with us to make the delivery passed a full Month, the Soldjery and my selfe lying aboard in the hott Sunn all the time, which was not a little troublesome,

Public Record Office, C. O. 77. Vol. IX, folio 221.

besides the severall abuses received from the Vice Roy, some of our Soldjers that had run away from Ange-Deeva were taken by our people in the Road of Goa going aboard a Portugall Vessell, and were brought to mee aboard the *Pinck*, the Captain of the *Castle* by the Vice Roy's Order would have Commanded them ashoare, which I refused being our Kings Majesties Subjects, upon which there was a greate broile, to advise the particulars would bee tedious: I was forced to deliver them that our bussines of Bombaim should not cease, the which I did to the Vice Roy himselfe, with caution, that hee should secure them and see them forthcoming at demande whenever our Kings Majestie should require them, but hee litle regarded that, but sent them aboard his Vessell that was bound for Europe, and tooke severall other Englishmen from the East India Compaines Shipps and did the like, which hath bin noe small affront to our Nation. Some tenn daies after this hee writes mee, that the persons were nominated, and in a redines to Embarque for Bombaim to make the Rendition, and sends mee a paper that containes severall Articles and Conditions made by him, that I should observe and signe after the Receipt of the Island, which to excuse disputes, promised I would, and did, as appeareth by said papers of the Rendition, for otherwise there would have bin one thing or other to have excused the delivery while further Orders from Europe. Our boates wee came in were rotten and ready to sinck, soe could not possibly have held out any longer, if there had bin made anie scruple or doubt in the delivery of the Island, But now I have the possession shall observe noe more his Articles then what is Convenient. Herin I remitt the papers of the said Rendition, by which you will see all the particulars therin, and may perceive his willingnes to bee troublesome, that wee might not have the surrender; in regard hee nominated noe person that shall receive the Island for our Kings Majestie but sait[h] that it shall bee delivered to the Gentlemen English. The persons that were to make the Rendition scrupled at it, soe cost some trouble to cleare. Wee set saile from Goa toward Bombaim in the aforesaid Boates the 7th January 1664 accompained with 10 Galliotts, that brought the Chancelor of Goa and the Viasor dafazanda, whome were the persons appointed to make the surrender of Bombaim; both were very antient men, by the way they fell sick, soe put into Chaule where wee staied 8 daies for their recovery: the 2nd February 1664 wee arrived at Bombaim, being there detained on board six daies more, while the City and Gentrey of Bassin came to bee present at the delivery as witnesses, the 8th February we Landed our men in Armes, to receive the Island in our Kings Majesties name, which was donne with all the Ceremony and honor could bee, what they deliver'd was onely two small Bulworks, some Earth and Stones (the Ceremony for the Island) as appeareth by the papers of the Rendition. The King of Portugall (as they say) hath neither house, Fort, Amunition nor foote of Land on it, onely the aforrowes or Rents, which is but small, importing about 700lb. yearely. The two Bulworkes they delivered (Donna Ennes da Miranda claimes to bee hers) and appeareth soe with the house. Our Kings Majestie hath nothing more then the Rents that the King of Portugall had, with the Island and Port, which being wholy unfortyfied will cost much monies to make it defenceable by Sea and Land, which must be donne if his Majestie intends to make any thing of it.

At present I shall onely make a Platforme for our security while further Orders from his Majestie, which with the two Bulworkes will hold all our Ordnance. It will bee very necessary two or three small Forts more (with a Wall about the Towne) For which shall want Guns and Orders, with effects to accomplish the same.

Public Record Office, C. O. 77, Vol. IX, folio 221.

In this Island was neither Government nor Justice, but all cases of Law was carried to Tannay and Bassin, now it is in his Majesties Jurisdiction there must bee a setlement of Justice, according to such Lawes as his Majestie shall think fitt. For the present I have nominated for the whole Island a Tannadar, which is a kind of an under Captain ; hee had the place afore with 300 Serapheems a yeare, I am to allow him as much, I have likewise nominated a Justice of peace, to examine all causes with a Bailiffe, that matters being brought to a head, they may make report to mee, to sentence as I shall see cause, I have likewise nominated two persons to take care of Orphants Estates, one for the white people and one for the Black, as it was formerly ; with other Officers under them. I have enordered a Prison to bee made to keepe all in quietness, obedience and subjestion, these people generally being very litigious. I have alsoe nominated two Customers, one at Maym and another at this place ; if our monies will reach shall build in each place a house for his Majesties Account, which will bee very necessary to recover his Customes. In the Island are five Churches, nine Townes and Villages, and upwards of 20,000 soules, as the Padres have given mee an Account ; the generall Language is Portugueez, soe that it will be necessary the Statutes and Lawes should bee Translated into that Language: the people most of them are very poore; as yet wee have bin here but a short time; as I find occasion shall nominate what other Officers shall bee necessary. I intend as soone as may bee to have a generall Muster, to know what Armes are in the Island, and by the next opportunity give you an Account therof.

This Island yeildeth at present nothing but a greate quantity of Coco Nutts and Rice with other necessary provissions. The Jesiuts are much troubled at our being here, and strives all may bee to make us odious to the people, and hath already attempted to take Orphants off this Island, of the Gentues, Moores and Banians, to force them to bee Christians which if should bee suffered wee shall never make any thing of this place, for the liberty of Conscience makes all the aforenamed desirous to live amongst us. I shall doe all may bee to give them encorougement, as his Majestie Commands in his Instructions. They desire to have Churches, but for the present I have not granted it, neither shall till I have further Orders for it. If I should the Portugalls will strange * in regard they looke on it as a scandall to their Church, for the present I have ordered they use their Ceremonies in their houses privately, but are not to give scandall to any. It will bee requisite that Orders bee sent what shall bee donne in this particular, finding how necessary it is to Fortyfy this place (according to his Majesties Comands) our monies being short to effect it, I writt to Sir George Oxinden to know his resolution whether hee will supply us or not, with monies to compleate the said Fortiffication, his answer herin I remit, that his Majestie may see how unwilling they are to doe any good Office for his affaires, notwithstanding the East India

* [sic]

Public Record Office, C. O. 77, Vol. IX, folio 221.

Company at home certifyeth him that they have enordered their President to supply us with all things that shall bee necessary; which Sir George Oxinden takes noe notice off at all, but on the contrary is troubled wee are setled here, saying theire Trade is now lost. According to his Majesties Comands, I have administred the Oath of Allegiance to all our owne people and some of the Inhabitants, herafter I shall tender it to all the rest that are of a Capacity to receive it, as yet have not found any deny to take it.

This Island lyeth excelent well seated for Trade, both for the South Seas, Red Seas, Gulph of Persia, Coast of Mallabarr, Cormondell, Bay of Bangaule, Pegu and other places; tis a very wholsome aire and pleasant, its some 8 Miles in length, and five Miles and a halfe broad, severall Merchants begins to Flock hither already from all parts, soe that I question not, but in a short tyme it may bee as beneficiall to our Kings Majestie as Battavia is now to the Dutch, it will cost monies to fortyfy it as it ought, but in a short time noe question it will repay its charges with proffit. Herein I remitt you a Coppy of the King of Portugalls Patent given for part of the Customes of Maym, a Towne and Port in this Island, for soe many lives as appeares in it, they paying onely 240 serapheens rent to the King for the Customes, which is but small in Consideration of what that Port rents. I shall desire to know whether the Patent is to stand in force now the Island belongs to our Kings Majestie, here are severall that holds Lands and other rents for lives on the same Terms, therefore it will bee necessary to know his Majesties pleasure herin. Since I had the possession of this Island I have writt to the Vice Roy at Goa, demanding in his Majesties name all the Rents that hath bin due to him since the arrivall of his Fleete here, with my Lord of Marlebrough, which was in September 1662, the said Vice Roy then constituting himselfe Governor of this Island for our Kings Majestie, soe noe question but he received the Rents to his use, what his answer will bee know not, but hope his Majestie will demand it of the King of Portugall in case hee gives not satisfaction here, which is to bee feared.

For the advancement of this Port it will bee necessary to procure from the Court of Portugall the priviledge of Navigating in that Kings currents and streames here, freely and without any manner of impediment, for all Boates and Vessells whatsoever that shall bee bound to this Island with Merchandize belonging to either English, Moores, Persians or Banian Merchants, from and to two places lying beyond Tannay upon the Terra firme in the Mogolls Dominions, the one called Cullian and the other Buimdy, where (if ever this bee made a good Port) all goods of Indostan growth and make, as well as those of Decan, Gulcondan and the Coast of Cormondell, must necessarily bee brought, which will make them cheaper by 15 or 20 Cent then those that are carried to Surrat, in regard of the great distance from it and vecinity to the two prementioned places. And wheras those goods, brought to the aforesaid Townes, must there bee Shipped off and pass downe the River by Tannay, in all probability (if provision bee not made to prevent the same) the King of Portugalls ministers there may lay imposition upon and take Custome for them, as the King of Denmarke doth in the Sound at Elsenore. And for the making this Port more Flourishing, Orders from his Majestie will alsoe bee necessary for the building six Briganteens or Galliots for keeping the Coast heraboutes free from Mallabarrs, who doe very much infest the same to the greate detriment of Trade.

Public Record Office, C. O. 77, Vol. IX, folio 221.

Herin I remit a generall Muster of all persons that are actually in his Majesties service on this Island, taken by Mr. Henry Gary, who is the person Sir George Oxinden, Knight, enordered to doe it (as his Majestie Comands), by which you may perceave our weake Condition to defend our selves and keepe these Islanders in obedience, out of which am forced to send 20 men to Maym to remaine there to keepe them under likewise, his Majestie will plainely see, how necessary it will bee a good recruit both of Officers and Soldjers, which, to save his monies, I have not made any, soe that my care hath bin the more in officiating my selfe all the Officers places that are wanting; which service I doubt not but his Majestie will please to consider.

Herin I send his Majestie an Account of all pay and other disbursements since Sir Abraham Shipman, deceased, entred the service, and myselfe, which is from February 1661 to the 3rd December, 1664, by which hee may please to perceave what greate husbands said Sir Abraham and myselfe have bin in saving his Majesties monies by not making Officers as they died, and in laying it out for other things necessary, as Account; which if had not donne, his said monies would not have held out neare soe long; by the said Account you may perceave the Monthly pay according to the Muster Rolls, which remaines in my Custody. I assure you they have bin duely and exactly taken every Month, as his Majestie hath Comanded, by the declining of the said Rolls, its plainely seene how our men died Monthly. The six Months they were at Sea on the Voyage could noe Muster bee taken, the Shipps being seperated nor upwards of three Months they were at Surrat, the Governor there not permitting them to Land with Armes or Drum, this my Lord Marlebrough knowes to bee true, soe doubt not but hee hath acquainted his Majestie therof; besides Sir Abraham Shipman was that tyme at Goa and Busseene, following the demand with the Vice Roy and Councell for the possession of Bombaim, soe could not bee donne. Our first Muster after wee came out of England was taken on the Island of Ange Deeva the 30th day of January 1662, and hath continued on exactly every Month since as per the Rolls and the Account appeareth in the said Account. Sir Abraham Shipman charges every private Soldjer *3d.* per day for the six Months they were aboard Shipp, the other sixpence being discounted for his Majestie for their Victualls, and is not charged in this Account, the *3d.* is for Clothes, Shirts, Stockings and Shoes to every one as it was ordered in England by his Majestie to bee given aboard Shipp, the which was observed, soe that what Soldjer died aboard, their *3d.* per day would not pay for their Clothes they received, which loss Sir Abraham Shipman sustaines.

The Carriadges wee brought out for our Ordnance, and those wee received from his Majesties Shipps in India, are all rotten and eaten with the Wormes, and fitt for nothing but Firing, as by the Certificate which herin remit for satisfaction. I have bin forced to make and buy all new ones, which otherwise our Guns would have stood us in little stead, they then lying on the ground at Ange Deeva,

Public Record Office, C. O. 77, Vol. IX, folio 221.

I doubt not but Sir Abraham Shipman gave his Majestie a large Account in his life of all things else wanting, therefore I shall not trouble your honor further, referring to what hee writt from Ange Deeva by the Shipp *Loyall Merchant* the last yeare. I hope when his Majestie seeth our sad Condition, he will please to Comand wee have Succour sent us in September next 1665, as well Commision Officers and Soldjers and all else that is wanting: for otherwise it will bee impossible to keepe this Island if wee should sustaine any tollerable loss these next Raines or any Enemie attempt to beate us off; herin I send an Account of all his Majesties stores, as well what is spent as what remaines in being, by it they may governe what to send of each for a Recruite. On Ange Deeva Island was much lost and spoild, which could not bee remedied, the Island being very moist and lodges as bad: besides the loss by Transporting too and againe.

According to his Majesties Orders Sir George Oxinden with much adoe hath paid some parte of the 14,550 peeces of 8 which his Majestie enordered us for a recruit the last yeare; hee promissed the remainder, when hee doth I shall give a receipt for the whole. I perceave his Majestie is to pay after the rate of 5*s*. 6*d*. per each dollar, here they goe in payment to the Soldjery for noe more then 4*s*. 9*d*. a peece, and will not pass in the Country for more then 4*s*. 6*d*. each. To raise them to the Soldjery in payment cannot bee, without particular Order from his Majestie, and if hee should doe that, at 5*s*. 6*d*. each Dollar they were not able to live on their pay, Sir Abraham Shipman never paid the same Dollars at more then 4*s*. 9*d*. a peece, and the Portugall *Crusadoes* at 4*s*. a peece, for mee to innovate and raise the price would cause Mutiny, and would not bee received at more then aforesaid. I see his Majestie will bee a greate looser by it, but it cannot bee remedied. The 14550 peeces of 8 computed to bee 4000*l*. at home, will not make here more then 3455*l*. 12*s*. 6*d*. according as I pay them to the Soldjery. I can assure you they loose 3*d*. in each Dollar at the rate of 4*s*. 9*d*. as they receave them, however when his Majestie Comands to the Contrary, it must be observed.

The bearer herof is Ensigne John Thorne, whome I send on purpose overland with this Pacquet to give advice to his Majestie of the possession of this Island, knowing how desirous hee may be to have the newes therof; the said party hath bin an eye witnes of all passages here, ever since wee came out of England, being alwaies in his Majesties service, so can verbally relate all our miseries and troubles past. Hee is Sir Abraham Shipmans Kinsman, I doubt but his Majestie will please to take Cognizance of his paines, care and services donne him as well here, as undertaking this Journey overland. Since the dispatch of the Shipps from Surrat, hath come hither severall Englishmen to bee entertain'd in his Majesties service, and in regard the generall Muster is already taken and sign'd I have bin cautious to entertaine any, while I have further orders from his Majestie for it, but our necessity being soe greate for want of Soldjers, I have ventured to entertaine some this day, and shall herafter list 40 or 50 men if can procure them, I hope his Majestie will not scruple their pay, they being to augment our force and for our better security here. I hazard these to Surratt, in hopes to find the Compaines Shipps there, to goe by that conveyance by Sea, herin goeth a Pacquet directed to the Portugall Ambassador from his Chancelor Major here, who was the person that delivered us the possession of this Island, and was very Instrumentall thereunto, hee having put a period to all scruples and doubts, desires it may safely bee delivered. Public Record Office, C. O. 77, Vol. IX, folio 221.

I had almost through hast and multiplicity of bussines, omitted to acquaint your honor that our Minister being dead, wee are in great want of an Orthodox Divine. Soe remaine ever

Your honnors most humble and obedient
servant at Command,

ISLAND BOMBAIM 3d *March* 1664/5. HUMFREY COOKE.

HONOBLE, Public Record Office. C.o. 77. Vol IX folio. 217

The Inclosed, is Coppy of what I formerly wrott you over land; since when by his Majestys second Orders after much troubles and many delayes, I have received the possession of this Port and Island of Bombaim which was delivered me in his Majesty's name the 8th february past 1664/5. It is a very pleasant place and a good ayre, yeldeth greate quantity of Coconuts and rice; His Majesty's rents at present imports little more or lesse 700 *li.* per annum; as trade and commerce encreaseth so will his revenue, It is cituated very convenient for trade and commerce for all parts, as South seas, redd seas, Gulph of Persia, Coast of Malabar, Chormandell, Bay of Bengala, Pegu and other places; It is some eight miles in length, and five and a halfe broad, in it are five Churches, nine townes and villages, and uppwards of 20000 Soules as by the Churches information; the generall langwage is Portugueze; Banians, Mahometans, and gentills about the mayne and neighbouring Islands begins to flock hither to reside, so that in few yeares I question not but that it may bee as benneficiall unto the King his Majesty as Batavia is now to the Hollander. At the first, his Majesty must expect to bee out of monys for Fortifications, it beeing at present not alltogeather deffensible; Shipping will bee also very necessary to incourage merchants to trade for all parts, which will much advance our Kings revenues and custumes; I have given a very large relation of all unto his Majesty by these conveyances boath by sea and land which latter I send on purpose for inteligence unto him in regard the shipps bound for Europe from Suratt at this seasone will bee forced to make a winter voyage, so that in all probabillity the messe may arrive some monthes before them into England, when I doubt not but Mr. Secretary will communicate unto your Honour the needfull.

I have sent his Majesty a list of a generall muster, as also an account of all pay and disbursments since Sir Abraham Shipman, and myselfe entred the service, untyll the 3d of December 1664, which I hope will give satisfaction;

I have received your letter directed to Sir Abraham Shipman, dated the 8th March, and have taken notice of its contents; I rest ever

Your Honors most humble and obedient servant,

ISLAND OF BOMBAIM HUMFREY COOKE.
the 3rd March, 1664/5.

[*Endorsed.*]

Bombaim,
H. Cooke from Bombaim,
3rd of March 64.

Public Record Office, C. O. 77, Vol. IX, folio 217.

Since the finishing and firming of the preceding, the Vicar of Parela, Padre Antonio Barboza (a Jesuit) presented mee with the paper which is herewith sent for your perusall, by which hee endeavours to make appeare that 2000 Sherapheens out of the Kings rents at Maim, which comes but to 26 Sherapheens more per annum, were given to their Company by the King of Spaine, Don Phillipp (then Lord also of Portugall), and confirmed unto them by the Vice Roys of India. But it seeming unto mee a thing most unreasonable that they should take away all the benefitts of the rents of the said Maim, and his Majestie nothing at all (hee being at soe vast a charge in mainteyning this Garrison) which is for the security of this Island, and consequently of the Lands and livings which these people enjoyeth I shall therefore secure the said 2000 Sherapheens by having it deposited untill his Majesties further Order, as I shall proceed in the same manner with him that hath the Patent for the Customes of 3½ per cent at Maim, conceiving that now our Kings Majestie is absolute King and Lord of this Island, and the King of Portugalls Dominion and Governement ceasing, all Merces as Donatives of the like nature ceaseth, alsoe with his Government many more such like matters I suppose may present themselves herafter, of all which I shall take such care as his Majesties interrest shall not in the least bee prejudiced: But being newly arrived and entred into this Government and these Christians that had Offices in it being most unwilling to discover unto mee the trueth of things, it is impossible to bee acquainted as yet of that which time will make manifest. When that I had proceeded thus far I was informed of a business of importance which is that the Bandarins of this Island, a sort of people who gaine a lively hood by drawing of Tody a liquor distilling from the Coco-Nut-tree paid formerly unto the Foreirors Mayores or Senhorios of the Severall Cossabeys or Townes a duty called Coito, that is for the knife wherewith they prune their trees, amounting unto about 700 or 800*li*. per Annum, which falls now to his Majestie, which together with what more may bee discovered and collected of his Majesties Rents, importing at present (which as yet is come to my knowledge) incirca to 1500*li*. per Annum, it will bee a helpe towards the payment and mainteynance of this his Garrison.

I have at last (after much enquiry made) obtained a coppy of the Forall of the Mandowin or Registring-house (a kind of a Custome house) of Maim, which I herewith send alsoe for your perusall, by the same you will discover how far the Limits of the said Mandowin reaches, and what places are subordinate and paies duties unto it as in folio 4 and Sections 54 and 55 of the said Forall appeares.

Whilst I shall receive further Orders from his Majestie for the encouragement of Merchants to come to habit and have commerce in this Port, I have imposed 4½ per centum custome uppon all Merchandize to bee imported or exported (vizt) 3 per centum to bee added to his Majesties Cash, and 1½ per cent towards the defraying of the charges of Custome house Officers but at Maim the duties that heretofore were paid to that Mandowin are (vizt) 3½ per centum which goes to Francisco Murzelo Coutinho aforementioned 2 per centum called consulado, 1 per centum imposition besides some other petty duties, wherof a just Account is kept in a Booke apart by the Customer. This being all at present I have to advise, desiring your honor to communicate to his Majestie the particulars herin, I subscribe as afore.

Public Record Office, C. O. 77, Vol. IX, folio 221.

Your Honors ever obedient humble servant
at all Commands,
HUMFREY COOKE.

ISLAND OF BOMBAIM,
the 15*th March*, 1664/5.

P.S.—Both by this, as likewise by an Overland conveyance the 3*d.* currant I wrote your honor giving you therin an Account of the Rendition of this Island, and of what else offered needfull Intelligence, to which referr you.

These at present are onely to certify, That Sir Oxinden hath paid mee on Account of the Bill [of] Exchange which Alderman Backwell gave his Majestie for a recruite to his Forces in these parts, value 14550 peeces ⅝ the following sums (vizt) 4000 peeces ⅝ at 4*s.* 9*d.* per peece is Sterling 950*li.* and 21,625 Rupees and 12 pice, which in payment to the Soldjery will not goe for more then 2*s.* 3*d.* per diem each is 2432*li.* 16*s.* 3*d.*, together amounting unto 33 or 2*li.* 16*s.* 3*d.*, which if hee had paid in the prementioned 14550 peeces ⅝ according to the bill of Exchange at 4*s.* 9*d.* per peece, as I pay them to the Soldjery,'t would have amounted unto 3455*li.* 12*s.* 6*d.*, soe that there is lost by the Rupees by not sending peeces ⅝ 72*li.* 16*s.* 3*d.*, which Alderman Backwell must discount out of what his Majestie is to make him good for the whole 14550 peeces ⅝. I make his Majestie good in Account 33 or 2*li.* 16*s.* 3*d.* which is what I have received and am to pay it at the rates above specified and noe more.

I am just now informed, that not onely the Jesuits but divers more that belong to this Island, have writt to their correspondents in England, to make friends to his Majesty to confirme their old Pattents, as alsoe the coito before mentioned, Taverns and Shopps, with other more exacting Tributes, not well look't upon by Tradsmen, especially the latter; which if hee grants, hee will not have any considerable matter left, towards the defraying of this vast charge hee is at of mainteyning this his Garrison and thus much I thought it necessary to make this airze that your honor might acquaint his Majesty accordingly, soe remaine

Your honors most humble
and obedient servant,
HUMFREY COOKE.

Public Record Office, C. O. 77, Vol. IX, folio 221.

[*Endorsed.*]

Bombaim.

The Governor of Bombaim letter unto the Principall Secretary of State 3 March, 64/5.

Mr. Humfrey Cooke, Governor of the said Island, 3. March 64 sends Ensigne Thorne by land, to his Majesty. To signify their sad Condition at Anchidiva in 1662 till the possession had of Bombaim 8th February, 1664. The Aversenesse and ill will of Sir George Oxinden to that Designe, as jealous it would hinder Trade at Surat that they lost 72*li.* by the money Sir George transmitted to them. That the Portugese would perswade him that 2 Forts belong to Donna Miranda : the Rents of Maim and the port to the Jesuites by letters patents; and others have like clayme to the Customes; soe that his Majestys revenue (thus) is not above 700*li.* a yeare. However, he secures the whole till his Majesties order; which he prayes, as alsoe officers and more Soldiers; and a chaplaine; and rules of civill Government in the language of the place (which is Portugese), money for the Fortification of the Island and port, to build 3 Forts, wall the Towne; (and more great Guns) and to build a Custome-House there, and at Maim. The Island rarely seated for Commerce: good ayre: the Island is 8 miles long 5 and a halfe, broad; hath 5 churches; 9 villages: 20ne [thousand] people in it: but poore: yeilds little but Rice and Coco's. Permits not the Jesuites now to take and educate the children: allowes liberty of Religion to Heathens and Mahumetans in their Owne Houses (which invites them thither) prayes 6 small ships to guard them against the pyrate-Malabars; and to passe the portugese castles in the Straits of Tannay and Buindy, custome free; (and soe, they may undersell Surat 20 per Cent: and soonn be as considerable to the King as Batavia is to the Hollanders) Hath done the duty of all officers, but made none, (to ease his Majesty of the charge) Sends Accounts of disbursements from 1661 to December 64 and of Stores spent and left. Hath made new Carriages for the Guns. Hath listed 40 or 50 men, for feare of the Raines and of Surprise. The King allowes Sir G. Oxinden 5*s.* 6*d.* a Dollar and hee payes the soldier at 4*s.* 9*d.* (in the Island they goe but 4*s.* 6*d.*). He hath discover'd a Taxe impos'd by the Portugese call'd Coito; that is, on the knife, us'd about Coco-Trees (which they doe tap for Toddy) which (with the former) will make a Revenue of 1500*li.* a yeare. Sends a Transcript (in portugese) of the Custome Booke at Maim. Hath (till further order) laid 4 per Cent. on all Goods exported or imported (1 and ½ is for the Officers that attend the Customes). All his soldiers have taken the oath of Allegiance and many alsoe of the Inhabitants; noe one hath as yet scrupled it.

To

[Inserted in top margin in another hand:—]

Mr. Cook's letter to the Earl of Arlington touching the Protest made by the Portuguese's Vice Roy upon Mr. Cook's taking Possession of Mahim. The Arrears of Rent due before the taking Possession of Bombaim and other matters relating to that Island.

Public Record Office, C. O. 77, Vol. IX, folio 308, No. 142.

RIGHT HONOBLE.

I writt your Lordshipp overland by Ensigne John Thorne, and by the Companys Shipps that went from Surat the *London* Commaunder Robert Bowen in February 1664, therein I give a large relation of our having possession of this Island for our Kings Majesty, and all else what then offered, one or boath of which I hope by this may bee arrived with you, that you may the better know our wants and necessity wee are in. These are to continue what since hath offered.

Portuguese Protest.

The Vizorey Antonio de Mello de Castro hath enordered his Captain generall, Ignacio Sarmento de Carvalho which resides in these parts of the North to make a Protest against me; for taking (as they pretend) the Island of Maim, saying it belongs to the Jurésdiction of Baçaim and so consequently appertaines to the Crowne of Portugall, with many other very frivolous fals things, (as you may please to perceive by the Coppy of the said Protest and my contra Protest to it;) They would have Maim and Bombaim to bee two severall Islands, but cannot well make it out, I never tooke Boate to páss our men when I tooke the Possession of it, and at all times you may goe from one place to the other dry shod; I cannot imagine how they cann make them two Islands; Maim is the best part of this Island and they thinke it to good for our Kings Majesty, but befor they have it againe (except his Majesty please to enorder it to them) it shall bee long enough by my consent; they since begin to bee sensible of theyr errors, and are very quiet, I thinke they thought to have frighted us out of what was his Majestys due with theyre greate words and threatnings, but seeing it doeth not prevaile, they find it theyr best way to bee quiet.

Arrears of Rents before the taking Possession of the Island.

I have writt the Vizorey Antonio de Mello de Castro, demaunding in our Kings Majestys name all what rents hee had recovered in this Island from the time my Lord of Marlebourgh arrived, to the day wee tooke the possession; hee answered me that what hee had receíved, hee spent in keepeing Garison in the said Island for our Kings Majesty; I demaunded, what orders hee had for that, our Kings Majesty having a Governor and souldjery of his owne for the said purpose? On this I have had severall letters to and againe, but I cann gett no monys.

According to his Majestys command I have made a Protest to him, the Coppy of which goeth heere enclosed, it was delivered by Mr. Robert Masters a Factor for the Company at Carwar, whom writes that he hath waited one whole month, and as yett cannot obtaine an answere; and concluds hee will give now, as appeares by the secretary of state of Goas note which I heerein remitt.

Public Record Office, C. O. 77, Vol. IX, folio 308, No. 142.

The Portugalls on the Maine and Neighbouring places in these parts, some have lands on this Island, and many Inhabitants heere, have lands there, so that I have been forced (to excuse a confusion) to settle the Civill law among them in this Island, the which hath hugely pleased boath partys; among our selves is marshall law, and for religion, liberty of Conscience is given to all.

This Island is hither to but a meere Fishing place, and as yett no merchant of quallity nor any else is come to settle heere, nor will not, while [until] a trade begins, which must bee done by his Majestys enordering all the Companys shipps to lade and unlade heere, and the Factory of Suratt to bee removed hither, theyre very Custume only will goe neere to pay the Garison and a greate animating for others to come to live heere, and noe question, in few yeares, will reape a large bennefitt for his Majesty in the interim, hee cannot expect but to bee at a yearely charge, by sending supplyes, in regard the rents of this Island are so small, all not ammounting unto above 1000*li.* per annum, and although in my last to your Lordshipp the last yeare, I writt about a rent that did belong to the King that might import to about 700 or 800*li.* per annum, for the Knife that was to prune the Cocer nutt tree, it hath proved incerte, for since by papers I find it belongs to the Owners or Foreiros of the ground for which they pay unto his Majesty what appeares by theyr Foralls, so that it proved a fals information.

These Past raines hath proved very pestilentiall to our menn having lost by death and runn away 51 as appeares by the enclosed list of theyr names, which in our small quantity hath much weakened us, allthough I entertaine all, what English, French, or Sweds that comes.

The last yeare I made an end of Fortifying this house towards the sea, by the building of a large platt forme 51 yards long, wherein cann play 18 peeces of large Ordinance, it hath cost his Majesty monyes, but is the best piece in India, and secures all the Roade, its made as strong, as lime and stone cann make it; and no question will last for many hundered yeares; I have likewise repaired the two slight Bulworks and made them substantiall against Battery.

I have one from your lordshipp directed to Sir Abraham Shipman, of date the 27th March 1665, with a contract made by the Commissioners of his Majestys Navy and the Easte India Company to tra[n]sport us for England in case wee were styll on the Island of Angediva, the which letter and Contract, I caused publiquely to bee redd in our Garison, that all might understand the greate care his Majesty hath had of us to bee at such a vast charge to transport us home after so greate a losse and not having don him as yett any service, whose most gratious favor hath so much obliged all in generall that I am comfident they will all venter theyr lives on theyr bare knees to do him service.

On the receipt of your lordshipps letter wee were in Possession of Bombaim for his Majesty so that Contract served to no effect, wee being now waiting for furder Orders from his Majesty.

In regard wee were ordered home; his Majesty sent us no supplys of monys this yeare, and its imposible the souldjery can live without its pay, heere beeing nothing to bee had, but for our monys and not one man that liveth uppon this Island, is able to trust us, for a dayes victualling, they have it not, beeing most of them Fishermen. Public Record Office, C. O. 77, Vol. IX, folio 208, No. 142.

I have had letters from the Vizorey Antonio de Mello de Castro and Ignacio Sarmento de Cavalho Captain Generall of the North, and severall others, that the warrs betweene us and Holand is broke out, and publiquely proclaimed, and that the Dutch for certaine entends to beate us off of this Island, the which hath putt mee at my wits end; the want of mony boath to fortify, Victuall for a Seige and for the soldjers pay and other necessarys for warr, I have made my addresse unto the President of Surat Sir George Oxinden, aleadging the afore reasones and others, and that of necessity without hee supplye us, wee must disband, and then his Majestys Interest will bee lost, Hee answered, hee had no order from the Company to supply us with any thing; then I desired him that hee would doe it out of his owne Stocke; Hee writes much of his zeale to his Majesty I wish it weare as much as to his monyes; I could not prevaile any thing from him, neither one way or other, so that I having a little mony of my owne and of some freinds in England, I hope I shall bee able to rubb out whilest [until] September next 1666 which otherwise this Garison could not have subsisted, and consequently his Majestys Interest lost.

All this sommer I have been ordering and makeing Fortifications to the landward, for a place of security, which as yett is not quite made an end of, heere inclosed your Lordshipp will receive Its ruff draught, which bee pleased to shew unto his Majesty Its all done with Turffe and Cocer nutt trees 14 foote hygh round; with little repayring it will last for many yeares, all beeing Cannon prooffe, this worke would have cost his Majesty 5000*li*. to have concluded it; but I hope it will not cost him 100*li*. for I have taken such care, to have all the Islanders to worke by turnes some dayes 1000 men, some dayes 800, without pay, only something to drinke, its much worke to bee done by force of hands, wee have bein about it upwards of three monthes, it hath nott cost me little trouble and care.

Wee are now dayly expecting the enemy, the greate want of the losse of those menn that dyed the last raynes, and the many sentinells wee have with our new workes hath forced me to entertaine in our fower Companys tenn menn in eache Company being in all forty Portuguezes white menn of Europe; they have the same pay our owne menn hath, I would entertaine more but our mony will not hold out to pay them.

I hope in September next 1666 his Majesty will not faile to send us supply of menn, mony, match, greate Ordinance, shott of all sorts, powder, and all other necessarys for warr, for this wee have heere, will suddainly bee spent, in a Siedge: Our mach wee brought out, is all spent, so that I have bein forced to have a quantity made heere which is very bad, and deere, our necessity is so much wee could not bee without it.

The *Chestnut Pynke* riding at an anchor in this Roade will runn a greate hazard to bee burnt by the enemy, therefor I have thought fitt to hall hir on shore under the command of our artyllery, the menn

Public Record Office, C. O. 77, Vol. IX, olio 3 No. 142.

are entered in his Majestys sirvice for privat sentinells whilest furder Order from his Majesty to dispose of hir, for as yett shee hath not don us any sirvice at all; hir Gunns, Pouder, amunition with tackling are all in his Majestys store. I hope by this, shall save the King 600*li*. per annum beeing hee is now ridd of that charge. John Stevens Commander stomacks it much, and hath a turbulent and mutinous spiritt about it, that maters not, at all, I doe my Duty.

Wee have had no medicines sent since wee came out of England, but have bein forced to buy out of the Companys stores every yeare, which cost deere enough, I hope heereafter, things will bee better husbanded in case this Garison remaynes; Wee want much a Chaplaine to Instruct our menn to doe theyr duty to God Allmighty.

My humble petition to your lordshipp is, that you will please to motion to his Majesty, how the ayre of this Country doeth not agree with mee, having bein very sick of a flux, and am desirous to end my old age in my owne Country, therefor most humbly desire his leave to goe home by the next shipps, I hope hee will send a Governor out befor this same cann come to your hands, but in case hee should not, then to minde him heerein for which your lordshipp will ever Oblidge me to bee

Your lordshipps most humble
and obedient servant
HUMFREY COOKE.

BOMBAIM
The 23rd December, 1665.

P.S.—The Vizorey Antonio de Mello de Castro was the first that writt mee of the warrs beeing broke out betweene the Dutch and us, and that for a certaine they entended suddainly to assault and beate us off this Island, I imediately writt him of our greate loss of menn, at Angediva, and therefor demaunded of him in our Kings Majestys name, that hee would assist me for our monys, or enorder his Captain Generall heere in the North to doe it with menn, Artyllery, pouder, or any thing els I should want, for the deffence of this place, seeing himself adviseth me the Hollanders might bee soone upon us; this I writt by fower conveyances, two of which I have answere by Englishmen that they delivered them to him, but could gett no answere to this day; so that it's plainly seene theres no trusting to any but our selves, the Portugalls proveing so treacherous which please to advize his Majesty.

The greate House with three small ones and the ground that is now in his Majestys possession fortified appertains unto (the Widdow of Dom Roderigo de Montsanto deceased) Donna Ignes de Miranda, who as yett will not agree to take what monys all was valued in unto hir at the death of hir said husband which is neere 350*li*. it must bee paid; I cann assure the Houses only, were never built for 4,000*li*. The Arabs hath don much hurt to the Houses espetially the greate one which will cost much to repaire.

There is one thing of much importance that I shall desire you please to advise his Majesty thereof; that is, in case hee please to bee absolute owner of all this Bay, Port, and rivers that the Portugalls hath, that runns out into the Bay, ther must of necessity be a Fort made with tenn or twelve good Gunns, and One hundered English men constantly to bee there to examine all vessells that goeth in or out it beeing much out of command of our Gunns from this Fort; Its a small Island that lyeth at the botome of this Bay cal'd by the Portuguezes Ilha das Pateias by Trumba, there is no Inhabitants on it, but belongeth to a subject of his Majesty on this Island. My Lord of Marlebourgh can give your lordshipp a large relation of it and how necessary it will bee to bee don, except which wee cann never expect any greate trade from the maine; the Portuguezes demaunding Custumes allready of any thing that cometh hither, and maketh theyr owne rates, and can noe wayes bee remedied, except the said Fort bee there to keepe them under.

Police Record Office, C. O. 77, Vol. IX, folio. 308, No. 142.

HUMFREY COOKE.

[*Endorsed.*]

23*rd December* 65. Received 19*th February* 667.

Mr. Cooke. Bombaim.

The Portugueez have protested against him for taking the Island of Maim which with his owne justification hee sends over: will keep it till his Majesties further Pleasure.

Wrote to Antonio de Mello de Castro Vizéroy for the arrears of Rents received before possession was taken of the Island, but without Successe, hath settled the Civill Law there and among themselves the Martiall Law: no merchant lives there yet, requisite his Majesty send supplies yearly thither, the rents yearly coming to but 1,000*li.*, about 50 of their men are dead, hath built a Platform upon which 18 ps. of cannon can play next the Sea: published to the Garrison his Majesties care of them, who will venture their lives in his Service, want pay for the souldiers this year: hearing of the warre with Holland and fearing they might attack the Island, sent to Sir George Oxenden for supplies, but hee had noe order from the Company to doe it, hopes out of his own stock to keep them till September 1666: fortified the House to the landward at small charge to his Majesty, hopes by September to receive supplies: detain'd the *Chestnutt Pink* for fear shee might bee burnt by the enemy and placed her under the Artillery: Want medicines much; prays hee may returne home, recommends that his Majesty would build a Fort at the Isle of Pataires which belongs [to] a subject of his Majesties.

ARTICLES BY WHICH BOMBAY WAS DELIVERED BY ANTONIO DE MELLO E CASTRO, VICEROY AND CAPTAIN GENERAL OF GOA, TO HUMPHREY COOKE, 14 JANUARY, 1665.

1st. The Island of Bombay should be delivered to the English Gentlemen with a declaration that whereas the other islands of the jurisdiction of Bassein have through the bay of the said island of

Bombay their commerce, trade and navigation with equal right, liberty, and freedom the said English gentlemen shall never prevent or cause any impediment, nor levy any tribute or Gabell neither on the importation of salt or any other merchandize of those islands and countrys, nor on any other articles which may be brought there from abroad ; and it shall be free for all vessels loaded or empty to navigate from the said islands and countrys of the Portuguese or other nations that might come to them, and the subjects of the King of Great Britain shall not oblige them to make their first discharge or pay any thing in their Custome House, nor by any other means whatsoever, nor shall they for this purpose make use of any pretence because it is thus declared from this time for ever ; and they shall not only have good treatment and free passages to our countrys, but to those of other parts as they have hitherto been in the habit of doing.

2nd. That the port of Bandora in the island of Salsette or any other of the island shall be impeded and all vessels from that port or ports and others coming to them shall be allowed to pass and repass very franckly, and the English gentlemen shall not alledge that they pass under their guns, because it is under this condition that the island is delivered to them and they cannot expect more than what is granted to them by the Articles of peace and the marriage treaty.

3rd. That they shall not admit any deserter from our country, be it for whatever cause, nor shall they under any pretence whatever pretend to conceal or defend them, as this is the most effectual means of preserving . . . . scandalous practice and future injuries, and in case of any person going to them they are obliged to send and deliver him up to the captain of the time being of the city of Bassein, and because many Gentoos who have in their charge goods and money belonging to the Portuguese and other subjects of His Majesty by way of retaining the whole it may happen that they may come to Bombay and shelter themselves under the shadow and protection of the colours of the most serene King of England, the English gentlemen shall not only apprehend such people till they satisfy what they may owe, and on their not doing it within two months they shall deliver them up to the captain of Bassaim in order to satisfy the parties as it may be just and right.

4th. That the English gentlemen shall not interfere in matters of Faith, nor will compell the inhabitants of the said Island of Bombay neither directly or indirectly to change their Faith or to go and attend their Sermons, and shall allow the Ecclesiastical Ministers the exercise of their jurisdiction without the least impediment, being a condition mentioned in the Articles of Peace, under which delivery of the island is ordered to be made, and making out any time to the country it is understood that the whole agreed upon and promised will be violated, and that the right of the said Island shall fall again into the Crown of Portugal.

5th. That too the Fleets of the King of Portugal our master both ships of the line and the small oared vessels and any other vessels of his, will at all time be free to sail in and out of the said bay without the least impediment, nor will they be obliged to ask any leave, because by the reason of the other Islands and countrys belonging to him a part of the said Bay belongs also to him, and it is free to him to make use of it as his own without any doubt or question.

6th. That all the inhabitants residing at Bombay as well as those who may have estates in the said Islands, when they should not like to reside in the said Island it shall be free to them to farm out their estates or sell the same on the best terms they may be able to obtaine, and if the English gentlemen should require them, it shall be for their just and equal value and not on any other terms, but if the English gentlemen should not chuse to buy them, nor the holders live in them, it shall be free to them to alienate the same, and untill thy do so, it shall likewise be free to them to enjoy and make use of the same as they have hitherto done without the least contradiction from the part of the English gentlemen.

7th. That the inhabitants of the said Islands of Salsette, Caranjah, and Baragao, and of other places of our jurisdiction shall freely fish in the said Bay and River and in the arm of the sea which enters and divides Bombay from Salsette by Bandora till the Bay; and the English gentlemen shall not at any time prevent them nor will they at any time and under any pretence whatever demand any tributes on this account, and the inhabitants of Bombay shall be allowed to do the same with the same liberty and freedom.

8th. That the Curumbies, Bandarino, and the rest of the people (Abunhados a set of people bound to serve the Landholders) or inhabitants of the villages of one jurisdiction shall not be ádmitted at Bombay and on their or any of them resorting thereto, they shall be immediately delivered up to their respective owners, and same shall be observed with respect to slaves which may run away, likewise with regard to the artificers that may go from our countrys to Bombay, such as Carpenters, Weavers, Turners, Joiners, Caulkers, Sayers, Drillers, and Smiths, and any other they shall be immediately deliverd up; and if the English gentlemen should at any time require those artificers they shall ask them from the captain of Bassaim, who will send them for a limited time, they keeping their familys in our countrys and on their being still wanted even after the expiration of the limited time they shall go and present themselves to the captain of Bassaim for the time being to whom the English gentlemen shall ask for them again, and know thereby that neither the capitulation nor the good neighbouringship, which we shall also observe, is not to be violated.

9th. That in case any of the deserters should be willing to change his Religion and to the confession of the English gentlemen to prevent them being restored to us, the English gentlemen shall not consent thereto, and the same shall be observed on our part with regard to those that may desert to our countrys.

10th. That although the manor right of the Lady the Proprietrix of Bombay is taken away from her estates if she lives in the Island, and they are not to be entermiddled with or taken away from her unless it be of her free will she being a woman of quality they are necessary for her maintenance, but after death, and her heirs succeed to those estates the English gentlemen may if they chuse take them, paying for the same their just value, as is provided in the case of other Proprietors of Estates, and should the English gentlemen now wish to take her houses to build Forts thereupon they shall immediately pay her their just value.

11th. That every persons possessing Revenue at Bombay either by Partimonial or Crown Lands they shall not be deprived thereof except in cases which the Laws of Portugal direct and their sons and descendents shall succeed to them with the same right and clause above mentioned and those who may sell the said Partimonial or Crown Estates shall transfer to the purchaser the same right and perpetuity they had, that the purchaser may enjoy the same and their successors in the like manner.

12th. That the Parish Priests and monks or regular clergy that reside in Bombay shall have all due respect paid to them as agreed upon, and the churches shall not be taken for any use whatever nor sermons shall be preached in them, and those who may attempt it should be punished in such manner as to serve as an example.

13th. That the inhabitants of Bombay and the landholders of that Island shall not be obliged to pay more than the foros they use to pay to His Majestey, this condition being expressly mentioned in the capitulations.

14th. That there shall be a good understanding and reciprocal friendship between both parties rendering one another every good office like good freinds as this was the end of the delivery of this and other places, and the intention of His Most Serene King of Great Britain, as appears by the treaty made and entered into by and between both Crowns.

Given at Pangin, the 14th January, 1665.

Letter dated 10th March 1676/7 from Charles II to the Viceroy of Goa repudiating Mr. Humphrey Cook's Treaty or Convocation of the 8th January 1665 :—

Charles the second, by the Grace of God, King of Great Britain, France and Ireland, King, Defender of the faith, etc. To the most illustrious and most excellent Lord Lewis de Mendoca Furtado, Count of Lauradio, Viceroy and Captain General of the Indian Affairs and Dominion, under the command and authority of the most serene Lord Peter, Prince of Portugal, Regent etc. our very dear friend, sendeth greeting. Most illustrious and most excellent Lord Viceroy, our very dear friend—Our subjects through the East Indies excercising trade have lately preferred their complaints to us that they had experienced little of that friendly behaviour which they expected from the Portugese nation, but, on the contrary, had met with much worse treatment there than the treaty of marriage between us and our dearest Consort seemed to promise. In order to remedy this evil our intention is shortly to elucidate and explain the 11th article of that treaty conjointly with our aforesaid brother the most serene Prince of Portugal, by whose justice we doubt not our sovereign rights in the Port and Island of Bombay and their Dependencies will be vindicated from that very unjust capitulation which Humphrey Cook was forced to submit to at the time when that place was first transferred to our possession, which capitulation neither he, Humphrey, was empowered to come into, nor any one else to impose upon him, in contravention to a compact framed in so solemn and religious a manner. We therefore are determined to protest against the said capitulation as prejudicial to our Royal dignity, derogatory to our right, which we hold in the higher estimation for coming to us in part of the dowery with our aforesaid dearest Consort.

We shall signify to our abovementioned brother the Prince of Portugal, with how much displeasure we have learnt that our subjects going by sea on the prosecution of their trade into the dominion of the Great Mogul and Savagee (between whom and us a good understanding exists, and who are not at variance with the Portugese, which obviates all pretexts for obstructing the free passage) are nevertheless, against the laws and customs of all nations, compelled to pay a tribute for sailing only through the open streights of Tannah as also for passing by Carinjah, though lying contiguous on the very waters of our said Port ; neither of which proceedings we can submit to ; nor do we doubt that the said Prince of Portugal will order to be refunded whatever has so wrongfully and so much against all precedent been exacted from our subjects, and besides other grievances which he will not fail to redress. That he will also take into serious consideration the affront offered to our person and the hardships and damages sustained by our subjects on account of the said island of Bombay, together with its dependencies, not being at first delivered to us faithfully and according to agreement as it ought to have been. In the mean time we have forbidden our subjects of the East India Company to submit to such arbitrary and unjustifiable exactions as paying the tributes at Tannah and Carinjah, which are not less inconsistent with our Royal sovereign right, than contrary to the laws and customs of all nations. For not even in the streight called the *Sound* on the coast of Denmark is any tax or toll imposed in an arbitrary manner, a moderate sum only being paid for lighthouses and beacons erected for the security of Navigation ; nor was this even levied before treaties and stipulations had been made between Princes for that purpose; while our subjects are willing and ready to pay the customary port duties and charges respectively settled in different places (which they refuse not to do when they trade in any part of the Portugese dominions) we do not see with what right anything further can be demanded of them. We have therefore thought it proper to signify all these particulars to your Excellency in an amicable manner, both on account of your exalted character and the authority you are deservedly invested with in those countries, next in dignity to Royalty itself, as well as in consideration of the great regard and respect which you profess for our person. Neither have we the least doubt that your Excellency will not only perform, to the utmost of your power, whatever is consistent with equity and with the aforesaid treaty; but will likewise, as occasion offers, treat our subjects with due benevolence, and act with readiness in whatever you may judge conducive to their service and interest. We, on our part, shall certainly be ready to render the like good offices to the Portugese and to all who are in friendship with your Excellency.

And here we should have ended for the present, but that our aforesaid subjects have further informed us that the one half of the customs which are paid at Gombroone in Persia belong of right to them in the same manner as the Portugese receive them at Cong in the same kingdom. It has been usual among the European settlers in India to grant passports or letters of safe conduct to the shipping of the Natives (which are called Junks) in order to secure the navigation to Persia and to other ports on those coasts. But it has lately happened (in opposition to the aforesaid practice) that such passports have, by your Excellency's direction, been denied to those that were bound to Gombroone. In consequence of which all those vessels were necessarily obliged either to proceed to Cong, or to expose themselves to dangers, which they are liable to who venture by sea without passports to Gombroone, where (as already observed) the English receive a moity of the customs. But as this unequel distribution of passports not only seems to indicate a sort of ill-will to the English nation, but to carry with it an appearance of injustice, and might very reasonably provoke our aforesaid company of merchants to commit retaliations; we therefore most amicably and most earnestly request it of your Excellency to withdraw that prohibition and all other order whatsoever delivered for that purpose, as repugnant to the aforesaid treaty of marriage, of which the principal and most essential intention was to unite both nations in the strictest bonds of friendship and to engage them to treat each other with the most brotherly affection and goodwill. This shall always be most cordially observed on our part and we hope will in like manner be observed on the part of your Excellency, whom we finally recommend to the protection of the Almighty. *Given at our palace of Whitehall the* 10*th day of March* 1676-7.

Your Excellencys good friend,
CHARLES R.

To the most illustrious and most Excellent Lord Lewis de Mendonca Furtado, Count of Lawradio, Viceroy and Captain General of the Indian Affairs and Dominion, under the command and authority of the Most Serene Lord Peter, Regent and Prince of Portugal, our very dear friend.

Though Dom Pedrode Almeida, who succeeded Lavrado, treated Charles' letter with scant respect, it cannot be denied that his arguments were based on the solid foundation of universal practice. Charles' Government showed the same culpable ignorance of geography as Clarendon had done, and his repudiation of Humphrey Cooke's Treaty after an ominous silence of twelve years makes us suspect the validity of his claims, and the sincerity of his purpose. Almeida's reply was as follows :—

" The Count de Lavradio, whom I have just succeeded as Viceroy, has handed me the letter your Majesty was pleased to address to him, regarding the question the Mandovis of Caranja and Thana. The Moors give the name of " Mandovis " to what we call Custom Houses. Caranja was always the Custom House of the whole *terra firma*, and Thana of part of the Galhana and Bumdi *terra firma* of the Moors, and Bombay of the district where everyone pays taxes in the form of the ancient "foros" of the time of the Moorish dominion; and, as the vassals of the Prince, my master, are not exempt from the payment of duties in Bombay, it does not seem right that the vassals of your Majesty should be exempt from paying duties in my Prince's dominion. As regards the "passes", we issue them to the Moors and Natives in the usual form." The letter was written on November 11, 1677.

In the following paper, we get a glimpse of the internal condition of India. The references to Sivaji are interesting, and Aurangzebe's untiring energy is the source of endless plots, intrigues, gossips, and wars.

INDIA, *November* 1666.

Since the *Africans* and *St. Georges* departure there hath been noe Conveyance from hence to Persia, nor 'tis thought will this yeare, for all these parts of the World are Imbroiled in war, as much as Eroupe; the Persian King hath entred for certaine above 500 miles into this King's Countrey, hath had two notable victories over Oranzeeb's army, and taken the great City of Caubell, in soe much that Oranzeebe hath throwne of his Dervis Coate, and gone with a vast army in person against him. The rebell Savaged* some 10 moneths Since yeilded himselfe a prisoner unto Rajah Jesson, on conditions that his life should bee secured, but at his appearance before the King, hee would have had him cutt in pieces, on which Rajah Jesson Solemnly Swore unto the King, that if Savaged died hee would Kill himselfe immediately in his presence, after which the King Spared his life, but committed him prisoner into the charge of Rajah Jesson's Sonne, who with his father having given their word to Savaged that hee should bee freindly dealt withall in case hee would Submit to the King, (for they could never have compelled him to it) and they finding the King contrary to his word endeavour to break their promise, tookit soe hainously, that the Son with the father or through his meanes gave Savaged opportunity to escape; After notice of which coming to the King's eare, hee in a rage discarded the Rajah's Son who Comanded 6000 horse, and posted Rajah Jesson himselfe with a great Strength to fetch him againe, in which time the King of Persia entring his Countrey, hee recalled the Rajah againe; and 'tis credibly reported in Surat that hee hath refused to come, and really thought that having for the most part Esdues† in his army, hee will prove a mortall enemy to Oranzeeb: Alsoe Savaged's coming to Surat is much feared againe, insoemuch that report hath given him Severall times to have been within a day or two dayes journey of the place, which hath caused Sometimes 5 or 6000 to pack up their Aules and run out of the towne, and when another report hath given the first the lie, then they have crept in againe, but if he comes 'twill bee when the ships arrive from Bussora.

Public Record Office, C. O. 77, Vol. X, folio 61.

[* *sic* for Savagee = Sivaji.]

[† *sic* ? a copyist's error for "Gentues."]

Public Record Office, C. O. 77, Vol. X, folio 61.

The report goes here alsoe that Sultan Suza Oranzeeb's elder brother the King of Bengalla residing in the Persian King's Court, was the cheifest instrument of his coming into this Country, and that hee is in person in the army. As alsoe that the King of Golgundaugh and the King of Vitchapore are preparing to goe upon Oranzeeb's back: We have had noe certaine newes out of the Gulfe of Persia this yeare, onely a small vessell from Musckatt, and they on her have reported that the Bashaw of Bussora was routed by him of Bagdat, that Bussora was wholy taken, and the towne on conditions redelivered againe to the Arab, and that the shipping were as high as Cape Bardestone, when understanding the trouble there they beat it back againe for Cong and that after the Bashaw of Bussora sent to Cong and invited them thither; and more the King here hath sent downe positive order that noe ship whatsoever shall bee suffered to goe into the Gulfe of Persia, as wee heare that the King of Persia hath stopt all the Junckes belonging to this port, which is the reason that they have had noe conveyance for their overland packett: here hath not been yet the least newes of a Dutch ship this yeare upon the Coast and 'tis certaine that the Dutch will not give a passe for any vessell to goe downe the Coast of India, by reason they will not have newes brought to Suratt of their bad succes: Wee heare here that they have lost Cucheene to the Natives; Wee heare for certaine they have not had a ship from Europe since the war began, they have not bought a penny worth of goods this yeare in India; they have called all their ships from all parts whatsoever to Batavie, and how they fare thereabouts wee know not, but 'tis Supposed that the Longhaired China men with others are on their backes.

In Sir Gervase Lucas' Despatch, printed below, Mr. Cooke's administration is denounced in scathing terms, while the "false dealings" of the East India Company are exposed in no measured tones. Lucas was an able and energetic administrator, and could not tolerate the culpable administrative methods of Cooke. The Jesuits, too, had begun to give trouble, and the miserable Governors found themselves harassed on all sides. The conflict between the servants of the King and those of the Company ought to have been foreseen by Charles' Government. The mutual recriminations in which they indulged were most unfortunate at this juncture. The Portuguese were only too glad to take advantage of these bickerings, and we are not surprised to find the original treaty interpreted with all their accustomed ingenuity. Nathaniel Herne's defence of the Company should be compared with Lucas' Despatch.

BOMBAIM 2*nd March* 1666/7.

Public Record Office, C. O. 77, Vol. XII, folio 273.

MY LORD

The East India Companies Factory deales so falsely here in all things concerns his Majesties Interest in these parts, that it is not possible for the most vigilent Person in the World to meet their motions at so great a distance as Bombaim is from Surat, and in a Country where is no better way of sending Dispatches, then by lazie

[Coppie, the original was sent by Ensigne Thomas Price.]

Footmen, which is the reason this I have now sent my Lord Arlington came two dayes to late to passe upon the Compaines Ship Returne; which I ever fearing, put his Majestie to the charge of sending 2 Pacquetts of the same tenour the 30th November by way of Persia, which I hope will arrive so timely at Whithall, as may free me from beeing thought growne either lazie or negligent in his Majesties Service. I have at large in those dispatches, and this now sent to my Lord Arlington, given my opinion which is the best way to Strengthen this place, and advance his Majesties Interest at least charge to his Majestie, and cannot add any thing to it; but that here is great resort of Bannians, who are the Merchants of these parts, who desire to build houses in this Island, in expectation his Majestie will order the Trade of these parts to this Port: which is the best harbour where Shipps may enter and ride safe all Seasons.

Public Record Office, C. O. 77, Vol. XII, folio 273.

At my arrivall here I found Mr. Cooke very weary of his imployment, haveing just at that time, run as Farr as his Majesties Treasure would inable him: and if not so seasonably relieved as by my arrivall; it had been very hazardous how his Majesties Island and people had been disposed of: for he had, by his imprudence and bribery, lockt himselfe up from justly advancing his Majesties Revenue: 250*li.* of which money he had received I have paid back againe, on purpose to redeeme his Majesties just Title to Fishing in the Salt waters, which cannot propperly belong to any other, beeing under protection of his Majesties Gunnes and cannot bee defended without them. I have taken it into Custodie, and hope to make 300*li.* a yeare of it. And some other duties, which through the corruption of the Portugueze Officers have been unjustly detained from that Crowne a long time. His Majestie and the Queen will have loud Outcries against me from the Jesuites, Barnardine de Tavora and Igius de Miranda, which 3 have almost the whole Island of Bombaim in their possession, with the Fishing in Salt water, and power of Tribute over the People, power of punishment, imprisonment, whipping, starving, banishment; all which since my arrivall, I have secured the Inhabitants from, allowing no power to any to punish but by order of his Majesties Governour upon the place, or by such Justice of peace as are appointed by the Governour; which hath put the whole Island into a secure and quiet Conditione as to their persons and Estates: and I dare Confidently aver to your Lordshipp his Majestie hath not in all his dominions a more obedient, peaceable and easie to be governd people then these, except the Jesuites and the other two, who have till this time governd the people, and lived by the rapine and spoile of the Inhabitants: and therefore I hope their complaints will not be able to obstruct my endeavours justly to advance his Majesties Revenue: nor will it seeme unreasonable to you, when their complaints come before you, to returne them to the Governour of the place with his Majesties command to doe them Justice, which if reason will satisfie them, they now have:

For my Lord, I will never give any thing under my hand at never so great a distance that is not truth: and for all those Lands and Royalties they have rob'd the Crowne of Portugall of, and have long enjoyed, there is not one of them can produce the Kings hand and Seale, and yet they will pretend they are alienated from the Govern

Public Record Office, C. O. 77, Vol. XII, folio 273.

ment without power of revocation. I am altogether ignorant of the Articles of Surrender of the Island to his Majestie except the 11 Article which reserves nothing to the Inhabitants but the free exercise of the Romane catholique Religion : and in terminus gives the King all Right, Title, Interest, power and dominion which the King of Portugall had : and I hope in time to discover it to be of more advantage to his Majestie then wee yet know ; and therefore it is necessary, I have a Commission sent mee, under the great Seale, of a larger Tenour, as power to let Leases in his Majesties name for certaine yeares or Lives, as his Majestie pleases, and to constitute and appoint all civill Officers and Magistrates for the decission of Controversies arising among the people, which they hourely trouble me in. I have at large acquainted my Lord Arlington how I parted with Mr. Cooke about his Accounts : and sent his Lordshipp a short abstract of them : by which, when Mr. Cooke arrives at Whithall, his Majestie and Councill will see in breife the disbursments of all his Majesties Treasure since Sir Abraham Shipmans setting forth till my arrivall here the 5th November 1666. I have received of Mr. Cooke 1700 and odd pounds which I have given my Lord Arlington an account, and I cut him of 1300*li.* he pretended his Majestie was indebted to him : all which your Lordshipp will see in my Lord Arlingtons Letter now sent him. I send for more security of his Majesties haveing intelligence from this place a Person who came out of England with Sir Abraham Shipman, and hath been upon the Island ever since his Majestie had possession of it, Mr. Price an Ensigne, a very sober man, and is able to give so good account of the place that his Majestie may take a better measure by his relation of his Majesties Interests in haveing this Island then by Letters can be given his Majestie. I am providing Lyme, Stones, and Timber for Fortifications : but cannot begin the worke till either his Majestie send us a recruite of money, or Trade Ships, whose customes may answer the same : For the monethly charge of the Officers and Souldiers comes to 206*li.* 7*s.* 6*d.* besides my allowance, and the charge of materialls for the worke and other contingencies are at present very great. I will use my utmost endeavour if his Majestie will give mee leave to advance his Revenue on this Island as much as I can towards the defraying the charge of the place which would not be very great if his Majestie had ended with the Dutch, the Fortifications raised, and Trade setled : I dare say it would yeeld his Majestie a better Revenue then now it costs. I have according to the Order your Lordshipp gave me when I last kissed your hand, drawne 3 Bills of Exchange upon my Lord Treasurer for 1869*li.* 3*s.* 8*d.* for value 1500*li.* received of Sir George Oxinden and Companies Councill at Surat : by which your Lordshipp may see the great losse his Majestie is at by sending Bills of Exchange or Letters of Credit into these parts. I have acquainted my Lord Ashley Cooper with it and any one of the Bills, beeing satisfied the other two are null.

I am endeavouring to get 20 Horse upon the Island which were of great Advantage both to his Majesties Service and security of the place. I hope his Majestie will not be offended at it : since there is no gocd corespondence to be held from the severall parts of the Island without them. My Lord there are many Troubles and difficulties I am engaged in betwixt his Majesties just Right and some of these peoples pretences in point of Title to those Estates they possesse : I hope I have Creditt with your Lordshipp to beleeve me so modest and just, and so well to understand the Honnor, as well as Interest of his Majesties Government in these parts, that I would not by force violate any man's just Title: and of the contrary, I will no more loose a penny I can discover that is due to his Majestie, then I will part with my eyes: I have good reason to beleeve I shall this yeare increase his Majesties Revenue to some considerable advantage, and if I live the next yeare more, and resolve not to give over till I have made the soyle of the whole Island pay his Majestie Rent. What recruites of Stores and moneyes we want Ensigne Price hath Lists of and will acquaint your Lordshipp with them. I hope his Majestie and Councill will consider that more then the Revenue comes to must bee supplied by his Majestie which if he please to send in Commodities, would turne to better account then Letters of Credit: for as they value money here, his Majestie pays above 40 per Cent for Exchange: I will not in this longer trouble your Lordshipp then whilst I begg your pardon for this tedious trouble, and as in duty bound subscribe my Selfe

Public Record Office, C. O. 77, Vol. XII, folio 273.

Your Lordshipps most obedient
and humble servant
GERVASE LUCAS.

[*Endorsed.*]
Duplicate of Sir Gervas Lucas' letter to Lord Chancellor March 2d. 1666/7 touching the fishry and the King's Lands.

[*Title inserted on first page*:—]
Letter from Sir Gervais Lucas to the Lord Chancelor.

MAY IT PLEASE YOUR LORDSHIP

Public Record Office, C. O. 77, Vol. X, folio 88.

According to your Lordships command, we herewith send you our letters to our president at Surrat, and our Agent at the Fort, in favour of the French. We have in several former letters recommended the same, and have an account from them, that they have on all occasions acted towards them as became them, and consonant to our orders, although the French have not been so candid towards us: For at Surrat they insisted very high to have our Ships strike to theirs, which our President fairly avoided. And by our last letters from Fort St. George, we have advise from our Agent, that the French General had seized two boats loaden for English accompt; and the Ship *Ruby* and her lading belonging to Mr. Jearsey, one of our Factors, and refused to restore the same, notwithstanding our Agent addressed to him to that effect. We therefore pray your Lordship would obtain for us letters to their Officers, that they may give noe occasion of future differences, and to restore the Ship and Goods taken: that so the desired amity may be preserved intire on their part, as it shall be on Ours.

We remain,
My Lord,
Your Lordships most humble Servant
NATHANIEL HERNE. [?] *Deputy.*

EAST INDIA HOUSE LONDON
23rd August, 1673.

[*Addressed.*]

For the right Honoble. the Earle of Arlington his Majesties Principall Secretarie of State These present

[*Endorsed.*]

August 23. 73.
East India Company.

The above account of the crooked devices, and devious methods of Mr. Humphrey Cook, whose subsequent conduct confirms honest Lucas' trenchant analysis of this adventurer's character, should be compared with the following narrative. Lucas paints the picture in sombre colours, but it is a faithful representation of reality; Wilcox describes in modest language the work he had accomplished. This is the first account of the system of Justice established in Bombay.

The following elaborate Report of the establishment of a Law in Bombay gives a very good account of Bombay. George Wilcox was appointed a Judge on August 8, 1672. (Bombay Council to Surat, July 12, 1672. *Selections.*) The Directors sent out the Statute Book and other law books in December of the same year, and Wilcox framed a rough Code of Civil Procedure. (*Forrest's Selections*, I, p. 64.) Portuguese Law was superseded by the English Law, and Wilcox was kept fully employed. He died of fever on August 9, 1774. A glance at the list of " Fees belonging to the Court" shows that justice was fairly cheap, though, of course, it was rough and ready. Bombay was divided into 3 hundreds, the hundred of "Bombay, of Maym, and Mazagon, each hundred to have a Justice of Peace and Constable." The Judge's salary was "pitcht upon Rs. 2,000 annually, and that to be paid out of fines, provided they were sufficient; if not, to be made up out of the treasury." This modest amount seems to have satisfied him, as the island was poor, and the pay of all officers, as " Clerks, Tipstaves, Messengers, Interpretors of the Portugal and Canary languages, and all charges belonging to the monthly sessions" was paid by him out of the fines. The "order of going to the Court of Judicature" is quaintly described, and a full report is supplied of the worthy Governor's eloquent speech on the English Law. It must have been an imposing ceremony, relieving the grey monotony of disease and poverty. He put down several drinking houses, and seems to have given general satisfaction.

Public Record Office, C. O. 77, Vol. XII, Folio 136.

According to the Governors command, I have drawn up a narrative of the establishment of the Law on the Island Bombay, as it is now setled, and confirmed by him, since his coming upon the place which is as followeth.

The watchful eye of our Honble. Governor being alwaies open to behold the things that belongs to our Peace, could never be satisfied, but in the prospect of that, which he hath now accomplished, to which end, after a most dangerous voiage from Surratt, it pleased the Almighty that he arrived safe amongst us, signifiing, though wee should be blest, yet it must be with difficulties. No sooner had his foot toucht our shore, but God toucht his heart, a fast was imediatly proclaimed, and kept, next a Proclamation issued out against the breach of the Sabboth profanness, drunkenness, and uncleanness, this rejoyct us at hoping when God was in the beginning, a blessing would be in the Conclusion. Having done this, divers petitions were brought in by the severall Cast for establishing the English Laws, upon which, his Honr. ordered me to bring in the forme and method of proceedings in a Court of Judicature, and the manner of setling al things as near as possible, according to the Custome, and constitution, of England, which having done in three several papers, he was pleased to issue forth his Proclamation for abolishing (from and after the first day of August next) the Portugal laws, and for establishing the English, and likwise to make void al Comissions of the Peace in the Portugal hands. The forme and method then offered is as followeth, vizt:

Public Record Office, C. O. 77, Vol. XII, folio 136.

A Summons to be left by an officer appointed for that purpose at the house of the Deffendant. In case of non appearance, Oath to be made in open Court that the summons was served by the messenger.

Forme of the Summons.

By vertue of an Action of trespass in the Case damages at the suit of you shal summon to appear at the Guild Hal of this Island on and in case of non appearence by his Atturney the Court will proceed to Judgment on evidence of the Plantiff.

The next Court day after summons the Plantiff to give in Declaration.

Two Court daies after Declaration to come to a Tryal, without sufficient cause shewed to the Contrary. A Court to be held every weeke if there be occasion.

Officers belonging to the Court.

A Judg, Councill, Clerk of the Papers, Tipstaffs and Clerks, besides Jury men.

Fees belonging to the Court.

	Rs.	Pice.
Summons and sealing of it	2:	00:
Entring the Action	0:	06:
Messenger for serving the summons	0:	12:
Councillers fee	1:	16:
Drawing a Declaration	1:	16:
Swearing wittness	0:	04:
Summoning a Jury	1:	00:
Jurys Verdict	2:	00:
Subpena	1:	00:
Joyning issue	1:	16:
Entring Judgment	1:	03:
Taking out execution..	2:	00:

Public Record Office, C. O. 77, Vol. XII, folio 136.

The party imprisoned if he hath a vissible estate, and wil not make sale of it towards paiment of his debts in six months time, sale shall be made for him and he released.

The second paper was reasons for setling an office for proving of wills and granting Administrations, which are as followeth.

The Law cannot have its current without this Establishment and what law can take hold of an executor, without he takes upon him the Execution of the wil, an executor in a wil is only nominal, 'tis the Probate makes him Legal.

If the Testator dies in debt, no Creditor can sue his Executor without he takes upon him the probate, should any bring an action against him ? how would he ground his Declaration, it must ly either as an Executor or Administrator, how can that be when he never did administer.

This settlement quiets the mind of al people they being in a capacity to recover their own. An Executor taking upon him the execution of a will has as much power to sue any man, as any man has power to sue him, here the laws has its current, and every man will injoy his right, and without this the best part of the law signifies litle.

Officers in the Office.

A Register, Clerke, and an Appariter.

Fees to be taken in the Office.

	Rs.	Pice.
The Probate and seale and swearing an executor	3:	08:
Ingrossing of a wil	1:	16:
For Registing it	1:	16:
This to the Register, and he to pay his Clerks and to be at al charges etce.		
For an Administration and Seale	6:	00:
Entring a Caveat	0:	12:
For warning a Caveat	0:	12:
For Coppiing a will	1:	16:

The Register to be at al charges in the Office for Pen, Ink, Paper, and bookes.

Al wills to be registed and bound up, and to be kept as records in the office, and the original wil to be there also.

Bookes to be in the Office.

A Booke of Probates, Administrations, Caveats, and a Calender, these to be renewed every Yeare at the Charge of the Register.

Al Inventoryes to be brought into the office, or the parties to be fined. The reason for this is because if Inventories are not brought, Estates wil be concealed, and so Creditors wil be defraued [*sic* ? defrauded].

The Charge of an Inventorye is two rupies a length, it being twice writt over, one for the partie, the other to remaine in the office.

An account to be likwise brought in the charge the same with the Inventory.

Public Record Office, C. O. 77, Vol. XII, folio 136.

The third paper was the manner of keeping a Sessions, and dividing Bombay into hundreds which is as following vizt.

Bombay to be devided into three hundreds. The hundred of Bombay of Maym and Mazagan each hundred to have a Justice of peace and Constable. A Sessions to be held every month, the Justices of every hundred to be there. The place Bombay and the Sessions to be kept where the Court of Judicature is kept, upon every complaint made to the Justices they to issue out their warrant, the crime to be incerted in it, the Constable to serve the warrant, if possible the Justices to make freinds, if not to binde them over to the Sessions taking security for prosecuting and appearing, sending the examination to the Clerk of the Peace, and he to draw up an Indictment, if no security can be found the partie to be sent to the Gaile til next Sessions, there to be heard before the Judg and Justices.

Two prisons to be ordered, one for debt, the other for felons, both to be in Bombay and the prisoners of each hundred to be brought thither by the Constable.

A sufficient Person to be chosen Keeper of the prison, he to put in security to the Judg against al escapes, and he to pay the debt of al escapes and to be recovered by Law.

Upon al escapes of felons and murders, the Keeper to be imprisoned and to be severely fined.

Officers belonging to the Sessions.

Clerk of the Peace, Clerks and Cryer and Interprotors.

A Constable to serve but one yeare, a new one to be chose every Easter Mundy by the major Voices of the Inhabitants, he to be sworne at Sessions, every hundred to chose their own Constable, and no Constable to serve any warrant but in his own hundred.

Church wardens to be annually chosen and sworn at the Sessions, they to see al people come to prayers mornings and Evenings, al defaulters to present them at the Sessions, as also al drunkenness, swearing, uncleanness and other Debaucheries that they may be fined according to their Crimes.

Overseers of the high waies to be annually chosen, they to act as neare as may be according to Law, Custome, and Conveniency of the place.

A Register to be made, to Register al mortgages, Sales, Deeds, Conveiances and alienations, &c.

A Coroner to be made to enquire after al murders and casual deaths, and to retourne them into Sessions, he to be an able man.

This method of law and Government thus delivered, was fully and freely debated where the Governor was pleased, weighing every particular with the Council, to approve of the whole, and ordered that

Public Record Office, C. O. 77, Vol. XII, folio 136.

the Island should be Govern'd according to this forme, and that every one should give obedience therunto.

His Honr. after this, fel upon the choise of fit persons to act in this great and weighty affair; where like a prudent and wise Senator, he discoursed very excellently upon the office and place of a Judg, declaring that a person qualified for that imploy should be prudent, knowing, grave and upright in his life and conversation, desiring, that they would likwise consider, that the honor of our English nation, depended upon the Choice of such a person, this being so wel performed, and he having received such satisfaction from the method brought in, was pleased to nominate me to officiate as Judg. I was so surprized: Knowing my inabilities to undertake so great a charge, desired his Honr. to make Choice of another, whose parts were more able to perform so great an imploy, but the whole Council approving of the Choice, imediatly voted me to stand, ordering that I should fit and prepare my self against the time appointed, and likwise find out a house where the Court of Judicature should be kept.

The next thing that offered was setling the office for proving of wills and granting Administrations, the Governor was pleased to conferr that upon me which I accepted as having been breed thre[e] years a Clerk in the Prerogative Office. His Honr. after this endeavoring to leave nothing undone, that might make the place happy, produces the Honble. Company orders for setling a Register, for Registring all Mortgages, Sales, Deeds, Alienations &ca. which Registry I have also accepted as belonging partly to the law, as likwise the establishing a Court of Conscience.

This being done, the Governor and Council tooke me off of al manner of trade and commerce appointing me wholy to the study of the Law, and to spend my time in reading such bookes as might advantage me to performe my duty in so high a place.

This disinabled me from improving that litle stock which was spared from my wife and Children, I must be no merchant, so that I can neither serve your Honr. in trade, nor advance my fortunes by commerce, I can expect no riches but what my salary wil make, and truly 25*i*. per Annum wil be but litle. A penny improv'd may turn to a pound, but when that is denied it will be just like the mans talent in the Gospel, it was the same when he tooke it out of the ground as when he put it in. This applied wil be just as I came out, so I returned, I hope I shal not gaine your Honrs. displeasure by this, I humbly throw my self and consernes at the Honble. Company's feet, not questioning, but if any thing be done to make my self and family somwhat happy, their Honrs. wil not be displeased with it, especially when their interest is no waies prejudiced.

My salary came next in debate: which before any thing like a proposal came, Several things were offered, it was thought convenient I should keepe house, and my Table should be so furnished, that their Honrs. should have creditt, and strangers entertainment, this tooke up some time, for the Governor debating the Honble. Company's interest, tooke care they should not be charged, yet something was to be done, that a creditt might go along with this new setlement, and it was agreed, that I should have an esteem put upon me by living somwhat answerable to my place. Things standing thus, a sume was pitcht upon, which was 2000 rupies annually, and that to be paid out of fines, provided, they were sufficient, if not, to be made up out of the Treasury, this past with some litle difficulty, because your Honrs. were wholy considered, before the Sume was concluded. I hope as the law has a repute upon the place, so it wil not be chargable to your Honrs. the Island is so poore, that *forma pauper* have been most of our Clients, but hitherto all Officers as Clerks, Tipstaves, Messengers, Interpretors of the Portugal and Cannary languages, and al charges belonging to the monthly Sessions, have been paid by me out of fines; As to my self, I had rather have your Honrs. favour with a litle, then abundance, with displeasure, but question not, as the Inferior Officers have their being from the Law, my self wil not be excluded. This being so, I humbly beg, that what hath past, your Honrs. wil approve, and that your great wisdomes wil be satisfied, that nothing was done, nor acted, before your Honrs. concernes were debated, which being truly considered, I am verily perswaded, that where your servants are made happy through honest meanes, your Honrs. wil rather encourage them, then be dissatisfied.

Public Record Office, C. O. 77. Vol. XII, folio 136.

The first of August drawing nigh, the President &ca. Council thought fit; that so great a day, should not pass without somthing of honor, for had there been no solemnity with this Change, the Peoples disesteeme of us, would have been greater then their satisfaction. Meddals were ordered to be made and flung among the people, and this to let them see, that what was done, could as wel be maintained.

The managment of this great business, was wholy left to our prudent and Worthy Governor, whose great wisdome appeared in this, that there was so great a Grandure with so little expensis. The day being now come, and every one in a readiness to attend the Governor, there fel so prodigious a quantity of raine, that his Honr was forct to put of the solemnity til the eight day. The order of our going to the Court of Judicature, and the works of the day be pleased to take as Followeth, vizt.

Fifty Bandaries in Green liveries marching two by two.

20 Gentues
20 Mooremen
20 Christians } each representing their several cast or sect marching two by two.

His Honrs. horse of State lead by an Englishman.

Two trumpets and Kettle Drums on horse back.

The English and Portugal Secretary on horse back carrying his Majesties letters Patents to the Honble Company and their Comission to the Governor tyed up in scarfes.

The Justices of the Peace and Council richly habited on horse back.

The Governor in his Pallankeen with fower English pages on each side in rich liveries bare headed Surrounded at distance with Peons, and blacks.

Public Record Office, C. O. 77, Vol. XII, folio 136.

The Clerke of the Papers on foot.

The fower Atturneys, or Common Leaders on foot.

The keeper of the prisons and the two Tipstaffs on foot, bare headed before the Judg.

The Judg on horse back on a Velvet foot cloath.

His Servants in Purple serge liveries.

Fower Constables with their staves.

Two Churchwardens.

Gentlemen in Coaches and Palankeens.

Both the Companies of foot (except the main Guard) marching in the Reare.

* [*sic*]

The whole as aforesaid marching through a guard of the militie* into the Bazar neare two miles in circumference, came to the Guild Hal, where the Governor entring the Court, tooke the Chaire, placing me next to him on his right hand, and the Gentlemen of the Council and Justices tooke their places accordingly. Proclamation being made and silence commanded, the Clerke of the papers read his Majesties letters Patents to the Honble Company for the Island Bombay, then the English Secretary read the Companys Comission to the Governor, which being done, he was pleased to give me my oath as Judg, as also my Comission, which was likewise read; afterwards I swore the several Justices of the Peace, the Governor giving them their Comissions, which were also read; next I swore the Publick notary and Coroner, then the Clerk of the Peace swore the Church wardens and Constables, and their staves were delivered to them by the Governor, with a charge to execute their respective offices and places honestly and uprightly, after this the Governor standing up (and the Court also rising) was pleased to make a most excellent speech in commendation of the English laws, which afterwards was Interpreted to the Portuguess in their own language by the Portugal Secretary, the speech is as followeth. Vizt.

My Worthy Countrymen, and you al good subjects of his Sacred Majesty and of the Honble Company. It is not unknown unto you that the first of August was Intended for the celebration of this solemnity, but it pleased God to send on that day and time soe great and almost prodigious quantity of raine, that I was forced to suspend it to this day. It seemes providence thought good to order some great and extraordinary accident to attend so great and extraordinary a worke, to render it the more remarkable to the advancement of his Glory; And seing it is now soe happely performed, I cannot doe less then in soe solemne a day of Joy to close up the Ceremony with a few words of consolation and advice.

In al great and publique alterations of Laws or Government wise men have observed that the minds of the People receive Impressions of satisfaction or disgust, according as their passions or Interests doe Incline them to like or dislike the Change.

I nothing doubt but in a body composed of soe many Casts of people as are on this Island, some though very few disaffected persons may be found, who more in regard to their owne ends then to the

publique good, doe privately wish this change had not bin, but that Public Re-
the old Custumes had bin continued. However in the maine I dare cord Office,
boldly affirme, that the best and most sober part of al the several C. O. 77,
Inhabitants, nay even of the Portuguess themselves are exceedingly Vol. XII,
satisfied and receive the establishment of the English Laws with much folio 136.
assurance of happiness and security therfrom.

Two things have caused some admiration in the minds of wise and considering men, as wel among our selves as of our neighbours.

First why the English having had possession of this Island now seaven years have not in al this time governed by their own laws.

Second why this Port and Island hath not thriven in trade and repute according to expectation, seing the English are knowne to be a nation soe happy and succeedful* in their enterprizes, that wherever they plant their foot, through the blessing of God on their Industry, Trade and riches doe attend them. As not only India but most parts of the habitable world can beare them wittness.

* [*sic*]

To the first consideration I shal say nothing at this time; But to the last I am free to declare my Judgment. That the only cheife reason why this Island Bombay hath not increased in trade and splendour, hath bin for want of the English laws. But in this my assertion I would not be misunderstood, for I speake not this in derogation of, or dishonor to the Laws of the Kingdome of Portugal, for I know and declare them to be excellent wise and pious Laws, But as it is manifest that all Countrys and Kingdomes are Governed by Rites, Customes and constitutions in the Execution of the Laws peculiar to themselves, soe tis an undoubted Maxime that those constitutions may stand with the good and Publique benefit of one nation which wil not square or beare proportion with the Interest of another.

This is the true State of the Case with us. The English Interest on this Island Bombay I may well compare to an hopeful Child fed with forreigne milke; which not agreeing with its natural constitution, hath hindered its groweth, and increased evill humors; But now being restored to the breasts of its own mother, there is no question, through the Providence of God, it will in time grow in Stature, good fortune and in favour with God and man.

And we may reckon the series of its good successe from the commencement of this happy day, I say this happy day, for it is a day of Joy and no mean consolation; A day of praise to God, and which wee ought to have in remembrance, and truly amongst many blessings which the Divine hand hath pleased to conferr on me: I owne this with a just devotion as a most remarkable providence over me, that God hath preserved me to this day to be a faithfull though a mean Instrument of soe good a worke.

Formerly the name of the English Nation was knowne to these parts only by the honesty of their traffique, but now I trust in God through the just execution of these laws, that our Neighbour nations will have cause to say of us, as Moses discourses of the Children of Israel, and their Laws in his Excellent speech which he makes them

Public Record Office, C. O. 77, Vol. XII, folio 136.

in the 4th Chapter of Deuteronomy. The nations, saith he, which are about you hearing of your statutes and Judgments will say,

Surely this great nation is a wise and an understanding people, for what nation is there soe great which hath statutes and Judgements soe Righteous as all these Laws which I set before you this day?

Many Nations have been famous for just and wholesome Laws as the Jews, the Athenians, the Lacedemonians, the Persians and Romans and others. As to our Laws, I shal not enter into a large emcomium of them, but in breife tel you, that these Laws, I say the nationall Laws of England, as also that Excellent Abredgement of them recommended by the Honble. Company are grounded on the Laws of God written in his holy word, and on the Laws of nature stamped on the heart of man, and they are compiled from the quintessence, or best part of all other Laws, especially those of the Roman Empire, which in their time were held as Sacred. But herein ours seem to have the advantage, in that they are free from the laborious ceremony of the one, and from the Intricacy and corruption of the other. I doe therfore pronounce you, the Inhabitants of this Island, of what quality soever, to be happy in them, and I doe require you all, in the name of his Sacred Majestie and of the Honble. Company, to acquiess therin, Assuring your selves of Justice and security in your lives, in your liberties, in your families, in your Estates, goods and prosperityes, and what ever you can in equity pretend to or call your owne. But Laws though in themselves never so wise and pious are but a dead letter and of litle force except there be a due and impartiall execution of them. I must now therefore address my discourse to you, Worthy Sir, who are appointed to be the Reverend Judge of this Court of Judicature, and the faithful Administrator of these Laws. I need not tell you what a great and important trust is Committed to you, nor need I bespeake your care and Integrity in your discharge of your Duty, for you are fully sencible of the one, and I am sufficiently convinced of the other, I shall only tell you that you have the Charge of God upon you, the Command of his Majestie and the Honble. Company, and by their order and authority from me to deal Impartial Justice to all with out fear, favour or respect of Person.

The Inhabitants of this Island consist of severall nations and Religions to wit—, English, Portuguess and other Christians, Moores, and Jentues, but you, when you sit in this seat of Justice and Judgement, must looke upon them all with one single eye as I doe, without distinction of Nation or Religion, for they are all his Majesties and the Honble. Companys Subjects as the English are, and have all an equall title and right to Justice and you must doe them all Justice, even the meanest person of the Island, and in particular the Poore, the Orphan, the Widdow and the stranger, in al matters of controversy, of Common right, and Meum and Tuum; And this not only one against the other, but even against myself and these who are in office under me, nay against the Honble. Company themselves when Law, Reason and Equity shal require you soe to doe, for this is your Duty and therin will you be justified, and in soe doing God wil be with you to strengthen you, his Majestie and the Company will comend and reward you, and I, in my place, shal be ready to assist, Countenance, honour and protect you to the utmost of the power and Authority entrusted to me; And soe I pray God give his blessing to you.

Public Record Office, C. O. 77, Vol. XII, foliol 36.

The Governor having ended his speech I delivered him a petition on behalf of al prisoners that they might have the benefit of this happy day by Injoying their libertie. His Honr. was pleased to grant me the petition, and Imediately liberty was proclamed with great acclamation, and the prison doores set open, this being done, Our Worthy Governor rises out of the Chair and was pleased to put me in, commanding that obedience should be given me by the Court, and al else in that place of Judicature, which concluded the ceremony and worke of the day with great shouts and acclamation of God save the King of Great Brittaine and the Honble. Company. His Honr. foreseeing that the concourse of people might hinder his passage in marching, appointed a master of the Ceremonies to keep good orders, and where he saw a great press to fling the meddals amongst them, which was coyned for that purpose. The Governor was pleased, with the whole Court, to march afoot to the fort, where he was received and saluted by the two Companies drawn up with three vollies of smal shot and 31 Great ordinance, and at night great Bonfires were made and the whole Island filled with rejoycing.

I doubt I have troubled your Honrs. in this tedious relation, but the time that is now spent I hope will prove happy because your Island is soe. Never was there a joyfuller day; the whole Island is become English; wee are incorporated and our Interest is al one, nothing striks them into a greater admiration then our Justice, the sound whereof remaines not only with us but hath reacht our neighbours eares; many being willing to come amongst us, there is no question but God who hath done this, wil give his blessing to it, and those who know him not in litle time may be brought to fear his name, for all kind of vice is discouraged, swearing and profaning the Lord's day punnished and al uncleanness severely chastised. I cannot omitt to give your Honrs. an account what passed at our Sessions (upon the account of rape the manner thus): one of your private Centinels, a Dutch man, enters a womans house, and offers incivilities to her, she refusing, he puls her forth by the hair of her head, draging her towards the Sea amongst a company of rocks, she made a great outcry caling out for help, but he drawing out his sword put it to her brest, swearing terrible oaths he would have his will or he would murder her, some of the Country people hearing a voise came to see what was the matter, they were no sooner espied by this fellow, but he makes to them with his sword drawn, and makes them al fley; the woman by this had means to run away, but he left persuing the people and overtooke her, draging her by the hair, and gaggs her, puting his sword to her brest, swearing being she would not consent to him willingly he would make her by force or he would kil her; she could make no further outcry he having ramed his hankerchief in her mouth, and he stil using this violence by drawing her amongst the rocks, with his sword to her brest, overcame the poore woman (being tired with strugling) and satisfied his beastiality; the woman and her husband complaining he was comitted, an Indictment was drawn up against him and the Jury, upon the woman's and

Public Record Office, C. O. 77, Vol. XII, folio 136.

witnesses' oaths, brought him in guilty, and accordingly had his sentence to be hanged, but execution day being the day after the agreement was made between your Honrs. and the people of this Island, they begged his life, which the Governor was pleased to grant but banished him imediatly of the Island. This gave a General satisfaction to the people, and has brought such a repute to our Justice, that they think themselves happy under our Government.

And that the Honble. Company may not be unacquainted with the whole proceedings of their Island, be pleased to pardon me if I trouble your Honrs. with what hath passed at our private Sessions.

A french man had his house puld down for seling drink and permitting publick gaming on the Lord's day in time of prayer, as also for harbouring lewd women, and suffering al kind of debauchery, and al this after warning given him to the contrary.

Several persons fined for their contempt and obstinancy in refusing to come to Church, spending their time in publick house to the scandoll of our Christian religion and contempt of Government.

The Butchers and Fishermen warn'd in to supply the markets with fish and flesh at moderate rates, that housekeepers may not be at a losse to provide for their families, nor Europe ships for fresh provissions at their arrival.

An Hospital to be provided for the sick, that care may be taken them by the Doctors (in one place *), and this to be done without charge to the Honble. Company.

* [crossed out in original].

Care taken for the mending and making publick high waies from place to place, and this to be done at the publick charge.

Several publick drinking houses put downe for permitting al manner of debauchery and wickedness and seling drink without license.

I shal not insert further for fear of being tedious, my Duty commands me to a just account, if in that I have been troublesome: tis my zeale to your Honrs. service, which as it requires my faithfulness, so I hope it wil beg my pardon, my conclusion shal be my prayers that God that hath made your Honrs. famous here wil likwise make you happy hereafter.

GEORGE WILCOX.

BOMBAY 30 *December* 1672.

[*Endorsed.*]

George Wilcox Narrative concerning the establishing the English laws on Bombaay.

No. 4.

Received 13 *August* 1673 *per the Rainebow.*

A Court of Committees holden the 14*th day of February* 1672 [1672/3].

On reading a letter from Sir Rob. Southwell with one enclosed written him by the Portugal Ambassador, desiring the Companys Orders to the President at Surat for reestablishing the Portuguez Jesuits in their Estates at Bombay; It is ordered that it be referred to the Committees for Suratt to peruse the Orders already made in this busines, and what hath been written by our Factors of the proceedings at Goa; and to make Report thereof, with their opinion what answer is fit to be given to Sir Robert Southwell touching the same: and the care thereof is referred to Maj: Thomson. Court Book, XXVIII, page 95a.

The following important document supplies us with very valuable information on many striking events of that stormy period. That the Company suffered from Sivaji's depredations is clear from the various accounts of its factors.

Wee come now to acquaint you with the Occurences of these parts since the last Monsoone. The Patans, a people bordering on Candaharr, are fallen into the Mogulls Territories, and taken the Province of Cabull, driving Mohobutt Cawne out of the cheife Citty, so named where they have seated themselves, and as yet, Wee heare not of any Army the Mogull hath sent against them to recover the Country. Sevagee hath fallen into the King of Visapores Country (who deceased this yeare) and rob'd divers places of Consequence, and taken some castles, among other places Hubely that Mart of our Carwarr Factory where wee sell and buy most of the goods that Port affords us. There the Honble. Company have lost to the amont of about £3500 sterling rob'd by Sevagee's soldiers, since which inrodes the Visapore King hath sent an Army against him, and on this side lyes the Mogulls forces, against both which he hath raised a Potent army. And hath so well fenced the Avennues into his Country, that he hopes to deale with them both, though wee beleive the Visapore Army may withdraw it not being the Interest of that King to destroy Sevagee who is the only Bullwark betweene him and the Mogull. And notwithstanding he is thus besett yett upon any rumour of an army being within 60 miles of Surrat the Towne is allarmd and ready to fly, as they were the passed month, when the Gates were shutt up for some time to keepe the people in. The French at St. Thoma beat off the Golcundah army, and raised the seige (this wee think wee advised the last Monsoone) afterwards Mounsieur La Hay the Vice Roy with two shipps of Warr went to Metchlepatam where he burnt 5 or 6 Jonncks and threatned the Towne if that King would not come to a peace with them. Haveing spent there some time in the Month of June he returned to St. Thoma where unexpectedly he found Rickleffe Van Goens with a Fleete of 19 men of Warr before it, he stood in for the Road but the wind chopt about and having discharged some broad sides with the outermost Shipps he stood off to Sea and fell in with some Port about 30 Leagues to the Southward where hee had not beene long but hee espied our Fleete of shipps bound from England which hee tooke to bee the Dutch Fleete pursuing him he sett sayle again and put for St: Thoma where it was his good fortune that the Dutch were gone from the place after they had discharged some broad sides against it, and he gott safe into his Goverment where not long before Mounsieur Baron one of the Public Record Office, C. O. 77, Vol. XII, folio 230.

Public Record Office, C. O. 77, Vol. XII, folio 230.

Directors Generall here was safely arrived with 3 Vessells from Surrat. The Dutch have bin using all their Interest in the Golcundah Court to draw downe their forces again to beseige it by land and they will beseige it by Sea, and promise to deliver the Citty to the King, but as to their further proceedings against St. Thoma wee have not yet advice And our Fleets arrivall on that Coast the 26th June might put the Dutch Gennerall upon other Counsells. The *Massingberd* spending her head and *Boltsprite* put back againe to England but blessed be God came safe into Madrasse road and Joyned with the Fleete the 30th July. Wee heard by Letters from thence in August that Van Goens with a Fleete of 22 Sail (but some of them crasy shipps and not very well manned, only his owne shipp had 65 brasse Gunns 250 men) were off Negapatam neare Ceilon, whence upon occasion he might drawe more men from his Garrisons, and probably attend the motion of our Fleete in passing about Ceilon, but Wee have no advice of any Actions nor heare not from Sir William Langhorne of their Departure toward us though he promised to dispatch them the 1st of September and send us advise thereof imediately, but wee beleive hee sent directly to Bombay, and the Army's lying in the way may have hindred the passage of the Cossetts. Wee are now hourely expecting newes of their Arriveall on this Coast, for Wee trust in God they were able by his protection to make their way through the Enemy.

[*Endorsed.*]

Occurrences in India from
May 1673 to November following.

The Company's petition to Charles, reproduced below, summarises the causes of its conflict with the Portuguese. A comparison of its grievances, with the rights enjoyed by the Portuguese by their Treaty with Humphrey Cook, leads me to believe that some of the actions of the Portuguese were permissible under the Treaty. The main fault of Charles lay in not repudiating that indefensible convention earlier. As regards the question of the dependencies, the cession of Bombay did not involve the cession of adjoining territories, and Bassein was no more a dependency of Bombay at that period, than was Thana. The Treaty, it will be remembered, had ceded Bombay and its "appurtenances". This term was in itself liable to endless discussions, and we are not surprised to find Charles insisting on the delivery of Thana. It is, however, clear that the Portuguese exceeded the limits assigned to their privileges, and that they made it impossible for the Company to prosecute their trade in safety. The Company requested Charles to examine the right and extent of its dominion in Bombay, and this, as we shall see, was done with characteristic thoroughness.

George Wilcox's quaint narrative of the establishment of Law in Bombay should be compared with the vigorous representations of the Company to Charles II. The one gives a vivid picture of the simple splendour and homely saws of the honest Governor, the other an energetic protest against the encroachments of their wily neighbours. That these encroachments were the inevitable outcome of their own cupidity and ignorance is complacently ignored by that eminently "just" institution; nor do they pay much heed to the original rights exercised by the Portuguese in that part. Of the legality of these rights there is no more doubt than there is doubt of their injurious effects on the Company's trade. Legally, the Portuguese were in a very strong position, and the Company's mistake consisted in trying to argue away all the rights secured by them under their treaty with Cook. Charles cut the Gordian knot by repudiating the Treaty altogether. This, it must be confessed, was the only possible step, as, of course, it was the logical deduction from the insecure legal position in which the poor Company was placed. The following petition sums up all the causes of this quarrel:—

To the Kings most Excellent Majestie.
The humble petition and Representation of the Governor and Company of Merchants of London trading to the East Indies touching the Rights of the Port and Bay of Bombaim.

Public Record Office, C. O. 77, Vol. XIII, folio 47.

SHEWETH

That your Majesty being by a Treaty with the Crown of Portugal seised of the Port and Island of Bombay in the East Indies, with all the Rights territories and appurtenances thereof whatsoever, aswel the property as the full dominion and sovereignty of the said Port and Island, with all the Royalties thereof; aswel in order to augment the Interest and Trade of the English in those parts (which are the words of the said Treaty) as to enable them to assist, defend and protect the Subjects of Portugal against their enemies: Your Majesty did in your Princely wisdom think it convenient (after several years governing that place by your imediate Officers) to grant and transferr the said Port and Island of Bombay, with the appurtenances, unto your petitioners, who having applied themselves with great expense to build, cultivate and fortify the said place, so as to make it for all ages beneficial to your Majesty and your Kingdoms, and even useful to your Allies of the Crown of Portugal, according to the original scope and intendment of the said Treaty, Your Petitioners have yet from time to time met with so much unkindness and such arguments of malevolence in the Portuguese Governors in those parts against the prosperity and settlement thereof, that they are constrayned now again to appeal unto your Majesty for justice and protection. And in truth, their grievances doe most peculiarly concern your Majesty to redress and vindicate, as relating to your Majesties Sovereignty and the Royalties of the place, which those people most despitefully endeavour to overthrow.

Public Record Office, C. O. 77, Vol, XIII, folio 47.

Your Majesty may vouchsafe to call to mind the difficulties which attended the first possession, even while the Treaty was fresh, while that Crown was involved in warrs, and your Majesties Troops in actual service in Portugal. How that by the perversness of a Governor (though carried over to that very intent) the whole voiage of the Lord Marlebrough and his Squadron was overthrown, to your Majesties great damage and the possession utterly refused, until fresh orders could come into India. In which time, of 500 English Soldiers sent over under Sir Abraham Shipman to enter and secure the place, 300 of them miserably died with want and extremities in a small desolate Island, which was the onely place of refuge they had. So that when at length the residue entred into Bombay, they were not in a condition to dispute, but minded at that distance their own preservation more than any Royalties or Dependencies of the place. And what by the death of some and want of vigour or capacity in others that commanded there, your Majestie's Rights were not asserted. After which, your Majesty was graciously pleased to grant the same to the Petitioners. They at their very entrance found the effects of this distraction, and all advantage taken by the Portugueses from the disadvantages they themselves created. And because your Petitioners heard it alleged, That if more indulgence were expressed by them to the Portugueses remaining in the place, all these hardships would be soon redrest, They did begin and so effectually apply themselves to the relief of the said Portugueses in all their interests and pretensions, as to leave none of them with any just cause of complaint.

The way being thus prepared, and that Article of the Treaty well weighed and considered, which did transferr the Sovereignty of the place and of its dependencies to your Majesty, some persons of account in your Petitioners service, were by them sent as Comissioners solemnly to treat with the Vice Roy of Goa, for the clearing up of these points : but after all the methods of fayr treaty and other perswasions were attempted, nothing could be obtained from him but a declaration of want of orders from Portugal. And so farr he appeared from admitting a trade or good correspondence, which was also insisted on, according to the cleer and express tenor of the said treaty, that he expressly forbade the setling of any English at Basseen or Damon, or even the intercourse of our own boats from Bombay to the Mayn, especially when they shall bring Tymber or Provisions, from whence onely those necessaries can be had.

Your Petitioners presume to annex hereunto the 11th Article of the said Treaty, and the cleer interpretation it seems to bear : which with the Mapp will plainly shew the natural dependencies of those small places adjacent, as the memory of former parties will also justify the whole Right of your Petitioners present demands : Yet contrary to so much justice do they obstruct the freedom of trade, and the progress of your Petitioners endeavours for a happy settlement, as may appear in the particulars following.

1. They doe not onely refuse to deliver to them those small Islands and Dependencies mentioned, but doe on some of them so strengthen themselves, as that for but passing by in the open stream and at a distance from them, sally out with their boats, and lay arbitrary impositions on our Trade.

2. They force your Petitioners to pay Duties for passing but* by some other places, which were known to depend absolutely on the Custom house of Bombay (Mayhem) and to pay themselves their Duties there. * [sic.]

3. They pretend dominion over the Portugueses and other Subjects remaining with your Petitioners, and to so much of Sovereignty in the very Bay, as in their Brigantines to wear their flag, in the defiance and dishonor of our Forts: Nor will they permit our own Ships to sail quietly in those parts, without the protection of their passports. Your Petitioners name not other affronts and depredations that are often susteyned, but these particular ones would probably all cease if the said Article were duly observed.

And seeing it is visible that in India the same Spirit of contradiction is derived† to all other Governors which was so prejudicial to your Majesty in the first, and that whatever it be that your Petitioners expend towards their happines they are never to thrive in that place, while they patiently submit to injuries, which the Governors there declare they cannot, or at least will not redress. † [sic.]

Your Petitioners therefore most humbly implore your Majesty first to cause the right and extent of your Dominion in that place, granted by the said Treaty, to be examined; and if they appear to have been thereby conveyed to your Majesty, that your Majesty would vouch safe to assert them, for your own honour and the protection of your Subjects, that your Petitioners may be restored to the sole dominion of the said Island, and that in the mean time till the said claim can be examined and asserted, as your Petitioners doe much esteem and in all things cultivate the friendship of the Portugueses (which your Majesties strict alliance with that Crown doth require) So they beseech your Majesty to procure from his Royal Highness the Prince Regent of Portugal, an effectual command to his Officers and Ministers in India. That noe Governor or other person may henceforth presume by erecting of a Blockhouse, to obstruct the English from passing by Tannah or Carinjah, or to impose or demand any Customs or Duties from the English, but that they may freely pass with their boats and vessels by the said places without any interruption, as the Inhabitants of Bombay have formerly done; and that the said Governors, Officers and Ministers may be enjoyned to live upon better terms of amity and friendship than hitherto they have done. Your Petitioners expecting nothing more than what the favour of the Treaty leads them to demand, and the publique fayth thereof binds the Portugueses to make good.

And they shall ever pray &c.

The following extracts from the *Court Minute Book*, Vol. XIX, in the India Office throw further light on this dispute :—

A Court of Committees holden the Third day of March 1674 [1674/5].

It is ordered, that it be referred to the Comtees. for Surrat (unto whom Mr Jollife Mr Boone and Mr Paige are added) to consider what is fit to be presented to his Maty. touching the opening of trade at Bombay, which is obstructed by the Portuguezes, or otherwise, for the advantage of that Island, and to report the same, and the care thereof is committed to Mr Rudge.

A Court of Committees holden the Nineteenth of July 1675.

It is ordered, that it be referred to the Comtees. for Surrat as also to Mr Jollife Mr Boone Mr Paige and Mr Houblon to consider of the late advises from Bombay touching the obstruction given by the Portuguezes to the Compa. trade, and to prepare a Memorial of what is fit to be presented to his Maty. touching that affayr, or any other particular that may be advantageous to the Compa., and to report the same to the Court, and the care thereof is committed to Mr. Houblon.

A Court of Committees holden 23 *February* 1675 [1675/6].

The several Members of Court now present were desired to accompany the Governor to Whitehall this afternoon to present a petition to his Maty..touching the obstruction that is given to the Compa. trade at Bombay, by the Portugueses in those parts.

The following document is a continuation of the preceding, but it enters, in greater detail, into the disputes with the Portuguese. The Company complained that " when their boats are sent by Caranja or Tannah for provisions, from whence onely such things must come, the fort in this place of Tannah, comands the Boats in, and the Governor levies 10, 12, or 14 p. c. as he pleaseth ; and because at Caranja the Stream is broad and no Fort on that side to comand, Boats are there armed out with soldiers, and such duty levied by them as they think fitt, unless when the English also put soldiers in their Boats, as they doe to resist it." These irritating proceedings could not fail to arouse anger, and the later documents describe at length the various forms which these squabbles assumed. Charles acted vigorously, and made a strong representation to the Portuguese. His letter to the latter, repudiating Cooke's Convention, has been reproduced above. (*See supra.*)

Bombaim described, how transferred to his Majesty, how afterwards to the Company, what Injuries suffered from the Portugees, what address made to the Vice Roy of Goa, what answer returned by him, what Opinion given by the President and Council thereon. And lastly the Soverainty of the whole Haven and Islands asserted.

The Haven of Bombaim lies neer 50 leagues Southward of Surrat in 19 Degrees of North latitude, and comprehends all the Sea or Water that enters between Colar, on the West point of the Island Salsett and the two small Islands of Hunary and Cunary on the South neer the Maine, which water is there above 20 Miles wide.

It is reputed one of the most famous Havens of all the Indies as never being choaked up by the Stormes or yearly Monsons, but affords at all Seasons reception and security to whole Fleets.

Within this Haven or Bay stands the Island of Bombaim (called aunciently Mahim) which gives Title and denomination to the whole Sea that enters, which is called the Port of Bombaim.

There are some small spotts of Islands as Trumbay Galean and others as Elefante and Patacas scarce worth the notice. But two others are of consideration Namely Carania, which is wholy encompassed by the Water of the Said Port, and Salsett, a much larger Island, in figure almost square, and against two sides whereof the Water of this Harbor Strikes.

The West side of Salsett is wholy exposed to the Ocean, and the North side is washed by an inlett of Water called the Road of Bazaim reaching as far as the East Point of Salsett, where wee may allow that the water of the Port of Bombay, neer the Streight at Tannah, does determine, Because though it flowes up from Bombay thorow here into the said Inlet, yet being now reduced into a narrow Channel, it may at that Point yeild up its name to the said larger Inlet of the Road of Bazaim.

On part of the Island of Bombaim stands Mahim, the name formerly of the whole Island.

There, in old time, was built by the Moores a great Castle, and in the time of the Kings of Portugall, this was the place where his Courts and the Custome house was kept, and here were the Duties paid by the Vessels of Salset Trumbay Gallean and Bundy on the Maine &c.

This was the place which by the 11th Article of the Treaty of Marriage was as freely conferred on his Majesty by the Crown of Portugall, as was the Citty of Tanger by another Article in almost the same words, though in performance and execution the difference proved very great. For when (as in the Petition is set forth) the voyage of his Majesties squadron was overthrown, and the Soldiers lay languishing for new Orders, when at last they came, Sir Abram Shipman, the intended Governor, was found dead, so that his Secretary, one Mr. Cook, took on him to receive possession of the place, and that even upon whatever conditions the Vice Roy pleased, violence on the one hand and necessity on the other made him agree (but without any Commission) to things which were imposed quite contrary to the Treaty; For in the Treaty nothing appeares in any part of it but favour to the English. They have Liberty granted of free Trade and habitation in all the Dominions of Portugall, whither of the West or East Indies, and particularly in Goa, Cochin and Dio, to remain as far as fower Families in each with all the priviledges of Portugees; Nothing seems to be the whole Scope of the Treaty, but that his Majestie should give protection to Portugall, and Portugall in liew thereof give extent of Dominion unto England. And as the present quiet and condition of Portugall bears witnes for his Majestie how intirely the Tyes of his said Protection have been accomplished. It were also to be wished that either in the said freedome of Trade, or in the Dominion of Bombaim, Portugall had but remembered the Treaty as well.

But so far short did the severall Governors fall from the obligations thereof, or of thinking to repair the Affront which his Majestie suffered by the non surrender, that his Majestie being tired out with such proceedings thinks fitt to transfer the place to his Subjects of the East India Company, in hopes that by their care and closer application to those Governors, the matters complained of might be negociated to a better Issue.

The Company enter and doe all things to make the place considerable; but (as in the Petition is sett forth) when their Boats are sent by Caranja or Tannah to the Maine, either for Merchandize Timber or provisions, from whence onely such things must come, The Fort in this place of Tannah, comands the Boats in, and the Governor Levies 10, 12, or 14 per cent as he pleaseth; And because at Carunja the Stream is broad and no Fort on that side to command, Boats are there armed out with Soldiers, and such duty levied by them as they think fitt, unles when the English also put Soldiers in their Boats, as often they doe to resist it.

But it neither consisting with the progress of Trade nor the Prosperity of the place to be thus in a State of Tribute, and contention, It was thought expedient to chose some fit persons to send unto the Vice Roy of Goa to treat for better Termes in this troublesome affair, and accordingly Mr. James Addams and Mr. Walker with a Portugees Secretary, and other Servants are sent with full and ample Instructions.

First, To pray liberty of Trade according to the Treaty and next an exemption from these duties, which were exacted against all reason, and even the Custome in all places, where the Navigable Passages are alwaies free.

But unto these demands, which were so modest in themselves and attended with all the deportment, which might make the application gratefull; for there was neither pressing for reparation of Injuries done, or restitution of what was past, which Justice did require.

The Vice Roy makes answer as followeth—

1. He saies he will cause entire observation to be given to the Treaty published in 1661.

2. He confesses it is just for him to give ear to what the Company desire about free Comerce in the Territories of the Prince of Portugall, But he hath no Order to yeild any such thing, It haveing been expressly forbid to other Governors, besides the French and Dutch, should he grant it, would claim the like, That it is a Royalty annexed to the person of the Prince, and must be immediately directed by himself,

onely he would to show his good will allow the English to trade in Goa, paying the same duties as the Portugees doe pay.

3. That as to their Second Point although it was true, all navigable Rivers were free to pass without paying of Tributes yet this rule did not reach unto the conquests made in the Indies whose Navigation did solely appertain to the Crown of Portugall. Besides that liberty was to be understood of Rivers that stood open to all by the Law of Nations, and not of Rivers that were lock't, as the English well know the Practice in the passage of the Sound; and with much more reason ought it to be in those of Tannah and Caranja, which with the Islands adjacent made a Barr that is lock't or shut up; And besides that as he cannot order anything in this affair, It being also a Royalty and out of his Power and Comission; so cannot he free even the Portugees from the Payments accustomed there, therefore the English are the less to wonder if they also must pay.

Yet in respect to the Honoble. English Company he will acquaint his Highnes the Prince with all, hopeing from his Benevolence such a Resolution as may be very convenient, and in the mean time if the Officers of Tannah and Caranja exact more then what hath been still accustomed to be paid, they shall be punished with rigour.

LUIS DE MENDOSA FURTADO.

3rd February 1673.

Upon receipt of this extraordinary, but finall answer, the Envoy returned to Bombay, haveing, either by the very ill aire of that place or some thing worse, lost 3 of his Company and himself and another at Deaths door.

But the President and the Councell there doe on the said answer make these following observations.

1. That notwithstanding promise is made to fulfill the Treaty of 1661, and the Vice Roy gives ear to the demand of free Trade (which is made but according to the Treaty) yet he wants orders therein, and saies that other Governors have had orders quite to the contrary, and takes on him to argue and shew inconveniencies against the express Articles of a Treaty; But at last he will as it were voluntarily allow a Trade at Goa, when it is just in the same manner as the Treaty does direct.

2. That after he allowes Navigable Rivers to be free from Tribute, yet the Indian Navigation is to know no such freedome having been conquered by the Portuguees to whome it solely appertaines, (This happily was the Strain in the reign of Don Emanuel, but now the case is altered and the argument quite worn out).

3. The difference made between open and shutt Rivers hath no application to Tannah and Caranja, where there are no Rivers at all, for it is the Sea it self flowes in, and though it grows Streighter in those two places, yet still the passages are open and navigable, as at Caranja the Water is two Miles over, and even at Tannah 'tis about half a Mile over, onely they have erected here a Fort in the middle of the Water, which commands Boats that pass, and here such Arbi-

trary duty is taken as pleaseth the Governor, who is but a Substitute to the Governor of Bazaim, to whose sole Profit this Revenue comes and nothing thereof paid to the Prince of Portugall. Nor hath it ever appeared to us that these Passages were stop't and obstructed by any Orders from Portugall, but a pure effect of the violence and oppression of the Government in India. Nor are the Shoares upon the Maine, opposite to Tannah and Caranja, in the obedience of Portugall, but inhabited by Moores, and under their own Moorish Princes, which overthrowes their pretence to Tribute.

4. It is true that the Portugees themselves who now pass at Tannah are made to pay, but they never paid there formerly. It appearing in the Forall or record for Regulation of the Custome House, which was kept at Mahim on Bombay, That at Mahim all duties were paid for the Trade of the Ports and Islands adjacent, and that no Merchandize or Provisions comeing from Calean, Bundy, or any of the Islands (in the Road of Bazaim) and passing by at Tannah to come to Bombay did ever pay; so that since the English are come there, here is a violence imposed by the Portugees on their own Subjects in order to give precedent and Justification to the like violence upon us. And the Vice Roy takes up this for his most forcible Argument, as if it was of auncient Custome, which the Records Shew plainly to be but since the English have planted there.

5. That although the Vice Roy pretends to lay this affair so before the Prince as that his favour may be expected in it, yet by credible advice, he so represents the matter, as to make the Prince inexorable, and that they there in India will oppose the English herein to the utmost, so that all application seems fruitless, and the whole will depend on his Majestie's asserting his Right even to the Islands themselves, for they justly belong unto him by his Sovereignty in the Port, and the dependance they have on the Capitall Island of Bombay.

If his Majestie or the Company give but Comission the whole work is feisible, at least when the Portugees should see they must part with the whole Islands, they would easily assent to the Just freedome of Trade, which hitherto hath onely been insisted on.

And thus they conclude attending orders from the Company.

Now as to his Majesties Right of Sovereignty to these Islands, which give all this trouble, tis necessary to consider distinctly, the words in the 11th Article of the Treaty of Marriage, which sayes, That the King of Portugall does (with the advice and assent of his Councel) grant and transfer to his Majestie the Port, and Island of Bombay, with all the Rights, Profitts, Territories and dependances whatsoever; and the direct, full and absolute Dominion, and Empire of the said Port and Island, and of the Premises, and all the Royalties of the same.

By which words it is plaine

1. That the Dominion of that part of the Sea, which enters and makes the port of Bombay is his Majesties cleer and undoubted right.

2. That the Islands which stand in this Port (as doe Caranja Elefante Patecos, etc.,) which are surrounded by the waters thereof and which cannot be approched but thorow this Dominion of his

Majestie, cannot belong to any other Sovereign then his Majestie. For if they did, then have those Islands right to give Law to the Port, which were to admit the exercise of two different Sovereignties in one and the same place.

3. But as to Salsett tis true; the case is not Just the same, for this Island is bigger in Circumference six times then the Island of Bombay, and but half surrounded with the waters thereof, However it is conceived that the Soverainty of this Island also belongs to his Majestie Because

4. That the Island of Bombay as the Capitall place gives Denomination to the Port, whose surface and extent is much larger then the Extent of Salset; if it imported any thing to Jurisdiction, which was greater then the Capitall Place or its dependencies.

5. Next, the Kings Courts and the Custome Hows were in the Portugees time held and established at Mahim (or Bombay) for all the places adjacent, and as such did Salset depend for Justice; and there also made Payment of its Custome Duties.

6. Besides the said Practice, the very dignity of the Port, Its usefullnes to Navigation, and its safty to mankinde, drawes to it a Naturall dependance and Subserviency of the neighbouring Shores; For had that inlett of Water in the Road of Bazaim (which washes but one side of the square) equall perfections with the Port of Bombay, it might have equall Prerogative, and so by way of an expedient, the Soverainty of Salset might be divided by a line drawn from the North Point neer Tannah to the South Point of Colar. But there being no Parity in the qualifications, there can be no competition about the Dominion.

7. On the Island of Bombay are more Soldiers, more Inhabitants, more Armes, Ammunition, Cannon and a better Fortress then on Salsett, and all the rest of the Islands together; besides the benefit of the Port to admit of all the Supplies his Majestie can give, which are beleived superior to those of Portugall.

Therefore what can the words of the Treaty mean otherwise, when in transferring the Port and Island of Bombay, It gives all the Rights, Profitts, Territories and dependances whatsoever; It grants the direct, full and absolute Dominion and Empire of the said Port, of the said Island, and of the Premisses; and that without any reservation, which had been absolutely necessary if Salsett and Caranja (which lie so in the bosom of the rest) had not been also granted.

Lastly his Majestie is the best Judge of his own honour and how far that may be concerned in this Question.

Which therefore is most humbly Submitted.

[*Endorsed in Pencil.*]

23 *February*, 1675/6.

[*Endorsed.*]

East India Company Petition and Case.
Read in Councill February 23rd, 1675.
Read at the Committee 2 March, 1675/6.
Read again 11th January, 1676.

The following reports of the Council will be studied with interest, as it is an extremely good example of the efficient way in which its work was performed. The Lords of the Council examined most carefully all the data, and framed their resolution only after a voluminous mass of material had been thoroughly gone into. Their progress would probably have been more rapid, if they had been able to find the old map of Bombay. But neither by Clarendon, who searched for, nor by Sir William Morrice, "who acknowledges the receipt of a small box of Plantation Papers from the old Lord Clarendon, at his Departure, nor by Sir Philip Warwick, who lived with the Earl of Southampton at the time the Council sate at the Earl's House, where the said map was exposed, can any manner of Tydings bee had thereby." The results of the Committee on Bombay are summarised in the document dated January 16, 1676-77; while the elaborate report of the Council, dated February 12, 1776-77, is contained in C. O. 77, Vol. 13, folio 165. Charles' letter to the Portuguese King, repudiating Cook's Treaty with the Portuguese Viceroy, was really based upon this Report. A comparison of the two documents will make this point clear. (*See* Charles' letter dated March 10, 1776-77 *supra*.) The Instructions to Sir Abraham Shipman, a copy of which is printed below, contained marginal notes in Clarendon's hand. Sir Robert Southwell's Report on the map of Bombay is instructive. The Company must have possessed an old map of Bombay. Even Davis' sketch would have been useful. This is surprising enough; much more surprising is the failure of the Government to procure another copy, or some other map, of Bombay. The Company, it is clear, lay claim to a territory to which it was not entitled under the Treaty, and the old map might have shown the absurdity of these claims. It is noticeable that Fanshawe had demanded Bassein, *in addition to Bombay*, as early as 1663, and that the demand had been resisted. It was but a short step from Bassein to Thana and Carinjah, and the Company returned to the charge in 1776. Their Report, dated February 12, 1776-77, should be carefully studied. It is a very elaborate document, and gives a lively account of the difficulties they experienced in the prosecution of their trade. But it is unconvincing, and we are not deceived by the arguments brought forward in support of their appeal. From Charles, however, they received a favourable reply, and the subsequent growth of Bombay is due partly to the strenuous advocacy of their cause by that monarch.

The Report, dated February 23, 1676-77, is supplemented by the document "touching the limits of Bombain and Maps" reproduced below from Folio 125, Vol. XIII, C. O. 77, Public Record Office. In the latter, an attempt is made to deduce the right to Carinjah and Tannah from Instructions and Commission to Sir Abraham Shipman, and the original Treaty itself is left in the background. The Company, it need hardly he added, could acquire only those rights which Charles II had secured under the Treaty, and this is admitted in the Report itself which states " they [*viz.*, Instructions and Commission to Shipman] are not the Rule of his Majesties Right . . . . but the Treaty is the Rule." It would have been better to have discussed Clause XI of the Treaty, and discussed the limits of Bombay in accordance with the spirit of the Treaty.

The clause is as follows :—" That for the better improvement of the English interest and commerce in the East Indies, and that the King of Great Britain may be better enabled to assist, defend, and protect the subjects of the King of Portugal in those parts from the power and invasion of the States of the United Provinces, the King of Portugal, with the assent and advice of his Council, gives, transfers, and by these presents grants and confirms to the King of Great Britain, his heirs and successors for ever, the Port and Island of Bombay in the East Indies, *with all the rights, territories, and appurtenances whatsoever thereunto belonging ; and together with the income and revenue, the direct, full and absolute dominion and sovereignty of the said port, island, and premises,* with all their royalties, freely, fully, entirely and absolutely. He also covenants and grants that the quiet and peaceable possession of the same shall with all convenient speed be freely and effectually delivered to the King of Great Britain or to the persons thereto appointed by the said King of Great Britain for his use. In pursuance of this cession, the inhabitants of the said island (as subjects of the King of Great Britain, and under his sovereignty, crown, jurisdiction, and Government) being permitted to remain there and to enjoy the free exercise of the Roman Catholic religion in the same manner as they do at present, it being always understood, as it is now declared once for all, that the same regulations shall be observed for the exercise and preservation of the Roman Catholic religion in Tangier and all other places which shall be ceded and delivered by the King of Portugal into the possession of the King of Great Britain, as were stipulated and agreed to on the surrender of Dunkirk into the hands of the English ; and when the King of Great Britain shall send his fleet to take possession of the said Port and Island of Bombay, the English shall have instructions to treat the subjects of the King of Portugal throughout the East Indies in the most friendly manner, to help and assist them, and to protect them in their trade and navigation there." (*Signed on June* 23, 1661.)

In this clause the interpretation of the words "appurtenances," territories," and "premises" will determine the relative claims of the English and the Portuguese to Carinjah and Tannah. There is no evidence to believe that Carinjah and Tannah were, *at that time*, regarded as an integral part of Bombay, and the representations to the Portuguese King, to which the document quoted from Folio 125, Vol. XIII, refers, met with resolute refusal on the part of the Portuguese King (*see supra*). The mere presentation of a Memorial to the Portuguese Ambassador cannot be held to be a recognition of the claims of the Company, nor is it correct to state, as the document explicitly asserts, that no reply was given. At the time of the signing of this Treaty, and a few years after, Bombay was regarded as completely distinct from the two places claimed by the Company. Legally, the Portuguese position was very strong, and the arguments adduced by the Company and the Lords of the Council are unconvincing. The right to the two places could be claimed only under the Treaty; it could not be deduced from the Instructions, Commission, etc., to the King's officers. The Instructions, it is clear, had reference not merely to Bombay, but also to other places. It is not necessary to point out that the other places were not the places claimed later on. The Commission referred to such islands and territories as might be *acquired* for the King, either by cession or by conquest. The question of tolls and vexatious dues levied by the Portuguese could be decided only after the claims of the Portuguese to Carinjah and Tannah had been determined. Moreover, their Treaty with Humphrey Cook had considerably strengthened their position, and it was not till after the repudiation of that Treaty by Charles II that vigorous measures could be applied for the removal of these dues. It will be noticed that Charles refers to the complaint of the Company with regard to Anglo-Dutch been a fruitful source of contention, during the passes. This had negotiations, and the remarkable report of the Counci lof Trade and Plantations, to which reference was made in No. I, Vol. I, of this *Journal* (*see my articles on the "East India Trade," in No.* 1), had voiced these grievances in no uncertain terms. Charles' decision to support the Company's claim for passes to Indian juncks or ships for security in their navigation to Persia and other parts was a logical deduction from this decision.

Sir Abraham Shipman's Commission and Charles' Instructions to him, should be compared with the elaborate Reports of the Committee on Bombay. Sir Robert Southwell's Report is important and should be compared with the letters of the Portuguese Ambassador quoted above.

MAY IT PLEASE YOUR MAJESTIE

Public Record Office, C. O. 77, Vol. XIII, folio 165.

There has been long depending before us a Complaint from the East India Company touching Injuries received by them at Bombaim, from the Portugeses. They set forth, and make it appeare, that Your Majestie's Dominion in that Port and Island is much infring'd; and their Liberty of Trade, to the Main Land, quite interrupted, by Arbitrary Taxes imposed on them at Tannah and Carinjah for but passing in the open streams. That they applyed themselves in due manner, for the Reparation of these Evills unto the Vice Roy at Goa, but without effect. Soe that we are prepareing a large adresse to Your Majestie with our humble advice that you would enter into some Negotiation with the Prince of Portugall, for the ascertaining Your Rights (by the Eleventh Article of the Treaty of Marriage) in the Port and Island of Bombaim and the dependencies thereof, whereby Your Subjects of the East India Companie may have a returne of the great expences of about Seaventy Thousand pounds laid out by them, as they affirme, in the defence of that Island; and Your Kingdome alsoe reape the lasting advantages thereof by Trade.

But forasmuch as the longer these Evills continue, the more incurable they will grow; therefore by the Ships which are now departing for India, wee doe thinke it adviseable, and humbly offer it to Your Majestie as our opinion. That some intimation of Your Majesties care of your Subjects, and Your Owne Sovereignty, in those parts bee given the Vice Roy at Goa by a letter to the effect following.

That Your Majestie hath lately taken into Consideration the Complaints of Your Subjects of the East India Company, who finde themselves much disappointed of the Freindship they hoped for from the Portugese Nation, in findeing many severities exercised on them, contrary to the Treaty of Marriage, soe that Your Majestie is now entering into an Elucidation of the Eleventh Article of the said Treaty with Your Deare Brother the Prince of Portugal, from whose Justice you cannot doubt but Your Rights of Dominion in the Port and Island of Bombaim and dependencies of both, will bee vindicated from that most injurious Capitulation forc't upon Humphry Cooke at the Surrender of the Place, which hee neither had power to submit unto, nor any one power to impose contrary to soe solemne a Treaty. That therefore you resolve to renounce the said Capitulation as a matter touching Your Majestie in point of Honor, and relateing to an Interest which is the more valueable unto you, as comeing in Marriage with Your Deare Consort the Queene.

That you intend to represent unto the Prince how greivious it is for you to heare that when Your Subjects Trade into the Countries of the Great Mogull and Savagie, with whome you are in Freindship, and the Portuguez Nation not in Warr (and soe void of all pretence) that for bare passing in the open streams by Tannah, contrary to the Law and Practice of all Nations; and by Carinjah in the very waters of Your owne Port, to bee subjected to pay Tribute, That it is a matter which cannot bee endur'd.

Public Record Office, C. O. 77, Vol. XIII, folio 165.

That Your Majestie does not doubt but that the Prince will Decree satisfaction for all that has been thus injuriously exacted contrary as well to former practice there, as unto Common Right, and that hee will not only remedy many other things which are to bee complained of, but allsoe take into his deep consideration the Injurie done to your Royall Person, and the calamity of Your Subjects, by the Non Surrender in the begining.

That in the meane time You have commanded Your Subjects of the said Company to refuse payment of those Arbitrary and unjust demands at Tannah and Carinjah, as prejudiciall to Your Rights of Sovereignty, and contrary to all the knowne Lawes of the world, there being noe arbitrary duties or Customes imposed at the Sound, but onely for the benefitt of Lights and Seamarks there is allowed a small Recompence which yett was never paid, untill by stippulation and Treaty betweene the Two Crownes it was soe agreed.

That therefore if Your Subjects are willing (as they are when they Trade to any of the Territories of Portugall) to submit to the duties and Customes of each respective place it is all that Justice can require.

That of all this You thought it a just respect to the character the Vice Roy beares in those parts, and to the Estimation you are told hee has of Your Royall Person, to give him Information; not doubting that whatever is of Right, and Consonant to the said Treaty, will not onely bee fullfilled by him, but that in all occations of Freindship hee will not faile to bee courteous and usefull to Your Subjects, which Your Majestie will bee ready to acknowledge upon all like Occassions.

All which is most humbly submitted.

COUNCILL CHAMBER

12 *February*, 1676/7.

Present—

Earl of Bridgewater.	Mr. Sectie, Coventry.
Earl of Craven.	Mr. Sectie, Willamson.
Mr. Vice Chamberlane.	Mr. Chancellor of the Exchequer.

[*Endorsed.*]

A Report about Bombaim.
Read in Councill 23 *February*, 1676/7.
And approved.

Entr: E.I.C.B. p. 190.

Public Record Office, C. O. 77, Vol, XIII, folio 125.

MAY IT PLEASE YOUR LORDSHIPS

In order to Redress Injuries complained of by the East India Company received at Bombaim, your Lordships directed inquiry to bee made first for the Map presented by the Portugal Ambassador, when that place was offered in the Treaty, which Map would certainly have cleared up the point in question. And next the Commission and Instructions given to Sir Jervis Lucas, when hee went to the Government of that place, to Rectify all abuses that had been offered in the non-Surrender, or in the Surrender but of part of what by the Treaty was intended.

As for the Map, neither by the Lord Clarendon, who has made search after it, nor Sir Wm. Morrice, then Secretary of State, who acknowledged the Receipt of a Small box of Plantation papers from the old Lord Clarendon at his Departure, nor by Sir Philip Warwick, who lived with the Earl of Southampton at the time the Council sate at the Earls house, and that the said Map was there exposed, can any manner of Tydings bee had thereof.

Public Record Office, C. O. 77, Vol. XIII, folio 125.

And as to the said Commission and Instructions (which doubtless contained the extent and purport of that Map) I can have noe news of them in the Offices. But hearing that Sir Jeffery Palmer then Attorney General, was consulted as to the powers of the Commission, I made enquiry with Mr. Johnson, then Clerke of the Patents, but hee can neither remember, or find, any footsteps thereof. Tis probable both are at Bombaim where Sir Jervis Lucas dyed, and soe in the hands of the Companies President there.

But as to the Commission and Instructions of Sir Abram Shipman, the first intended Governor, I have the drafts of those given mee by Mr. Cook, in the Original Papers, as they were prepared by direction of Mr. Secretary Morice, in whose own hand I find interlined, in 5, or 6 places of the Commission where Bombaim is mentioned these words. *And other the Premisses*, as if it were an omission not to understand that more than the bare Island was granted, and to bee possessed by the said Governor. Yet to leave unto your intire Judgement of this Inference, the preceding words of the Commission are these—Wee constitute and appoint you Governor and Commander in cheife, in and upon our said Island of Bombay, and of all our Forts and forces raised, and to bee raised there for our service either in the said Island or in any other Island, or part of the firme land in the East Indies, which shall bee either conquered by us, or bee rendred or delivered up to us. Now whether these last words of rendring and delivery, following that of conquering, doe not relate to what might bee done on the Indians, or what the Indians might Voluntarily doe, rather than what the Portugeses, by the Treaty, were obliged to doe, your Lordships will best determine. And as your Lordships understand this, soe will the Instructions bee understood.

For the second Article thereof directs thus—Being there arrived you are, as Our Governor of the Island and Country within the extent of your Commission, to demand and receive the same, with the Artillery, Ammunition, etc. These are the words of most scope and Remarque, for the Title of the Instructions is barely thus, For Sir Abraham Shipman Knight Our Governor of Bombay in the East Indies. And in all other the Instructions Bombay, and the said Island, is only mentioned, without Reference to any Map, or particular direction as to extent and meaning of the Treaty, though, in several places, these Instructions have amendments in my Lord Clarendon's own hand. All which is mentioned to your Lordships to give a faithfull account of what that Commission, and those Instructions, doe containe; for they are not the Rule of his Majesties Right, if they were as redundant as they seeme scant, but the Treaty is the Rule and I suppose the true Interpretation thereof would much better appear in the tenor of that Commission and Instructions which was given to Sir Jervis

Public Record Office, C. O. 77, Vol. XIII. folio 125.

Lucas, where all the circumstances were fresh, the persons in authority, who had framed the Treaty, and sufficient provocation given to assert His Majesties Right.

And yet what greater elucidation in this matter seems necessary to Your Lordships then one Article of a Memorial presented the Portugal Ambassadoı at that time (unto which there seems never to have been made any Reply) dated the 25th of July 1663, in the words following

" Moreover His Majesty insists very earnestly that not only Justice bee done upon the Vice King in the Indies, who hath soe falsly and unworthily failed in the Surrender of the Island promised to his Majesty there, but that Reparation bee made for the loss hee hath sustained in sending Ships and Men to take possession of it, the charges whereof are valued by the Officers of His Majesties Navy to amount unto at least One hundred thousand pound sterling and that likewise more effectual orders bee reiterated thither for the Surrender of the said Island to the full extent, exhibited formerly to His Majesty in the Map containing not only Bombaim, but Salzede and Taan, and soe promised to His Majesty, for the possession of which the Troops are yet detained there, suffering much inconvenience in the expectation of it."

After this I shall only presume to acquaint Your Lordships that Sir Abram Shipman dyed before hee could obtaine possession of Bombaim, and one Cook his Secretary pretending a power delegated to him by the Governors Will to take possession, as on the one side hee was impatient to have it, either for his own ends or to bee in better aire than the Infectious place, where 300 of the 500 Soldiers sent over, did dye, in attending the surrender; or that on the other the Portugeses were now become more sensible of the wrong, or that they might better impose on him any conditions, hee having now not Men enough left to fill up the extent of what, by the Article they were to give. But the conclusion was hee entred not till hee had very solemly signed a particular Capitulation with them to the effect following, vizt.

1. The Portugeses or others may freely come sell buy and trade at their Islands and Countries through their Port of Bombaim and be free of all payments.

2. The said freedom of Trade shall be particularly understood at Bandora and other the Creeks of Salsett though under the English Artillery.

3. The Runaways to be protected.

4. The English are not to meddle with matters of Religion on pain of forfeiting their Right in the Island of Bombaim.

5. The Fleets and Boats of Portugall to have free egress and Regress without asking leave because part of the Bay belongs to them in respect of their other Islands and Countries.

Public Record Office, C. O. 77, Vol. XIII, folio 125.

6. The Inhabitants to enjoy or sell their Estates.

7. That the Inhabitants of Salsett Carinjah Baragaon (which is Trombay) and the rest of the Islands of the Portuguese Jurisdiction may freely fish in the Bay and River, even in the Arm which enters and divides Bombaim from Salsett by Bandora up into the Bay, And the Inhabitants of Bombaim may do the same without Tribute or Custome on the other side.

8. That Workmen may be hired from the Portugeses but not detained.

9. No runaways to be admitted and detained upon pretence of changing their Religion on either side.

10. That the Lady in whom the Government of Bombaim was may yet freely enjoy her estate.

11. That no Inhabitants shall loose their Right either Patrimonial, or what is held from the Crown but it shall descend, and they may alien unless they forfeit according to the laws of Portugall.

12. The Ecclesiastics not to be molested but to have their churches free.

13. The Inhabitants who pay Tribute to the King shall pay no more to the King of England.

14. That all reciprocall friendship and good Offices shall pass from side to side as being the intention of the treaty, dated in Pangim or Goa 14th January, 1665.

ANTONIO DE MILO DE CASTRO.

From which Unwarrantable proceeding on either side the Portugeses have taken colour to restraine and disturb the prosperity of His Majesties subjects as much as possible they can. And as it seems a good Argument that they were to part with all which, by this sinister way, they thought to regaine, Soe is it now before your Lordships (as many other things) to judge whether His Majesty may not make this a fit ground of complaint to the Prince of Portugal, that His subjects should soe unjustly and presumptuously take upon them to make Articles contrary to the public Treaty betweene the two Crownes, and to constraine the execution of such private ones before the performance of the public.

All which is most humbly submitted.

[*Endorsed.*]

Report touching the limits of Bombaim and the Maps as also of the first surrender to the English.

Read to the Committee
16 January 1676/7.

Public Record Office, C. O. 77, Vol. XIII, folio 143.

RESULT OF THE COMMITTEE IN THE BUSINESS OF BOMBAIM.

16 *January* 1676 [1676/7].

1. Upon the whole Matter Their Lordships rather than insist farther on the demand of Salsett and Carinjah think fit to consider what is the Right and extent which His Majesty hath by the Grant of the Port. Whether it draw not with it the other Islands that stand therein soe as that they pass together with the Water.

2. How farr the English are freed by common Right even in the Portugese Streams when they land not on their shores, but drive their Trade with Strangers: And more especialy if such Impositions are grown up new, and since the time of Surrender.

3. In case his Majesty should now forbid the Company to submit to those Impositions, and should write to the Prince of Portugal to forbid his subjects to lay them on, but should not succeed herein; How are the Company provided to Right themselves by the same way of Impositions on the Portugeses.

[*Endorsed*].

Result of the Committee
touching Bombain.
16 Jannary 1676/7.
Entred B. p. 165.

February 23rd 1676/7.

Public Record Office, C. O. 77, Vol XIII, fol. 205.

His Majestie haveing by Order of this Board bearing date the 23rd of February 1675 reffer'd a Petition (from the Governor and Company of Merchants tradeing to the East Indies, relateing to Bombaim), unto the Right Honble. the Lords of the Comittee of Trade, and Forraigne Plantations. Their Lordships did this day make a Report in the words following

MAY IT &C.

[Blank]

His Majestie being graciously inclined to promote the Interest of his Subjects of the East India Companie, and considering that the impediments of their Trade doe lie in the arbitrary Duties which are imposed at Tannah and Carinjah, Hee hath thought fit to approve the said Reporte. And the Right Honble. Mr. Secretary Coventry is not onely to prepare a Letter for his Majesties Royall Signature according to the effect thereof; but the said Company are hereby required to forrbeare, and refuse, the payments demanded in the said Places, and even to resist the same in the best manner they can.

And whereas upon reading of the said Report, the Company did then present unto his Majestie, an humble Petition prayeing for an additionall Clause to the effect following.

That whereas his said subjects had further represented unto him. That they haveing a Right to halfe the Customes which are paid at Gombroone in Persia, as the Portugeses have the like at Cong in the same Kingdome; and that it hath bin the anntient practice for European Nations in India, to grant passes to the native Junks or Shipps for security in their Navigation to Persia and other Parts: It hath hapned of late (contrary to the said Practice) that refuseall is made, by the said Vice Roys orders, to give passes, unto any Junkes that would sayle to Gombroone, thereby obligeing all shipps to a necessity of goeing unto Cong, or else exposeing them to the perrills they would avoyd if they goe to Gombroone, where the English are concern'd in the duties as aforesaid. And whereas this refusall seemes to beare not onely the markes of some unkindenesse and disrespect, unto the English Nation, but a sort of Injustice, which may deservedly draw on a like practice and refusall, on the Companies part: Therefore his Majestie does earnestly desire the said Vice Roy to recall the said Prohibition, or any other orders given to the Like effect, as being Contrary to the Treaty of Marriage, which aimes at nothing more than the Union of both Nations, The muttuall affection, and Brotherly friendshipp which, on all Occasions is to bee exercised towards each other; and which is soe heartyly desired by his Majestie. Public Record Office, C. O. 77, Vol. XIII, folio 205.

Upon reading of which Additionall Clause, his Majestie was gratiously pleased to approve the same. And Mr. Secretary Coventry is to take care to see the same added accordingly.

[*Endorsed.*]

23rd February 1676/7.
Bombaim Order.

To be Right Honoble. the Lords of
the Committee for Trade and Plantations.
The humble representation of the Governor and Company of Merchants of London tradeing to the East Indies. Public Record Office, C. O. 77, Vol. XIII, fol. 206.

SHEWETH,

That the said Company have a Right to the one half of the Customs that are paid at Gombroone in Persia, and the Portuguez have the like at Cong in that Kingdome.

That it has been an auntient practice for European Nations in India to grant passes to the native Jounckes or Ships for their Security in their navigation to Persia and other parts. But of late the Company understands from their president and Councell at Surratt, that the Portuguez doe refuse to give their passes to any Jouncks that goe for Gombroone, thereby to force all ships that formerly paid Custome at that Port to go unto Cong, which is not onely an Act of great unkindness, but of contempt to the English Nation and contrary to the Articles of Peace and is highly resented by the Governour Shawbunder and Merchants of Surratt as Injurious to them in their Commerce, which refusall of the Portuguez if they should persist in, they may in reason expect the like retaliation from the Company.

And therefore the said Governor and Company humbly represent the same unto your Lordships That such course may be taken for redress of this greivance as to your Lordships shall seem fitt.

[*Endorsed.*]
The East India Company's humble address to the Rt. Honble. the Lords Comittees for Trade.

Read in Councill. February 23rd 1676 [1676/7].

SIR ABRAHAM SHIPMAN'S COMMISSION.

Public Record Office, C. O. 77, Vol. XIII, fol. 129.

Charles the Second by the Grace of God King of England, Scotland, France and Ireland, Defender of the Faith, &c.

To Our Trusty and Wel-beloved Sir Abraham Shipman, Knight, one of the Gentlemen in Ordinary of Our Privy Chamber, Greeting.

Whereas Wee are willing to give all protection encouragment and assistance to Our Subjects and people in and upon Our Island of Bombay in the East Indies, and that Wee have thought fitt effectualy to provide for the security and Government thereof. Know Yee therefore that Wee reposing Special Trust and confidence in the ability, direction, fidelity and experience of you the said Sir Abraham Shipman, have Assigned, Constituted and appointed, and by these present do Assign, constitute and appoint You To be the Governor and Commander in Chiefe in and upon Our Said Island of Bombay, and of all Our Forts and Forces raised and to be raised there for Our Service, either in the said Island, or in any other Island or part of the firm land in the East Indies, which shall be either conquered by Us, or be rendred and delivered up to Us, untill Our farther pleasure be known, and the Commands of the same be otherwise disposed of by Us, and to do and execute all things in due manner to the said Trust and Office appertaining which may tend to the defence security and good Government of Our said Island, and other the premisses, and to the Orderly and peaceable conduct and preservation of the Soldiers, Planters, and other Inhabitants there residing, according to such powers and Authorities as are now by this present Commission and such Instructions as are now, and shall from time to time be given unto you by Us, and according to such good, just and reasonable Customes and Constitutions as are exercised and setled in Our other Colonies and Plantations, or such other as shall upon Mature advice and consideration be held necessary and proper for the good Government and security of Our said Island of Bombay, and other the premisses. Provided that they be not repugnant to Our Laws of England nor to the late Treaty concluded between Us and Our good Brother the King of Portugall; And Wee do hereby give full power and Authority to You, the said Sir Abraham Shipman, to Muster, Command and Discipline All the Millitary Forces of Our said Island and other the Premisses at all convenient times, and to fight, kill, slay, repress and subdue all such as shall in an hostile or mutinous manner by insurrection, or invasion disturbe the peace or attempt the Surprize of Our said Island of Bombay or other the Premisses, And for the better Suppression of mutinees, and actuall Insurrections, and Invasions, when the ordinary course of Justice cannot be well and safely attended and applyed to, That then you the said Sir Abraham Shipman do put in Execution the Laws Martiall according to the practice and constitution of a Court Martiall upon Soldiers only, And you are hereby also impowred and authorized to Nominate and Constitute all Officers in the places of those that dye, or such places as otherwise shall become void. And wee do hereby require the severall Officers, Ministers, and others, the Soldiers and people of Our said Island and other the Premisses, to acknowledge You for Our Governor thereof, And all the said Soldjers and people are to be Obedient unto you as Our Governor and

Commander in Cheif in and upon Our said Island of Bombay, and other the Premisses, in pursuance of this Our Royall Commission, and the Instructions which you shall receive from Us.

INSTRUCTION FOR SIR ABRAHAM SHIPMAN, KNIGHT, GOVERNOR OF OUR ISLAND OF BOMBAY IN THE EAST INDIES.

Public Record Office, C. O. 77, Vol. XLIX, folio 131.

1. You are by virtue of your Commission under the great Seal, and such warrants, and directions as you have had from Us, or Our Councell, to receive under your Command the Forces of Foot raised in England for Our Service in the East Indies, and from the Rendez-vous at * Wind and weather serving, to Sail directly to Our Island of Bombay aforesaid.

[* blank.]

2. Whether the Earl of Marlebrough be not by His Commission to take Possession of the is land and to deliver it to Sir Abraham Shipman.

This was in My Lord Chancellor's hand.

2. Being there arrived, you are as Our Governor of that Island and Country within the extent of your Commission to demand and receive the same with the Artillery, Amunition etc., into Your Possession from the Governor of our Brother the King of Portugall.

3. You are not to apply any of the Provisions, or pay of Our Forces for support of any the Inhabitants not in pay, but in all cases of their want or straits, you are to dispose of them so (any thing to the contrary notwithstanding) that Our Towns and forts in Our said Island may not be endangered thereby.

4. Our maine design in putting Our Selfe to this great charge for making this addition to Our Dominions being to gain to Our Subjects more free and better Trade in the East Indies, and to enlarge Our Dominions in those parts, and advance thereby the Honour of Our Crown, and the General Commerce, and Weale of Our Subjects. You are with all convenient speed and advice to make use of the best ways and means for incouragment and invitation of Our Subjects and Strangers to resort and Trade there, and you are especially to give all manner of incouragment, helpe and assistance to the Subjects of the King of Portugall in the East Indies, and to protect them as much as in you lyeth in their Trade and Navigation there ; you are also to keep a very good Correspondance with the Vice King of Goa, and all other Portugall Governors, and likewise with the Natives of the Country, and to do all you can to settle a Trade amongst them.

5. You are to administer the Oath of Allegiance unto every person in the said Island capable by law to take the same. And We do hereby give and grant you full power and authority to Administer the said Oath.

Quaere. Whether he shall hand power to Erect Judicatories for Civil Affairs and for the Admiralty.

The present business being to Settle the Garrison you can hardly give him other then generall Instructions, till you receive some account from him.

6. You are Principally to take care that drunkeness, and all debauchery be discountenanced and punished, and that none be admitted to any publick Trust or Employment whose ill Conversation may bring scandall thereupon, And that the Protestant Religion

Public Record Office, C. O. 77, Vol. XLIX, folio 131.

according to the profession and practice of the Church of England may have due Reverence and Exercise among them; The Treaty made between us and Our good Brother the King of Portugall being nevertheless Observed and kept inviolable.

7. You are for the better defence of Our said Island and security of Our good people to use all possible care and expedition for the Compleating of Fortifications and rendring them defensible, for the effecting and finishing whereof you are to command all fitt and able persons to work by turns, and to punish such as being duly Commanded do refuse or neglect to do the same.

8. You are to give such Encouragment (as securely you may) to such Natives and others as shall submit to live peaceably under Our Obedience, and in due submission to the Government of the Island. And you are to suffer them to enjoy the Exercise of their own Religion, without the least Interuption or discountenance.

From this place to the end of the article it was written in My Lord Chancellor's hand.

9. You shall from time to time, as often as opportunity can be had, give an Account to Us of the Condition of Our said Island, and of the Affairs and Inhabitants thereof, and such other Intelligence as you can collect of any other places or things relating to the East Indies, and which may concern Our Service.

This was also in the Lord Chancellor's hand.

I think it will be necessary to give him very particular direction to keep a good Correspondence with the Vice King of Goa, and all other Portugal Governors, and likewise with the Natives of the Country and so do all he can to settle a Trade among them.

This was in My Lord Chancellor's own hand.

You know what Instructions My Lord Marleborough hath, but it will be very fitt and indeed necessary That the King write a Letter to the Vice King or Governor of that Country under the Portuguese, That this is the Person to whom he is to deliver that Island, the directions from Portugall being that he should deliver it up unto such Person as the King of Great Brittaine should appoint to receive the same, in the same manner as you did for Tangier.

[A pencil endorsement on a duplicate of this document (in C.O. 77/13) reads as follows :—] "These Instructions to Sir A. Shipman were dated March 1662: he died at Bombay in April 1664, but the whole matter was before the Council of Trade 16 January, 1676/7 and these seem to be the very papers then read and entered in S.P. East Indies 15, p. 131 etc. Hence they are placed here. E.S."

Public Record Office, C. O. 77, Vol. XLIX, folio 134.

On the 16th of January 167$\frac{6}{7}$ Sir Robert Southwell made a Report unto their Lordships touching the Mapp of Bombaim which could not be found, as also concerning the foregoing Commission and Instructions of Sir G. Lucas as followeth.

MAY IT PLEASE YOUR LORDSHIP

In Order to Redress Injuries complained of by the East India Company received at Bombaim, Your Lordships directed Inquiry to be made first for the Map presented by the Portugal Ambassadore when that place was offered in the Treaty, which Map would certainly have cleared up the point in Question. And next the

Commission and Instructions given to Sir Jervis Lucas, when hee went to the Government of that place, to rectifye all abuses that had been offered in the Non-Surrender, or in the Surrender but of part what by the Treaty was intended. Public Record Office C. O. 77, Vol. XLIX, folio 134.

As for the Mapp, neither by the Lord Clarendon, who has made Search after it, nor Sir William Morrice, then Secretary of State, who acknowledged the receipt of a small Box of Plantation Papers from the old Lord Clarendon at his departure, nor by Sir Philip Warwick, who lived with the Earl of Southampton at the time the Council sate at the Earls house, and that the said Map was there exposed, can any manner of Tydings be heard thereof.

And as to the said Commission and Instructions (which doubtless contained the extent and purport of that Map) I can leave* no news of them in the Offices. But hearing that Sir Jeffrey Palmer, then Attorny Generall, was consulted as to the Powers of the Commission, I made Inquiry with Mr. Johnson, then Clerke of the Patents, but he can neither remember or find any footsteps thereof. 'Tis probable both are at Bombaim, where Sir Jervis Lucas died, and so in the hands of the Companies President there. * [sic ? learn]

But as to the Commission and Instructions of Sir Abraham Shipman, the first intended Governor, I have the Drafts of those given mee by Mr. Cook, in the Original Papers, as they were prepared by direction of Mr. Secretary Morrice, in whose own hand I find interlined, in 5 or 6 places of the Commission where Bombaim is mentioned, these words, *And other the Premisses*, as if it were an omission not to understand that more then the bare Island was granted, and to be possessed by the said Governor. Yet to leave unto your intire Judgment of this Inference, the proceeding words of the Commission are these. Wee constitute and appoint you Governor and Commander in chief in and upon Our said Island of Bombay, and of all Our Forts and forces raised, and to be raised there for Our Service, either in the said Island, or in any other Island, or part of the firme Land in the East Indies, which shall be either conquered by us, or be rendered or Delivered up to Us.

Now whether these last words of rendring, and delivery, following that of conquering do not relate to what might be done on the Indians, or what the Indians might voluntarily doe, rather then what the Portugueses by the Treaty were obliged to doe, Your Lordships will best determine. And as Your Lordships understand this, so will the Instructions be understood.

For the second Article thereof directs thus. Being there arrived you are as Our Governor of the Island and Country within the extent of Your Commission, to demand and receive the same, with the Artillery, Amunition, etc. These are the words of most scope and remarke for the Title of the Instructions is barely thus. *For Sir Abraham Shipman Knight Our Governor of Bombay in the East Indies.* And in all other the Instructions, Bombay, and the said Island is only mentioned without reference to any Map or particular direction as to the extent and meaning of the Treaty though in several places, these Instructions have amendments in My Lord Clarendon's

Public Record Office, C. O. 77, Vol. XLIX, folio 134.

own hand. All which is mentioned to Your Lordships to give a faithfull account of what that Commission, and those Instructions doe containe, for they are not the Rule of His Majesties Right, if they were as redundant as they seeme scant, But the Treaty is the Rule, and I suppose the true Interpretation thereof would much better appeare in the tenour of that Commission and Instructions which was given to Sir Jervis Lucas, where all circumstances were fresh, the persons in Authority, who had framed the Treaty, and sufficient Provocation given to assert his Majesties right.

And yet what greater elucidation in this matter seems necessary to Your Lordships then one Article of a Memoriall presented the Portugall Ambassador at that time (unto which there seems never to have been made any reply) dated the 25th of July 1663, in the words following.

"Moreover His Majestie insists very earnestly that not only Justice be done upon the Vice King in the Indies who hath so falsly and unworthily failed in the Surrender of the Island promised to His Majestie there, but that repairation be made for the loss he hath sustained in sending Ships and men to take possession of it, the Charges whereof are valued by the Officers of His Majesties Navy to amount unto at least One hundred thousand pound Sterling. And that likewise more effectual Orders be reiterated thither for the Surrender of the said Island to the full extent exhibited formerly to His Majestie in the Map containing not only Bombaim, but Salzede, and Taan, and so promissed unto His Majestie, for the possession of which the Troops are yet detained there, suffering much inconvenience in the expectation of it.

After this I shall only presume to acquaint Your Lordships that Sir Abraham Shipman Dyed before he could obtaine possession of Bombaim, And one Cook, his Secretary, pretending a power delegating to him by the Governor's will to take possession, as on the one side he was impatient to have it, either for his own ends, or to be in better aire then the infectious place, where 300 of the 500 Soldjers sent over did dye in attending the Surrender, or that on the other, the Portugeses were now become more sensible of the wrong, or that they might better impose on him any Conditions, hee having now not men enough left to fill up the extent of what by the Article they were to give. But the conclusion was he entred not till he had very solemnly signed a particular Capitulation with them to the effect following :—

1. The Portugeses or others may freely come, Sell, buy, and Trade at their Islands and Countries through their Port of Bombaim, and be free of all payments.

2. The said freedome of Trade shall be particularly understood at Bandora, and other the Creeks of Salsett, though under the English Artillery.

3. The Runaways to be protected.

4. The English are not to meddle with matters of Religion, on paine of forfeiting their Right in the Island of Bombaim.

5. The Fleets and Boats of Portugall to have free Egress and Regress, without asking leave, because part of the Bay belongs to them in respect of their other Islands and Countries.

Public Record Office, C. O. 77, Vol. XLIX, folio 134.

6. The Inhabitants to Enjoy, or sell their Estates.

7. That Inhabitants of Salsett, Carinjah, Baragaon (which is Trombay) and the rest of the Islands of the Portugese Jurisdiction, may freely fish in the Bay and River, even in the Arme which enters and divides Bombaim from Salsett by Bandora, up into the Bay, And the Inhabitants of Bombaim may do the same without Tribute or Custome on the other side.

8. That Workmen may be hired from the Portugeses but not detained.

9. No Run-aways to be admitted and detained upon pretence of changing their Religion on either side.

10. That the Lady in whom the Government of Bombaim was, may yet freely enjoy her Estate.

11. That no Inhabitants shall loose their Right either Patrimonial, or what is held from the Crown, but it shall descend, and they may alien unless they forfeit according to the Laws of Portugall.

12. The Ecclesiasticks not to be molested, but to have their churches free.

13. The Inhabitants who pay Tribute to the King shall pay no more to the King of England.

14. That all reciprocall friendship and good Offices shall pass from side to side, as being the intention of the Treaty, Dated in Pangim, or Goa, the 14th January 1665.

ANTONIO DE MELO DE CASTRO.

From which unwarrantable proceeding on either side, the Portugeses have taken Colour to restraine, and disturbe the prosperity of his Majesties Subjects, as much as possible they can.

And as it seems a good argument that they were to part withall, which by this sinister way they thought to regaine, So is it now before Your Lordships (as many other things) to Judge whether His Majestie may not make this a fit ground of Complaint to the Prince of Portugall, that His Subjects should so unjustly and presumptuously take upon them to make Articles contrary to the publick Treaty between the two Crowns, and to constraine the execution of such Private ones, before the performance of the Publick.

All which is most humbly Submitted.

The following petition of the Company gives a very vivid account of the state of Bombay, and raises most interesting points of International Law. The Company was, I believe, perfectly right in their contention that there was no analogy between Elsenore and Bombay, and the dues exacted by the Portuguese did undoubtedly subject them to very grave hardship. Their commerce was affected no less than their relation to the Indians. The account of Bombay will be read with interest by her citizens to-day. Mr. Humphrey Cooke's unfortunate treaty with the Portuguese is still the object of their dislike, and we have a few pointed references to that unlucky bargain. The chief arguments adduced by the Company may be summed up under six headings :

(1) In the first place, there is the inevitable question of Freedom of Trade. This is by far their strongest line of defence, and if they had adhered to, and insisted upon, the observance of this fundamental right, it would have solved many of their difficulties. They had also asserted this principle against the pretensions of the Dutch, and their history during the first sixty years of the seventeenth century is nothing else but a record of their struggle for the maintenance of this principle. It must be confessed, however, that its application to the particular case was hardly justifiable. Freedom of Trade did not imply negation of customs duties, and if the Portuguese claim to the places in dispute is acknowledged, then the Company's assertion of this principle is meaningless.

(2) If, on the other hand, duties are enhanced to such an extent as to amount to an "Interdiction of Commerce" then it is clear that the Company have justification for their refusal to pay them. This was alleged by the Company, and there can be no doubt that the commercial development of Bombay would have been impossible if all the implications of Cooke's Treaty had been mercilessly deduced to their logical conclusion.

(3) Moreover, if duties are charged for a "bare passage in a streame of the Sea" and the stream is a "work of nature" and (4) no lights or buoys are maintained for the security of the passage of the ships, it seems unreasonable to demand an exorbitant duty.

(5) The Company were prepared to pay "a moderate thing", but they denied that (6) any analogy existed between Elsenore and Bombay.

So far we are on safe ground, and it may be conceded at once that the Company were justified in their complaints. The Despatches of the Directors, and the frequent complaints of their servants, show clearly enough the hardships, and even humiliation to which they were subjected.

The other claims of the Company were more doubtful. They contended that (7) they knew " nothing that gives bounds or limits to this Bay, but the Circle of the Main Land round about, unto which it flowes, part whereof being claimed by the King of Portugall, his grant of this water ought there to bee carried on as far as may be most beneficiall to his Majesty who received the grant." If followed, (8) that, the other part of the main land, belonging to the Great Mogull, not being a matter of dispute, " the whole body and surface of water that flowes in and the whole Fundus bellow even up to the high water mark is the King's, and the Land between the high and Low water mark is among the Rights of the Admirall."

They asserted (9), moreover, that if this "water were given to His Majesty as port, It was given as a place of safety from stormes, and for relief of the Damages, which are received at Sea, and asked pertinently if the Moguls will not be justified in levying all sorts of dues, should any English ship " come into port wanting Timber and other necessaries to refitt." Moreover, (10) " The Sea where it is mastered, seemes to carry with it a right of Dominion whithersoever it goes." " The first conquest of those Islands were made from the Sea, and where the Sea overflows any Territory of the neighbouring Land, all that space of Sea (*and in virtue thereof all the Land below it*) belongs to that Prince, who had the sovereignty of the Sea before." This, it must be confessed, is rather a shaky foundation on which to build an imposing edifice, and we can only marvel at the ingenious devices of these supple Directors. Their incursions into International Law would have been more successful if they had been backed by reliable authorities.

Our East India Merchants were apparently men of principle, and here, as elsewhere, principles are liberally sprinkled over a moderate amount of facts. They champion Mercantilism, Freedom of Trade, Commercial wars, and Free Trade with the same facility and verve as they champion the war against Aurangzebe, or the Interlopers. Witness their development of this theory: " Therefore wee cannot think the Portugueses would know how to Complain, should wee by his Majesties permission, strengthen Our hands, and by a Rule of retaliation stop all their shipps comeing into the Port, that are bound to Tannah, Bassain or Carinjah, levieing as arbitrary duties on them as they impose upon us." Their grounds for this startling deduction were expressed in the following, " Ought not the Main Land bee as free for the English as the Main Sea to the Portugueses? Will they give us a port and forbid us the use of that Land which makes it a port?"

The documents reproduced below show the extent of the influence of the East India Company on the policy of Charles.

Public Record Office, C. O. 77, Vol. XIII, folio 168.

To the Right honble. The Lords of the Committee for trade and Plantations.

The humble Representation of the Governor and Company of Merchants of London tradeing to the East Indies.

MAY IT PLEASE YOUR LORDSHIPS

Being encouraged to lay before your Lordships such informations and matters of Fact relateing to the buisness of Bombaim as suted most to your Lordships debate on the 16th January last, and which might best promote the Points that were in Issue before you, Wee presume in the first place to informe your Lordshipps what wee are in possession of; what it is wee want; and what wee think under his Majestie wee have Right unto.

Wee hold the Island of Bombaim and that spot called Mahim as a part thereof, on which part there has at all times beene a head Custome house, and particularly at the time when this Island was delivered to his Majestie, and there did all the Boates and Vessells belonging to Bombaim, as a dependent on the Custom house of Mahim, Salsett, Barragone or Trumbay, Carinjah, Elefante and the Patecoes, pay their dutyes, and never did any of these pay at Tannah, but alwaise at Mahim. No nor did the Boates of the two Moorish Cittyes Galiana and Biondi for their passing or repassing at that Streight either pay Custome or for Passage, but allwaies paid duties at Mahim, as manifestly apeares in both cases by the Forall which is the Custome-house Record of that Place, much less was anything paid by those of Bombaim at Carinjah, which it selfe was dependent on the Custome-house of Mahim, Mr. Humphry Cook, notwithstanding his Infamous Capitulation to the contrary, did retain many of the duties payable from the Port Townes in Salsett, so that when Sir Jarvas Lucas arived as Governor at Bombaim he imployed two Commissioners to receive and improve his Majesties Customs there, One of which, Mr. John Evans, attended your Lordships the last day, shewing the Accompts of his Collecting the duties of Colai and Bandora Vessava and Murr by a Substitute from Mahim, and that he farmed out those of Trumbay at a publick Outcry, continueing in the Office from November 1667 to August 1668 when the Company entred and Imployed Officers of their owne; But by Our Letters of January 1674 The President sayes that he was threatned to be deprived of the Customes of Trumbay, and had actually for three yeares been denied those of Vassava and Murr, two small Ports on the West side of Salsett, which in the King of Portugalls time did allwaies pay to Mahim, and the Portugees doe own that in the Island of Salsett there being 130 Villages which are devided into three districts, one of them paying their duties to Basaim, the other to the Custome house at Tannah, that the Third (consisting of 70 Villages) did still pay duties for all thinges exported or imported at the Ports of that District, which is alsoe suteable to the said Forall of Mahim, And Mahim was indeed formerly the name of the whole Island, and here in former times the Kings Court was kept and a great Castle Built in the time of the Moores Government.

Public Record Office, C. O. 77, Vol. XIII, folio 168.

Wee are in possession of the small Island of Pategos, which onely serves in the Winter Season for the Feeding of Catle. But Wee are not possessed of Elephante nor Sevine Nevine, and much less of Carinjah, tho' they all stand in the Port of Bombaim surrounded by the salt water thereof.

Wee doe not know by what infallible signes and markes to chalke out the Boundaries of the Harbor of Bombaim, But it seemes part of an argument That it extends to all the Bay of Water within ; seing the Vice Roy Antonio De Melo (who perverted all things) did (in his injurious Capitulation forct on Mr. Cooke) insert this fifth Article as followeth.

"Item, That the Fleets of the King of Portugall as well Ships as Boats with Oares and all other his Ships whatsoever may at all times enter into and depart from the said Bay without any impediment to bee given them or askeing any leave, for as much as on accompt of other Islands and Territories which he hath, part of the said Bay belongs unto him, and thereof he may have the free use thereof as a thing which is his owne without doubt or Question."

For a second Argument, wee can asure your Lordships that our President and Councell living upon the Island of Bombaym doe soe farr understand the whole Bay to be the Port of Bombaim as that in Virtue of the grant thereof by the Treaty (when they did in 1672 send Agents to the Vice Roy of Goa, touching the abuses at Tannah, and Carinjah) they did sett up a title to Carinjah upon Accompt of its Scituation in the Bay, for their Instruction runs thus, As to Carinjah you are to urge that it lies within the Bay or Port of Bombaim and by consequence does belong as an undoubted Right to his Majestie.

And in their Letters to us of the same yeer, they prest us to Consult here with some Eminent Civillians, to know whither the grant of the Water does not draw with it the Right of Dominion over all the Islands that stand therein and over those small Streights and Passages which make it. And in another place they farther add that the Portugueze are very injurious for detaining all the Islands within the Bay, which doe all by Right and Justice belong unto Us (excepting Salset) even by the Confession of many among themselves, and that in Salset alsoe wee have right and Dominion to all the Port Townes which ought to pay Customs at Mahim, as formerly in the Portugall time they did, etc.

But wee are now onely on that Point which Concerns the Extent of the Bay, nor doe wee hear the Portuguez oppose better Arguments why the whole is not the Port of Bombaim then that in some places within there are Variety of Names, as the River of Trombay, the River of Tannah, and the River of Carinjah, as the same Water washes or comes nigh the Banks of those places, whereas wee think these Names

Public Record Office, C. O. 77, Vol. XIII. folio 168.

are but given as the subdivision of Streets in the same Towne, or as if a Vessell should not bee said to bee in Falmouth or Milfordhaven because shee Road in some Creek thereof, that went by another Name, though supplied from the Water of the Common Bason.

Lately in consulting the ancient writeings and descriptions of the Portuguezes and particularly a Survey taken by Order of the Vice Roy of Goa about 1636, wee finde the Port of Bombaim to bee described for the largest and deepest in India, two Leagues wide at the Entrance, and so spatious further on within as not to admitt of the Fortification which was earnestly designed for Security of the Port.

Then in the very bottom of the Bay,. Water and appurtenances neer Tannah, is a Fort called the Bullwork of the Sea, which being three Leagues up from the Harbors Mouth, Imports the Continuation of the Sea, and Wee supose the Extent of the Harbor, and in no other part does the Water reach so farr, so that Wee cannot doubt of Our property in the whole Bay, but the Occasion of our present greivance and Complaint arises from the Impositions laid on us by the Portuguez for tradeing with the Moores (subjects of the Savagee and of the Mogul) even for those things which none but the Moores can furnish. And because the Injustice of proceedings by the Portugalls Ministers may bee made the more cleere and evident, Wee shall bee obliged to give your Lordships minutely an account of some things that serve them for the Grounds of their Injustice, and so describe the Situation of those places where wee are constrained to pay Tributes, That your Lordships may see how a Fort of two Gunns is compared to Elsinore, a River broad as the Thames unto the Sound, and either the Harbor of Bombaim or the Road of Basaim unto the Baltick Sea. To begin therefore by the small Inlett of the Sea which is caled the Road of Basaim.

First Basaim is a Citty of very good Consideration, and the Seat of a Governor, that has many Leagues thereabouts within his Jurisdiction; It stands on the main Land on the North side of the Road, about half a League up from the Sea, and about two Leagues higher is the River of Biondi, and about a League higher that of Galiana, haveing seated on them two considerable Cittyes of the same Names about two Leagues up in the Countrey, which belong to the Prince Salvagee, who is revolted from the Mogull, and these afford great plenty of Trade, nor can wee buy Wood or Timber or scarce Provisions for our occations elsewhere; the Land all adjoyning to the Road of Basaim, and which turnes away Northward is, towards the shoar at least, claimed by the Portugeses, but for the Southside of this Road of Basaim It is made up by the Island of Salsett, whose East side comes up close to the Main and makes the Passage, which is not there much broader than the Thames, so that for about the length of two Miles it is caled in that streight the River of Tannah, and perhaps for a good way lower from a Village of the same Name that appeares in the Map. But a litle further on beyond Tannah the Water widens, and there onely begins (as has been said) the Inner part of the Port of Bombaim when the tide is out, and that all the Channell further up about Tannah is left Quite dry, But when the Tyde flowes in, then alsoe doe the Waters of the Port of Bombaim shoot into that Streight and encounter the

Tyde that flowes up by the Road of Basaim, as shall presently bee said; But first it will be fitt to give a particular accompt of the Three Forts which stand in the length of this Streight; Whereof the First that stands towards Basaim is caled Belgrado, situated oposite to the two Rivers of Galliana and Biondi, and about half a League from Tannah. The second is called Passo Secco, built in the middle of the Stream just by Tannah, and the Third is a Gunshott lower towards Bombaim, and called as before the Bulwark of the Sea.

Public Record Office, C. O. 77, Vol. XIII, folio 168.

In this narrow are severall turnings of the River which is fitted with mighty stones that all ly dry to the bottom for above a Miles space, when the Tide is out, so that when the Tide flowes in (as it does by both these waies at once) there is in all that space so mighty a noise, and such furious contention of the Waters for neer an howers time, that all Boates and Vessells are fain to attend till the Tide be full, and then the Rage and motion thereof ceases, as it is at London Bridge, so that Vessells from 20 to 30 Tunns doe pass with their ladeing, And at the returne of the Tide the Noise and Motion of the Waters is much (tho' not so great as before) untill all be left dry for the space of a Mile as has been said.

Belgrado, as standing neere on the side of Salsett, is alsoe then left dry, but the Bulwark of the Sea is never so. Belgrado was erected (as the auntient Narratives sett forth) to guard against any incursions that might bee made on Salsett or Tannah from the opposite Rivers of Galiana and Biondi; The middle Fort was to guard the passage against the Moors from the other side the passage when the Tyde was out, and to defend Tannah which was a place unwalled; and the Third Fort was not onely to help herein, but to keep off from Tannah the Pyrates that might enter by the Port of Bombaim. The Charge and Expences of these Forts to the King of Portugall are as Followeth.

In Belgrado there are two or three small Gunns, a Commander, Eight Souldiers, a Gunner, a Lamp tender and four Mariners, The yearly expence 687 Pardoes which makes 52*li.* 4*s.* 9¾*d.* sterling.

In the middle one, called Passo Secco, there are two small Gunns, a Commander, Four Souldiers, a Gunner, a Lamp tender and four Boat men, which makes the yearly Charge of Five hundred Twenty Two Pardoes that is 39*li.* 13*s.* 10*d.* sterling.

In the Bullwark of the Sea, where there are 5 or 6 small Gunns and Chambers, an Officer, Eight Souldiers, a Gunner, a Lamp tender and four Boatmen, which cost 747 Pardoes a yeare, vizt. 50*li.* 16*s.* 0¾*d.* sterling.

Soe that the designe, importance and expence of these severall places being here sett forth, all of them point directly att the defence of Tannah without any fruit or benifit unto Bombaim, or the Security of the Ships rideing in the Port, but on the contrary Bombaim is indeed a Frontier and a Buckler on the Sea to All these Inner Parts.

The Main Land opposite to Tannah is by the Portugeses reputed to bee under their Jurisdiction, which they maintain by protecting a Moorish Captain or sort of Prince revolted from his Superior, who lives about the River Saboio, and has an allowance for 20 hors[e] and

Public Record Office, C. O. 77, Vol XIII, folio 168.

500 Foot, which hee is to raise and scoure the Country withall in times of Trouble, but there are no Portugeses that live upon this Tract.

The next place to bee described is the Island of Carinjah (two sides whereof front the Main Land of the Mogull) from whence when the Tide is out, one side of the Island is exposed to the incursion of the Mooreish horsemen, who by layeing Faggotts on the Mudd make a shift to gett over and committ great spoyle, wherefore, for the defence of the Island, there is allowed Pay for A Captain, Six Souldiers, a Gunner and some other help which cost the King yearly 480 Pardoes that amount unto 36*li*. 10*s*. 0*d*. sterling. But the Militia of this Island is considerable, and there is a good Fortification in it with Severall Gunns. The Fruits of the Island are Rice and Salt, from whence the Revenue ariseing to the King is Farmed at 2200 Seraphims which is under 200*li*. sterling.

At the South End of this Island are some Gunns which Comand in all Our Boates as they ever goe to, or come from Pennah or Magillan, to Trade with the Moores in the Country of the Mogull. And if our Boates keep off, because the Streame is so wide as that their Gunns cannot reach them, then doe they Arme out Small Boates with Souldiers and Levy on us what they please, not for the King of Portugall, but for the Commanders owne Private Use, as is affirmed, so that when wee putt armed men in Our Boates (as often wee doe) and resist this Payment, the resistance is Quietly borne and no Complaint is ever made thereof.

But at Tannah wee have not hitherto taken upon us to resist, because their Forts stand thick, and require us to Call in at Tannah and there to pay what the Custome Officers demand, which is on some goods 10, on some 12, and some 14 per Cent as they think fitt, which is very hard that when we have paid one duty for them to the Moores at Biondi or Galiana (whose duty is there as generally in other parts among the Indians, but 3 and ¾ per Cent) that so heavy a Tribute should bee forced on Us, for but bare passage in the open Streames, and forced to come in and pay the same; for wee refuse not where wee Land and Trade to pay all dutys of the place, as wee freely do to the Portuguese when we Trade at Basaim, or have our buisnesse at Tannah. If wee buy at *goods at Basaim then have wee a Certificate of the duties that are paid, upon the view of which at Tannah we are suffered to pass free, and not otherwise, The Customs at Tannah are computed at 4200 Zeraphims which is about 370*li*. a yeare.

* [*sic*]

And notwithstanding there is no wood, or Shipp Timber for use growing any where but in the Savagee's Country and none of it with the Portuguez, yett by a monopoly of Timber granted antiently to the Governòr of Basaim by the Kings of Portugall, on pretence of building shipps in the time of Warr for the Kings Service, and so to the end the Timber might not bee diverted, no man must buy Timber from the Moores and bring it downe by the Streame of Tannah, but it is Seased and Confiscated without the Governour's licence; which Licence doth cost more than is paid for the Timber to the Moores; And it is alsoe said that the duties on other goods so unjustly taken are Cheifly converted to his owne use, there never haveing apear'd any Order from Portugall to levy the same; For it is certaine (as hath bin said) that the Inhabitants of Bombaim, never paid any duties for passing here in the open streames in the King of Portugall's time, but the Practice began upon Us on pretence of Injuries by his Majesties Governors, in turning the Portuguez proprietors out of their Lands and houses, and tho' the Companie, when they enter'd did signall Justice in restoreing all with Universall applause and Consent, yett this Violence is still exercised upon us. Public Record Office, C. O. 77, Vol. XIII, folio 168.

'Tis fitt your Lordshipps should alsoe know, that as in Virtue of the Capitulations imposed on Mr. Cook they Claime a share in the Bay, so doe they exercise their usurped Dominion therein by Sayling with their Collours flying and their Flaggs aloft in theyre small Armadoes or Brigandines, to the shame and dishonour of his Majesties Colours on the Fort, where there are mounted no less than about 100 Gunns.

It is usuall, at some Season of the Yeer, when the Seas are trouble some, that all the Trade of Bassaim comes thro' this Port, and the Gallions, and other ships of the King of Portugall come alsoe from Goa and winter at Trombay, where the Water is deep, and the Bottom very Oazy.

But as the Portuguez throw on us upon all Occasions markes of their disrespect, so among other things they will not bee perswaded, but that they have a right of Dominion over the Portuguezes and other Subjects that live upon the Island. The Capitulation with Cook is all wayes insisted on, but the Root of all their Insolence comes from the impunity of that high disservice and affront given to his Majestie upon the Non Surrender whereby the Nation sunk Low in esteem even of those who did escape the punishment they soe notoriously deserved for the same. Yett notwithstanding all these discouragments and vexations, wee having an earnest desire if it were possible to reverse our Ill Fortune, to make the grant of Bombaim valueable to the Nation, and to answere the vast expences wee had been at in Fortifieing and improveing the Place. And all this by one single expedient of opening and drawing downe a Trade from the Inland parts, by the way of Galiana and Biondi, which being a Shorter Cutt, and of less expence, would divert much of what now goes to the Scale of Surratt. Wee did therefore send a very solemn address unto the Vice Roy at Goa, imploying 4 or 5 persons of Consideration therein, and Furnishing all the Inducements as of Reason and Justice on our side, so of Conveniency to themselves. But Our desire of prosperity in those parts, were so invidiously regarded, that wee could obtain no other answere then an Excuse for his incapacity to remitt any thing of those payments at Tannah and Carinjah. That the practice of the Sound justified those impositions, and that the Capitulation of Mr. Cook ought to determine all things between us, as to that Island and Port. Whereas it is manifest that at the Sound they take but one per Cent for Buoyage and Beaconage, and when attempt was made to raise this to a Custome of 4 per Cent all the Princes of Europe unanimously opposed it, denying any Customes to bee due in open streames, and even this one per Cent was stipulated for in the Treaty made then with Queen Elizabeth.

Thus your Lordships have as well the narrative of Severall proceedings, as the matters of Fact from whence, wee doubt not but

Public Record Office, C. O. 77, Vol. XIII, folio 168.

your Lordships will bee best able to deduce such Arguments as may concern our Right.

1. And heerein alsoe (if your Lordships will pardon the offerring what occurs to us) wee cannot but say That the Freedome of Trade bettween Allies seemes to bee so founded in Right that none can interrupt the Same without the highest provocations to either Side.

2. That enhanceing of Duties may amount unto such an Interdiction of Commerce as that the Freinds of a Prince may bee made as uselesse as if they were his Enimies.

3. That where goods are exported and where imported, the duties of each Country are to bee observed, But for a Third Prince to impose duties as high as both, for but bare passage in a Streame of the Sea is most unjust.

4. If the Streame were not a worke of nature, but of Charge; If the Forts that Stand therein were in the nature of Convoys to give Shelter from the Moores, or were as Frontiers to guard the Shipps being at Anchor within, If they maintained Lights or Buois for Security in Passage, then indeed might something bee demanded in proportion to the Expence and the benefitt received. But those Forts cannot bee said to guard or defend us from those whome wee desire to Traffick withall. They were not built but for the safety of Tannah, not for the Island of Bombaim, or the Shipps at Anchor, because as to both these, the Insecurity lies from the Sea, and Bombaim is rather the frontier, from Pyratts and Rovers unto all.

5. If some moderate thing were demanded in proportion to the Three lamps that burn on those Forts, It were but a thing of Course and ought to bee submitted unto, but to pay dutyes where there is no Traffique; to bee stopt in the Course of a Voyage and forced to the Shoare is a thing of Violence.

6. That the King of Denmark doth take Custome of all Shipps which pass the Elsenore is a mistake in the Vice Roy; since what is paid is a small recompence for Lights and Buoys laid, at certain distances, for the better security of Shipps in passing or comeing to an Anchor in the Night. And this alsoe is paid in manner and proportion as is before exprest; yett from this pretence (and without considering the disparity of being admitted to the benefitt of a Copious Trade within Severall Ports of the Baltic, where alsoe Pyrates are hindred from following and may bee stopped at their comeing out), will the Vice Roy needs inferr a like Institution in a poor Narrow inconsiderable Channell, where the Dominions of his Majestie may probably reach or at least come very neere it. And this not onely contrary to the former practice of the Place but contrary to the Former Practice at Mallaca, which, when in the Portugueses hands, they never demanded Customes of the English Shipps passing those streights, as being a thing against the Articles establish't between all Nations which is to have the passage of their Streames and Harbors free.

7. As to the Port wee know nothing that gives bounds or limitts to this Bay, But the Circle of the Main Land round about unto which it flowes, part whereof being claimed by the King of Portugall, his

grant of this water ought there to bee caried on as far (in any doubtfull case) as may bee most beneficiall to his Majesty who received the grant.

Public Record Office, C. O. 77, Vol. XIII, folio 168

8. The other part of the main land, belonging to the Great Mogull, does not afford matter of dispute, so that wee conclude (by what has bin said before) that the whole body and surface of Water that flowes in, and whole Fundus bellow even up to the high water mark is the Kings, and the Land between the high and Low water mark is among the Rights of the Admirall.

9. Next wee presume to think, That if this water were given to his Majestie as a port, It was given as a place of safety from stormes, and for releif of the Damages, which are received at Sea, so that if his Majesties Navy Royall should come into this Port wanting Timber and other Necessaries to refitt, could any Law forbid the buying the same from the Moores, and being bought, might not a Toll bee as Justly laid for the Anchorage of the Shipps as for the use of this Timber or the use of Provisions, or any thing Else that was needfull.

10. The Sea where it is mastered, seemes to carry and Convey with it a Right of Dominion, whithersoever it goes. The first conquest of those Islands were made from the Sea, and where the Sea overflows any Territory of the neighbouring Land, all that space of Sea (and in Virtue thereof all the Land below it) belongs to that Prince, who had the Soveraignity of the Sea before, so alsoe New Islands riseing up in the Waters of any Prince, doe become his Right, as doe all Islands standing in his Seas without inhabitation belonging unto him just as Wrecks in the Sea.

11. 'Tis probable that the Islands not named in the Grant to his Majestie but Inhabited, may have their private Rights and properties retained to the Owners, but tis not probable their dominion can remaine since they are so closely girded by the dominion of another Prince, and Cannot submit but by the benefitt of his Waters, soe that while the Question is so probable whither his Majestie should not have the soveraignity of [the] whole, how absurd is the practice to make him a Tributary in Part. That an English man might have lived and traded on better Terms at Bombaim before it was his Majesties, and that his Portuguez Subjects should bee put into a State of Servitude they never knew before, are not surely the things for which his Majestie made the Treaty, and sent his Fleet to the Indies to take possession.

12. Therefore wee cannot think the Portugueses would know how to Complain, should wee by his Majesties permission, Strengthen Our hands, and by a Rule of retaliation stop all their Shipps comeing into the Port, that are bound either to Tannah, Basaim or Carinjah, levieing as arbitrary duties on them as they impose upon us.

For ought not the Main Land bee as free for the English as the Main Sea to the Portugueses, will they give us a port and forbid us the Use of that Land which makes it a port ?

It is therefore evident That as the thing granted was at first refused, so now' tis given, they mean to take it away again. For if wee have not liberty of Trade, wee have nothing but a poore limitted

Public Record Office, C. O. 77, Vol. XIII, folio 168.

and expensive spot of Ground to support and neither fitt for his Majesties honor nor our profitt to bee retained.

What therefore, in most humble manner, Wee doe propose unto your Lordships as a fitt expedient in this afair is this, That you would please to advise his Majestie to make a Solemn representation of this Matter to the Prince of Portugall, by letting him understand the Extent of Dominion and Commerce promised and proposed by the Treaty; That after a Vast Charge in sending a Squadron to take possesion of this place, how the same was refused, The Voyage overthrowne and 300 of Subjects perished for want of Shelter.

That want of resenting this Indignity in the manner it deserved, drew on a presumption among the ministers in India, when possession was afterwards given to Humphry Cook to compell him to accept it, injuriously, under conditions quite contrary to the publick Treaty, and in him as treacherously accepted, haveing had no power for the same.

That instead of enjoying Salsett and the pass at Tannah as exhibited to his Majestie in the Map, and so promised by the Portugall Ambasador, as it was afterwards notified and objected to him when all these things were fresh by a Memoriall of the 25th of July 1663 as appeares, and that with much more reason the Island of Carinjah ought in justice to pass as being surrounded with the waters of this Port, there are severe Tributes imposed on all the Inhabitants of Bombaim, for but passing in the open streames by Tannah and Carinjah, contrary to the practice of the former times before the Surrender, and contrary to the Rights of Soveraignty granted his Majestie together with that Island, and contrary to the Law of Nations for passing in open streames. That by these Injuries the Place growing very Chargeable to bee maintained by his Majestie Hee thought fitt to transferr the possession thereof to his East India Company knowing they would redress all particular complaints; that if these duties were laid on in animosity, and revenge of particular wrongs they would soon be removed; But though it is apparent that they did all things immaginable for the gratification of particular men, and restoreing them to their Rights; Yett upon application solemnly made to the Vice Roy at Goa, they have not been able to obtain any sort of redress, so that if such Injuries be any longer submitted unto, the grant of that place will in all its advantages bee totally subverted and come to nought, which as it was not the intention of the Treaty on the one hand, so upon an impartiall reflection how his Majestie performed his part thereof, in the assistances given that Crown nearer home, It may not bee possible but his Majesties friendship in that part of the World may alsoe produce some suitable Effects.

That his Majestie being therefore excited in his Own honor to see this matter determined according to publique Justice, and sorry that hee should invite his East India Company into so vast an expence by improvements and Fortifications of the Place without seeing them reape the just benefitt in freedome of Trade that belong there unto, but seeing that they rather languish in the expectation thereof, than that they hitherto enjoy it, Hee cannot any longer forbear to express his resentments herein. And although upon all these provocations and the insuccesse of all endeavours in India, His Majestie be importun'd to permitt the Companie to right themselves by laying equall impositions on all Vessels bound either for Tannah, Basaim or Carinjah by the way of that Port; Yett hee Rather Chooses to suspend his Finall Answer herein untill the goeing of the next yeares ships. However that his Majestie doe declare it as a point of selfe defence (which no Law can forbid) that hee had already directed and commanded his said Companie to refuse and resist the Imposition of those Tributes in the best manner they could, and that his Majestie does hope before the next spring and the goeing of the Ships that then depart, to have this matter fairly composed to the satisfaction of all that are concerned, by a redresse of all the Evils past and restitution for what has bin unjustly exacted. And therefore to desire of the Prince to enter imediatly into an elucidation of the 11th Article of the Treaty of Marriag[e], to ascertain the Rights intended by that Treaty, and to insert the same into the Treaty of Commerce which is now intended to bee renewed with that Crowne. That his Majestie would in particular declare against the unjust capitulation forced upon Humphry Cook, to have it quite laid aside and mortified, because as hee neither had Power or Comission to accept such a thing, soe nobody had power to impose anything contrary to the Treaty, as that notoriously appeares to bee. That in the next place, the Trade into the Countryes of the Mogull and Savageé or any part of the Main may bee open and free; not onely to the English but all the Inhabitants of Bombaim, and all other Merchants tradeing to and from that Place, as well for Timber and Provisions as for all other sorts of Merchandizes whatsoever.

Public Record Office, C. O. 77, Vol. XIII, folio 168.

And Lastly as to the other Points that soe muc bee insisted on as apeares to bee the plain sence and scope of the said Article, when the same was treated and adjusted between the two Crownes. That so by a Cleere understanding of what has for so many yeers bred and will every day create new disputes and Contentions between the Subjects of either Prince, that they may at last learne to correspond and live in mutual Offices of Freindship and assistance to each other.

All which is most humbly submitted unto Your Lordships.

12th February 1676.

[*Endorsed.*]

Copy of a Report from the East India Company touching the reparations they demand in the Business of Bombaim.

Read at the Committee 13 February 1676/7.

A Court of Committees holden 24th April 1677.

It is ordered that a gratuity of 100 Guinies be given to Sir Robert Southwell one of the Clerks of his Mats. most hon. privy Councel, for his great paines in drawing up the state of the case relating to the Compa. interest in the port & Island of Bombay & the Dependencies thereof, and in manageing that affayr with the Lords Comtees. for trade, for removing the obstructions given to the Compa. trade by the Forts of Tannah & Carinjah, as also by the Portugals refusing

Court Book X X X, page 126.

Court Book, X X X, page 126. to give passes to the Natives jounks for Gombroon: and the Governor Depty. & Mr. Houblon or any two of them are desired to present the same accordingly.

The following documents deal with another phase of this controversy. Mahim is now the bone of contention, and the Company's efforts are directed towards securing a foothold on that Island. It is instructive to compare the documents quoted above with the following copy of an important petition from the East India Company. The petition is couched in the blunt, forcible way characteristic of the homely wit, maudlin humour and pugnacious temperament of the Directors. Their task was rendered much easier through the support of all the important officials of the King. His Majesty and his servants were frequently granted substantial gratuities, and the extract quoted above shows that Sir Robert Southwell himself accepted a gratuity of £100 from the Company.

A COURT OF COMMITTEES HOLDEN 11TH JULY 1677.

Court Book, X X X; page 141.

It is ordered that the narrative of the proceedings of the Captn. Generall of the Portugueze at Basseim against the English at Bombay mentioned in the last advises from Suratt be drawn out and presented to the Rt. honble. the Lords Committees for trade and plantations; that busines of Mahim being now depending before them.

Public Record Office, C. O. 77, Vol. XIII, folio 252.

Portugueze General at Basseim, Narrative &c.

To the Right honble. the Lords of
the Comittee for Trade and Plantations.

The Governor and Company of Merchants of London tradeing into the East Indies doe most humbly answer.

MAY IT PLEASE YOUR LORDSHIPS.

Haveing received your Lordships directions of the * to returne our farther Observations on the Memoriall of the Portugall Ambassador recited in our last answer of * touching his pretensions to Mahim and the Rights of the Prince his Master therein.

* [Blank.]

Wee are at a great Loss to think what sort of Title he can sett up, though wee doubt little of the Motives he may have to attempt it.

1. Perhaps he will argue That Mahim is a distinct Island from Bombaim, and that this later is onely mentioned and given by the Treaty.

2. Hee may pretend that Mahim does belong to particular men, whose properties the King of Portugall could not give away, and that even the Customes and publick Revenues of the Crowne were morgaged out for severall Lives unto particular men, which ought to be made good.

3. Hee may hope by disputeing the Title to discourage our Improvements there. Or at length by yeelding this, to Stop and conclude our pretensions to any more. Or to gain some Sanction to the Injurious capitulation imposed on Mr. Humphery Cook upon the Surrender, for they take a liberty of hopeing any thing since they have been able to get over the Offence of the first refusall of Bombaim with Impunity.

Public Record Office, C. O. 77, Vol. XIII, folio 252.

4. The Ministers of Portugall may have been in deep Meditation how to get back Bombaim, for of a Long time they have openly discoursed of repurchaseing it from his Majestie. But untill they doe by such fair Method compass it, tis very probable they will ever maligne and endeavour to obstruct our prosperity in that place. And how far this their temper is predominant in them may plainly be inferred from the following observations:

1. They did in the very beginning overthrow the Lord Malboroughs voyage, who in 1662 carryed in his squadron a Portugueze Vice Roy called Dennis de Melo de Castro to deliver that place, and 500 English Soldiers to possess it, who being kept out and forced to attend New Orders 300 of them, with their designed Governor, Sir Abraham Shipman, died miserably in a desolate Island. And the fitting of that Squadron cost his Majestie 100m *li.** which was all lost.

*[= £100,000]

2. When in February 1664/5 the said Vice Roy did think fitt to Surrender the Island to the surviving English, it was under various conditions, quite altering and retrenching in Severall Points the plain sence of the Treaty.

3. They proceeded presently after this to lay on a New and arbitrary Tax on our Trade in the Streames of Tannah and Carinjah, and have Still continued the same with great Severity.

4. They make a Monopoly of all manner of Timber not to be purchased but at their own Rates.

5. They Secretly perswade the Inhabitants of the place, that they are Still under the Allegiance of Portugall.

6. They brave it with the Flaggs up in the Port of Bombaim, as it were in defiance of our Castle, and the Flag of his Majestie there Erected. And when wee complain of any Outrages on our Ships at Sea, and other abuses suffered by Land, there is no redress to be had in those Parts.

7. Wee are denied by the Vice Roy of Goa liberty of Trade in their Ports, though the 12th Article is expressly for that End, his answer being that he must first consult the Prince, this being a Royallty which neerly touched his own Person, and wherein all Vice Roys were absolutely restrained etc.

Public Record Office, C. O. 77, Vol. XIII, folio 252.

8. They have lately refused their Customary Passes to any of the native Jouncks that would goe to Gombroone in Persia, where the Company have half the Customes, thereby to oblige them for Security to Trade unto Cong, where they have the Like part of the duties, whereof complaint was made to his Majestie in February last.

* [£80,000]

And now that wee have raised a Fort in Bombaim with 100 Gunns mounted thereon, setled the Government and expended 80m £* on the place to make it usefull for the Trade of the Nation, And after 13 Yeers possession since the Surrender, They

9. Put in a New claime, and would now rend away a Principall Member of the whole, alledging a Protest made for saving their Right Whereof wee never had any notice before.

10. And while the Ambassador is here negotiating for this Limb of that Island, the Governor of Basaim is takeing it by force, Insulting the place with a Body of 1200 men, as by the Letters of April 1676 may appear.

So that what they gave his Majestie for his Protection in their distress, while his Armes and Mediation was of use unto them, they would pull away and undermine now that they are at Rest. But how by any Colour or pretence of Right they mean to Justify this demand wee cannot see, for

1. Bombaim and Mahim were alwaies united under one governor, and both excluded out of the Government of Basaim. In auncient time Mahim was the name of the whole. There was a great Castle, and the Residence of a Moorish King. It has ever since continued to be the place for the head Custome house, it had dependent on it, and within its district, not onely 70 villages of the Island Salsett and the whole Isle of Caranjah etc., but that also of Bombaim, as appears by the Records and Lawes of the Custome house there preserved to this day. So that if the Prince has any Title to the Lands of Mahim, he has it also to the Sovereignty, the Rights, priviledges and dependancies thereof, and which if true then is his Majestie tributary in Bombaim to an adjacent Spott, and the Sovereignty of that Port and Island mentioned in the Treaty is but an Empty Sound.

2. There is little doubt but that both those places are, in the Generall Stile and way of Speaking, comprehended in the name of Bombaim, as the Denomination is taken usually from the Greater part. For can it els be imagined that a Spott so contiguous, nay that is united to Bombaim (but onely when the Waters of his Majesties own Port doe wrap it round and that the Tide is in) could be excluded from the Grant of the rest without words of particular reservation to that Effect.

What meaning els can be given to the Words of the Treaty, if this part at least be not comprehended? For to the Grant of the Port and Island of Bombaim tis also added, Together with all the Rights Territories and dependencies whatsoever, And then upon repeating again the things granted, Tis not onely said the Port and Island But also the premises and all the Regalia thereunto appertaining. In the very same words is the 2nd Article of the said Treaty relateing to Tangier, where nothing is particularly named but the Citty and the Castle. Yet the general words of Regalia did pass the Harbor, the Mole, the Arsenal, the Cannon, the Custome house, the Courts of Guard, and all the Territory serving for Forage which was within defences.

Public Record Office, C. O. 77, Vol, XIII, folio 252.

The whole Scope of the 11th Article declares a purpose for the enlarging our Trade and Territory, and the 15th is again expressly full of the same. Nothing indeed was then thought too dear for his Majesties allyance, But now, by the course of Time, the onely Scope and intention of our Allies seems to be to dismember us, so that if protesting and a different name from Bombaim be sufficient, when any Spott is separated from the rest (as Mahim it self seems to have been by the Tydes) every Storm may beget a New Title, and his Majesties Dominion of the Land may be destroyed by what he holds in the Sea.

Wee doe presume to observe That the Ambassador mentions onely the Treaty, and the 11th Article thereof, and saies nothing of the Capitulations imposed on Humphrey Cooke, though in the Indies, at every turn they are insisted upon, and imposed as the Rule, and were doubtless by the Tenour of them framed in Portugall to that end. But as to the present question they make more in our favour then otherwise as by these following Instances will appear.

The Second Article is in words thus.

1. That neither the Port of Bandora in the Island of Salsett, nor any other of the same Island, shall be obstructed, but that all the ships, as well those that shall goe out of the said Port or Ports as those that shall come to them, may freely pass, and the English shall not alledge that they pass under their Artillary, because with this condition the said Island Bombaim is delivered to them, and they shall not desire more then is granted them by the Article of Peace, and Treaty of Marriage.

The 7th Article begins thus.

2. That the Inhabitants of the Islands of Salset, Caranjah, Baragnas and the rest (which are of our Jurisdiction) shall freely Fish in the said Bay and River, and in that Arm that enters, and which divides Bombaim from Salsett by Bandora up into the Bay etc.

Public Record Office, C. O. 77, Vol. XIII, folio 252.

So that tis but looking on the Map, and it will appear that their own Capitulation does condemn them.

1. Bandora, which stands on the other side, was not thought Secure without this Salvo.

2. Remoter Islands are named, but no mention of Mahim.

3. The same Arme which divides Bombaim from Salsett, divides also Mahim from Salsett, and therefore Bombaim and Mahim are allowed to be the same thing.

Thus wee have promiscuously set down what occurs unto us in this matter, as not knowing by what Arguments or in what particular Method the Ambassador will proceed to support his claime, which perhaps a short question made him touching the time of that protest, and the Motives of it, or rather a demand of the Protest it self, might discover.

But wee doe here most humbly beg of your Lordships to lay hold on the Negotiation that is Offered by this Memoriall, that wee may thereby attain the Ends of our Representation made your Lordships on the 12th of February last, unto which wee desire to be referred, It being a Matter of Great Importance to our Trade, and wherein by your Lordships favour, wee have made one considerable Step, by obtaining his Majesties Letter to the Vice Roy at Goa, and shall need farther applications to the Prince of Portugal, in order to compleat that work, the whole consisting in a due explanation of the 11th Article of the Treaty of Marriage, into which affair the Ambassador seems qualified with powers to enter, and wee hope so good an overture will not be lost.

All which is most humbly Submitted unto your Lordships.

4th September 1677.

[*Endorsed.*]

The East India Companies answer to that part of the Portugal Embassadors Memorial concerning the pretensions to Mahim.

Court Book XXX, page 156.

A Court of Committees holden 5th September 1677.

Mr Parry lately representing unto the Court, that he was going Envoy for his Maty. to the Court of Portugal, † and that having attended Mr Secry. Coventry for his instructions, Mr Secry. told him that he wanted information touching this Compa. affayrs at Bombay; and therefore directed him to acquaint this Court therewith: On consideration whereof had, it is ordered that Maj. Thomson be desired to cause a copie of the Compa. last address to the Rt. hon. the Lords Comtees. for Trade and Plantations to be transcribed, and the Comtees. for Suratt are desired to attend Mr Secry. Coventry with the same, and that Mr. Parry have notice of the time.

COUNCILL CHAMBER,
25th of October 1667 [*sic, i.e.* 1677].

SIR

The Right Honble. the Lords of the Committee for Trade and Plantations upon consideration of the Business of Bombaim as it lyes before them by Petition from the East India Company did this day agree to Report unto his Majestie in Councill that as His Majestie has already been pleased to signify by His Royall letters unto the Vice Roy of Goa his Commands given unto the East India Company to refuse payment of those unjust demands at Tannah and Caranjah, So it is now time that the Prince of Portugall do receive the same intimation, that he may give his positive Orders to His Officers in India to exact no more duties of the English Nation which Report will be presented unto His Majestie at the first meeting of the Councill; Their Lordships have at the same time perused the East India Companies Answer to that part of the Portugall Ambassadors Memorial that concerns the Oppressions of the Portugueses, and particularly of Alvaro Pires de Tavora ; of which they have not only expressed their full approbation, but have likewise Ordered that it be shew'n unto the Portugall Ambassador when he shall insist upon the said Memoriall.

Public Record Office, C. O. 77, Vol. XIII, folio 268.

Their Lordships having dispatched so much of this business do now think fitt that the East India Company do bring in their Answer to the other part of the Ambassadors Memoriall, which Questions their right to Mahim, and the extent of His Majesties Soveraignty in those parts, that so their Lordships may be fully enabled to satisfy his Excellency upon the whole Complaint. All which by their Lordships Commands I signify unto you. And am with all respect.

Sir
Your Most Humble Servant
WM. BLATHWAYT.

To the Governor of the East India Company.

[*Addressed.*]

To Sir William Tompson Knight
Governor of the East India Company.
These.

[*Endorsed.*]

25 October 1677.
Mr. Blathwaite's Latter.

20 *October* 1677.

There being this day presented to his Majesty in Councill a Report from the Right Honble. the Committee of Trade and Plantations in the words following.

* MAY IT PLEASE YOUR MAJESTIE.

Wee did by Our Report to Your Majestie in Councill on the 23rd of February last past, Set forth the many hardships which Your Subjects of the East India Company did Sustaine in their Possession of the Island of Bombaim being in perticuler constrained by the Portu-

* [The full text of this quoted document appears at fol. 270.]

Public Record Office, C. O. 77, Vol. XI:I folio 274.

guezes there adjoyning, to pay certain Arbitrary Tolls and duties contrary to all Right. So that Your Majestie thereupon thought fitt, to command Your Said Subjects to refrain submitting to such Payments, and ever to resist the same in the best manner They could, and hereof Your Majestie was pleased by your Royall Letters to make signification to the Vice Roy of Goa, with the motives Inducing the same and hereof alsoe wee think it high time, that Your Majestie doe by Letter Intimate to the Prince of Portugall, the Grounds and Progress of this matter, to the Effect following.

That Your Majestie having thought fitt to deposite into the hands of your Subjects of the East India Company the care and Possession, of Your Island and Port of Bombaim, together with all the Territories and dependancies thereof, They have exposed to Your Majesty the state of severall Injuries susteined by them from the neighbouring Portuguezes, and that notwithstanding They have frequently and in all due manner, offerred Their Complaints herein to the Vice Roy of Goa, yet noe redress was given, or can be hoped for.

That the particuler Greivance now to be mentioned, is of an unjust demand, made by order of the Governor of Basaim, of certaine Arbitrary Tolls and Taxes imposed on your Majesties Subjects, as They Trade and pass in Boates, in the open Streames, by the Forts Tanah and Caranjah, in Their way to the Territories of the Great Mogul and Savagée, with whom Your Majestie is in Friendship. Nor is the Prince of Portugall in Warr.

That if Your Subjects shall remain thus burthened and perplexed in their Trade, the Grant of Bombaim will prove altogether fruitless; which as it cannot be imagined was the Intention of Portugall, soe neither can Your Majestie easily part with an advantage that is the more valuable to You, as coming in Marriage with Your Deare Consort the Queene.

That these Tolls, and Impositions, were never practised or laid on, in any former times, under the Crown of Portugall.

That the Treaty is contrary to Them; and their exaction utterly disavowed in all like cases by the Law of Nations. Soe that Your Majesty has thought fit to forbid Your Subjects to submitt unto the Payment of Them in the future; and if any Acts of Compulsion be made, That they resist the same in the best manner They Can.

That Your Majestie by the Ships that last departed, has hereof given full intimation by your Royall Letters to the Vice Roy of Goa, signifying also your Purpose of acquainting the Prince his Master with the same as now you doe, Not doubting but That his Highness would be more inclin'd upon hearing the nature of the Complaint to order restitution of what has bin for soe many yeares unjustly exacted, than to give Countenance to the Continuation of such a Wrong.

That therefore Your Majestie does desire his Highness to issue forth speedy orders to his Vice Roy of Goa, as also to the Governor of Bassaim, that a stop be put immediatly unto the Levying and forcing any Tribute from your said Subjects, in their Trade and Passage in the Streames aforesaid, it being a Thing not onely Injurious in it selfe; but even wounding the Right of Your Majestie's Soveraignty in that Place.

And lastly To the end That not onely this and other Complaints and difficulties which have arisen, But even the memory of that grievous violation and the Consequences thereof, Committed in the begining about the non surrender, may be buried in oblivion; Your Majesty does propose that full and ample Powers be sent by his Highness, unto his Ambassador Extraordinary residing in this Court, for the better Elucidation and cleering up the Eleventh Article of the Treaty of Marriage, which is the onely Rule hitherto subsisting that can limitt or enlarge Your Majestie's Rights of Possession and Soveraignty in those parts. This being the onely meanes to have a lasting foundation of friendship and good Correspondence, between the Subjects of either Crowne in these parts and to make Bombaim of that Importance to your Kingdom, as by the Grant thereof, was doubtlesse intended on either Syde. Public Record Office, C. O. 77, Vol. XIII, folio. 274.

All which is most humbly Submitted.

FINCH.
ANGLESEY.
ESSEX.
CRAVEN.
J. WILLIAMSON.
J. ERNLE.

COUNCILL CHAMBER

25th of October 1677.

His Majesty upon consideration thereof was gratiously pleased, to Approve the same; And the Right Honble. Mr. Secretary Coventry is accordingly to prepare a letter for his Majesties Royall Signature. And to Instruct Mr. Parry his Majesties Envoy in Portugall to sollicite the effects thereof. But in the said letter the word elucidation in the last clause of the Report is to be Omitted, least thereby the Court of Portugall should thinke that they were let into the makeing of a New Treaty, Whereas the Article of the old one does containe his Majesties Rights, and needs onely some explanation and assertaining of the same. As also to exclude and extinguish, certaine abusive practises on the other Side which have no Countenance from the said Article, but are rather contrary thereunto. Court Book XXX, page188.

[*Endorsed.*]

26th of October 1677
Order upon a Report
concerning Bombaim.

[*Inserted Title.*]

Order of Councill on a
Report concerning Bombay.

A COURT OF COMMITTEES HOLDEN 1ST NOVEMBER 1677.

On reading a Letter from Sir Robt. Southwell directed to Sir Nath. Herne, and of an order of his Matie. in Councell touching the duties exacted from the Inhabitants of Bombay by the Portugueezes at the Passes of Tannah and Carinjah It is ordered; That it be referred Public Record Office, C. O. 77, Vol. XIII, folio 278.

Public Record Office, C. O. 77, Vol. XIII, folio 278.

to the Comtees. for Surrt. to consider thereof and to attend the Rt. Honble. Mr. Secrie. Coventry touching the Letter to be written to the Prince of Portugall, mentioned in the said Order, and to proceed in the managing of the said Affaire as they shall thinke fitt.

MAY IT PLEASE YOUR MAJESTY

A few dayes after my arrival in this State to execute the place of Vice Roy, which the Prince my Master was pleased to intrust me with : the Count de Laurader to whom I succeeded, delivered me the letter your Majesty was pleased to write him, concerning some differences touching the Duties of Carinjah and Tannah. And that your Majesty may see alwaies with how great a regard to his service we act, in what concerns your Majesties Subjects, which is so much recommended to us by the Prince my Master, I shall represent to your Majesty what I have been able in so short a time to understand of this affayr.

The Indians call Mandeins that which we term a Custom house Carinjah hath alwaies been the Custom house of the whole Terra firma ; Tannah of this part of Galiana and Biundi, terra firma of the Indians, and Bombay of its district In which place every one payes the duty according to the order of the ancient assize ; and the Custome established in the time of the Government of the Indians : And since the subjects of the Prince my Master are not dispensed with from paying the duties due at Bombay, it seems not just that your Majestie's Subjects should be exempted from paying the duties belonging to the places which depend of the Prince my Master, whose Subjects suffer great prejudice by those of your Majesty, who have got into possession of a greater extent of ground then was setled by the treaty made in Portugal. And hereof advice hath been given to the Prince my Master, to the end that neither we on our side may be wanting in anything that hath been agreed by the said treaty, nor the Subjects of your Majesty extend themselves further. There have been some passages that would have greatly scandalized us, but that we are sure it is not done with your Majesties permission nor come to your knowledge, which makes us hope your Majesty will cause all things to be reduced to the terms established by the said treaty. As to the Passports, we give them to the Indians in the accustomed form, and in Persia since the loss of Ormuz we never have had peace with that King but for the Port of Congo by an accord made fourty years agoe by General Ruy brother of Andrade, with promise to pay half duty to this Custom house, and never to give passport except for this onely Port. And this hath been alwaies continued so and we have peace in noe place of Persia but that : and nothing hath been innovated lately which may give cause of complaint to your Majestie's Subjects, who in all the ports of the Prince my Master do alwaies meet with friendship and good correspondence, not onely for the common advantage, but even for the advantage of each particular. And your Majesty may be assured, that in whatsoever you shall be pleased to command me for your service, I shall employ my self with all kind of affection, as the Prince my Master recommends to me. God preserve your Majestie's person many years.

Goa 11th November 1677.

Signed,

DON PEDRO DE ALMAYDA.

[*Endorsed.*]

Translate of the Prince of Portugal's Ambassadors Letter to his Majestie touching the differences about Customes at Tannah and Carinjah.

11 November 1677.

WHITEHALL
December 1*st* 1677.

SIR

The East India Company of London having made their Complaint to his Majestie of Divers Injuries done them by the Portuguezes at or neer the Island of Bombaim, and perticularly about their demanding and exacting from his Majesties Subjects certain arbitrary Tolls and duties for their passage in the open Streames, contrary to all right as well as to our Treaties with the Crowne of Portugall, His Majestie hath written at large upon that Subject to dis highnes the Prince Regent, which Letter is herewith sent unto you together with a Copy of the same, for your better information in the case. It is his Majestie's pleasure, That having received his said Letter you forthwith demand an audience of his said Highnes to whome you are to deliver his Majesties Letter, and then, and from time to time afterwards by Memorialls and all other diligences earnestly to solicite the Effects thereof as a matter which his Majestie takes very much to heart; giveing an accompt of your success therein, and of the Orders sent or to be sent to the Vice King of Goa, and the Governor of Bassaim if you can obtaine any, which is all at present, from

Public Record Office, C. O. 77, Vol. XIII, folio 284.

Sir
Your most faithfull humble Servante,
H. COVENTREY.

For Fran: Parry Esq., Envoy from his Majestie of great Brittain to his highnes the Prince Regent of Portugall.

[*Endorsed.*]

1st December 1677.

Mr. Secretary Coventryes Letter, to his Majesties Envoy about Bombaim and the Complaints of the Portuguese there.

A COURT OF COMMITTEES HOLDEN 7TH DECEMBER 1677.
AFTERNOON.

Court Book XXX, page 203.

A letter was now read prepared to be sent to Francis Parry Esq. Envoy from his Maty. to the Prince Regent of Portugall, which was approved and the Governor desired to sign the same.

The following documents deal with the claims of Don Alvaro Pirez. They throw further light on the Company's administration of Bombay, and its policy towards the Portuguese. The quarrel dragged on for years, and Pirez's incorrigible loquacity involved the harassed Directors in tedious negotiations. The volume of data on this subject is very large, and I have not deemed it necessary to reproduce *all* the documents here. They are of interest only in so far as they throw light on the administration of Bombay.

Court Book XXX, page 203.

A COURT OF COMMITTEES HOLDEN 4TH JULY 1677.

Upon reading a letter from the Secretary attending the Rt. honble. the Lords Committees for trade and plantations, wherein was enclosed the copy of a Memorial presented to his Maty. by the Portugal Ambassador touching the Island Mahim claimed by the Prince of Portugal, and also concerning the complaint of Don Alvaro Pirez, To which their Lopps. expected the Compa. answer on the 5th instant: On consideration thereof had, the Court finding the said Memorial to agree verbatim with that which was transmitted from their Lops. in Febry. last; It is ordered, that the Committees for Suratt, as also the rest of the Members of this Court be desired to attend the right honble. the said Lords Comtees. to morrow morning, and to present their Lops. the copie of the Compas. representation made in the busines of Bombay in February last, and of the order of his Maty. in Councel touching the busines of Don Alvaro Pires de Tavora.

Court Book XXX, page 140a.

A COURT OF COMMITTEES HOLDEN 13TH JULY 1677.

The Committees for Suratt reported unto the Court, that having attended at Whitehall the 5th instant to give answer to the Memorial presented to his Majesty by the Portugal Ambassador now depending before the Rt. honble. the Lords Comtees. for trade and plantations, there was nothing done, in regard the Lords Comtees. mett not, onely the Lord Privy Seale and the Lord Falconberge being present, the Lord Privy Seal recd. from the Secry. a copie of the Compa. representation made in February last touching the busines of Bombay and its dependencies, and was minded of what his Maty. in Councel had done in the busines of Don Alvaro Pires. That his Lop. desired the Compa. would give their Secry. copies of the Charters granted to them by his Maty. and also that what occurrences came from India of publick concern (wch. usually are sent to the Secry. of State) might also be given to the Secry. attending the Lords Committees. On consideration whereof had, the Court directed that the same should be done accordingly.

Court Book XXX, page 149a.

A COURT OF COMMITTEES HOLDEN 10TH AUGUST 1677.

Mr Parry his Mats. Envoy extraordry. for Portugal acquainting the Court That Don Alvaro Pires de Tavora being now sensible of the error of his proceedings is desirous to make his submission to the Compa., and to pray their favour in restoring him to his estate on the Island of Bombay; Answer was returned, that the Court would consider of his motion and acquaint him with the resolution they should take therein.

A COURT OF COMMITTEES HOLDEN 15TH AUGUST 1677.

Court Book XXX, page 150.

On consideration had of Mr. Parry's motion made the last Court on behalf of Alvaro Pirez, Resolved, that answer be given him, That when the Court doe see in what manner the said Alvaro Pirez will make his acknowledgment and submission, they will take the same into further consideration: And Mr Boone is desired to communicate this resolution of the Court to Mr Parry.

A COURT OF COMMITTEES HOLDEN 7TH SEPTEMBER 1677.

Court Book XXX, page 156a.

Upon the motion of Mr Parry that Signor Alvaro Pirez might have leave to omit some words out of the addresse that he is to make to the Compa., It is ordered that it be referred to the Comtees. for Surrat to peruse the advices and consultation books recd. from the President and Councell touching the absenting of himselfe from the Island of Bombay when the Dutch Fleet were in the road and report the same unto the Court.

A COURT OF COMMITTEES HOLDEN 17TH OCTOBER 1677.

Court Book, XXX, p. 183-183a.

This day Alvaro Perez de Tavora late an Inhabitant of the Island Bombay presented his humble petition unto the Court both in the English and Portugall language, with [his] name thereto subscribed acknowledging the Justice of the proceedings of the Govr. and Councell of Bombay agt. him for withdrawing himself from the Island contrarie to his dutie without leave from the Govr. and his refusall to obey the proclamation made and published for his returne, and alsoe his misdoeings in wrongfully complaining agt. the said Govr. and Councell, and in seeking redresse where he ought not, And humbly begging pardon of this Compa. for his said misdemeanors, and submitting himselfe unto the Court, beseeching to be restored to their favour, and to the Estate wch. he (Then) possessed on the said Island; Promising that at his arrivall at Bombay he will make the like acknowledgment with this to the Govr. and for the future be obedient unto this Compa. and the Govrs. which shall be by their authoritie established in that Island; On consideration thereof had, the Court being willing to make it manifest, that the proceedings of the Govr. and Councell at Bombay, have not been for any advantage that might arise to them by seizing his Estate, or for any other sinister respect but for maintaining the honor and upholding their Government on the said Island, doe order that a Letter be written by our next Shipping to the Governor and Councell at Bombay directing that upon the said Alvaro Pirez de Tavora his appearing before them and making the same acknowledgemt There as he hath afore Us here, they forthwith issue out a pardon to him under Our Seale of Bombay of all his said Delinquencies, and thereby to restore him to the possession of all such lands and Estates as did then rightfully belong to him, and were sequestred into the hands of his Mother.

At the Court at Whitehall 17th of January 1677-6.

Public Record Office, C. O. 77, Vol. II folio 201.

Upon Reading this day a paper presented to the Boord signed by Alvaro Pires de Tavoras by way of reply to the Answer of the East India Company to his petition,* complaining of the hard usage he had received from the said Company at Bombay. It was Ordered by His Majesty in Councill. That this Paper

* [see fol. 209.]

(together with all others relating to this business) bee referred to the Right Honble. the Lords of the Committee of Trade who are to consider thereof, and Report the true State of the whole matter, With their opinion thereupon to His Majestie in Councell.

To the Kings most Excellent Majestie

Alvaro Pires de Tavora Gentleman of the house of the most Serene Prince of Portugall and Subject of Your Majestie in Your Island of Bombain, humbly presents That hee and his Predecessor alwayes possessed in the Islands of Bombain and Mahim severall lands and Estates very considerable, which in recompence of their Service they received from the Grandeur of the most Serene Kings of Portugall.

And amongst others the Villages of Mazagan and Vazella with their Appurtenences and Orchard of Palm trees, all which amounted to a very important Revenue, of which he had the pacificall Possession when the Islands was delivered to your Majesties Commissaries.

And whereas by vertue of the agreement concerning the Surrender of the said Island and conformable to the 11th Article thereof. Your Majesty obliged Your selfe to the preservation of the Portugezes who would remain in the saide Island in the possession of their Estates in the same manner as they had before enjoyed them under the Government of the Crown of Portugall. A little after the Surrender Your Petitioner was deprived of his forementioned Estate by the English Officers (which bore command) against reason and Justice, and he having recourse to the Honble. Company of East India Merchants they issued out an Order by their Commissaries for the restoring his Estate and goods with Justice and Equity.

But the Governor Gerardo Aungier executed this Order so ill, as he would restore no more then a small part of the said Estate and Goods, dividing them as he pleased, and seperating from them the most considerable Rents against reason and Justice. And because your Petitioner is a poor Gentleman, destitute of all fortune, with the charge of a Widdow Mother and Maiden Sisters, without any releify he accepted the said restitution as he pleased to make it, protesting notwithstanding against, and reserving the Right of his pretence to the remainder denyed him, as is manifest by his protest.

And besides this Violence the Governor committed a greater against him, making him consent and sign to a new Tribute which he put upon the people, taken* from them more then a 4th part of their incomes which were restored them, whereas he should have took no more then that certain Tribute they and their Ancestors before paid to the Factors of the most Serene King of Portugall, against which unjust dealing he made a protest before the Ministers of the Councell. And last of all not content with all these oppressions making use of this pretext that Your Petitioner, against the Orders of the said Governor, absented himself from the said Island at the time when the Hollanders were there expected, the Governor absolutly deprived him of all his Estates, prohibiting his return from thenceforward to his own house. Whereas this pretext was so much against truth, that the said Petitioner was not absent from the Island more

* [sic]

then 3 hours to carry over his goods to a Neighboring Island, as did also all the English Inhabitants and Officers of the Councill which were then resident in Bombaim. Moreover Your Petitioner had leave from the Governor to do what he did, and being farr from absenting himself for fear of the Hollanders, returning presently to the said Island, he did all he could to be admitted by the Governor again, not only offering himself to the said Governor's commands by a letter, but also making use of the intercession of Mr. Barron, Director of the French Fleet, which then hapned to ride in that Port, that the Governor would permit him to live there as before; who notwithstanding would [n]either admit him, nor this Intercession for him, nor the letter he sent, nor the purgation of the false Crime laid to his charge. Whence clearly may be gathered the malice and passion with which the Governor hath proceeded in all these affairs, and that his intent was only to expulse Your Petitioner from the said Island, in order to more secure enjoyment of his fortunes to himselfe, which in reality he doth enjoy for Your Petitioner being destitute of all humane remedy and outed of his proper habitation, and all his goods, it was proper for him to repair to the City of Goa, to seek there some remedy, not being able to compass it either by his own industry, or by the intercession of the Vice Roy of India; departing* at length to find Justice and Benignity of Your Majesty he resolved at length to come over to this Kingdome.

* [sic? despairing.]

Where prostrate at the feet of Your Majesty he humbly implores (that what is already asserted, being made manifest to be true) by authenticall Papers which he hath, and will present. Your Majestie will be pleased by express Order to the Governor of Bombain to Command restitution of the lands, Goods and fortune, Jurisdictions and places as belonged to Your Petitioner as he enjoyed them, and his Predecessors, before the Surrender of Bombain, in the form and manner of the 11th Article of the Treaty, to which Your Majesty obliged Your selfe. And that Your Petitioner may be paid the profits, and incomes of all as is owing him from the time of the unjust seizure of his Estate, That by this example of Your Majesties piety and Justice not only Your Petitioner may continue his Zeale to serve Your Majesty but all the other Portugueze Your Majesties Subjects in those parts may be animated in their Loyalty and faithfullness to their Protector and Defender.

And Your Petitioner as in duty bound shall ever pray.

The Answer of the Governor and Company of Merchants of London trading to the East Indies to the Petition of Alvaro Pires de Tavora.

Public Record Office, C. O. 77, Vol. II, folio 205.

MAY IT PLEASE YOUR HONOR,

The said Governor and Company upon perusal of the said petition presented to His Majestie by the said Alvaro Peres have endeavoured to inform themselves out of their advises and dispatches from India of the truth of all matters relating to the Petitioner and his concerns; And do finde—

That upon the Delivery of the Island Bombay to the Company, there were some disputes (and those grown to some heats and great dissatisfaction) between the Governor of the said Island, His Majesty had before placed there, And divers of the Inhabitants, especially the Portugall Inhabitants thereof, touching their Title to severall lands claimed by them. The Portugall Inhabitants, under Colour of the 11th Article in the petition mentioned, seting up severall titles to several lands and Estates, which His Majesties Governor did suppose (and we beleive had reason to suppose) they had no Right unto, at the time the said Island was surrendred unto his Majesty.

That matters standing thus when His Majesty was pleased to make over the Island unto the Company, their President of Surrat and Governor of that Island Gerald Aungier Esqr. And Council (who were directed by the Company not only inviolably to keep the said 11th Article, and to do the Inhabitants all Justice in reference to their Rights and Possessions, but also by all reasonable kindnesses to sweeten the Government to them) Did, in the first place, make it their business to settle that matter touching their claims to any lands, and to quiet them in the possession of what was their just Right, and for that purpose had severall meetings with the cheif of the Portugal Inhabitants (chosen by the rest for their Representatives) amongst whom the Petitioner was one.

And at a meeting in November 1672 a full agreement was made touching all matters, and concluded between them, A Copy whereof We present Your Honor herewith.

That this settlement being made at their own request, was so fair and so well resented, that it gave a general content and satisfaction to the Inhabitants, And the petitioner himself was so well pleased with it, that he made his request to Our said Governor to have a command in the Militia of the Island, And the Governor presuming that he had put such an obligation on all the Portugal Inhabitants, that now they could not but be faithfull and true to the Goverment, and joyn heartily upon all occasions in the defence of the Island, Gave him a Commission to be a Commander in the Militia of Masagoan. But in March 167$\frac{2}{3}$ (there being then Warr betwixt his Majesty and the Dutch) the Dutch coming with a great fleet before the Island, and it being hourly expected that they would make some attempt upon it, And the said Governor having thereupon put the Island in the best posture of defence he could, and raised all the forces thereof, the petitioner among the rest being then in Arms, as Commander of the Militia of Masagoan (notwithstanding the former kindness shewed, and Trust now reposed in him) did on a sudden, either cowardly or treacherously desert his Command, and abandon the Island, and that by his example above tenn thousand of the Portugall, and other Inhabitants likewise deserted the Island in that time of iminent danger, whereby the Island and the lives and fortunes of all the English therein were manifestly exposed to hazard. And how great a crime it is for a Commander in a Garrison (as the Island Bombay alwayes is) in a time of Warr, in the very face of the enemy, and when the Island was in such iminent danger to desert his Command and trust, and by his pernicious example to draw off such a number of Inhabitants from so small an Island, Wee leave Your Honor to Judge.

That the Governor upon this unworthy desertion of the said Alvaro de Peres issued out Proclamations commanding all the Inhabitants who had deserted the Island, to return to their habitations there within 24 hours upon pain of confiscation of their Estates, and because it was a time to act with resolution, he caused the doores of all their houses to be sealed up. Upon which Proclamation, all the Inhabitants (except the Petitioner) better bethinking themselves, returned to their habitations within the time of the Proclamations, and stood by the Governor in the defence of the I sland.

But the Petitioner being conscious of his unworthy carriage in that business, did not return, whereupon a Summons was issued out for him to return in 40 days: but he never appeared there since, but instead thereof he gave the Governor great trouble by clamorous complaints against him to the French Admirall, the Dutch Admirall, the Portugal Admirall, the Portugal Vice Roy at Goa, and other great persons in India (and upon such untrue Suggestions as are in the petition) obtaining their Letters by way of intercession, and sometimes of expostulation on his behalf, Unto all which full answers were given.

Notwithstanding all which the Governor did not nor hath deprived the Petitioner of his Estate (as the petition suggests) but hath put his own Mother in the possession thereof, and still permits her to enjoy the profits thereof, for the maintenance of herself, and of her and his family, who there live on it to this day, Nor hath the Governor prohibited the Petitioner to return to his house, but on the contrary hath constantly required his return to the Island, and to stand a fair and legal tryal for what should be layd to his charge, (as good Subjects under every Goverment ought to doe), and he should be justly dealt with, the failing wherein having been the cause of proceedings against him.

This being the true matter of Fact, as appears by Our advises from India, we humbly conceive, that it would be destructive to the Government of the Island, and consequently in a short time to the loss of the Island it self, if his Majesty should so interpose as to prevent proceedings against a person who hath been so eminently failing in the discharge of his duty, especially when he hath been already so tenderly dealt with, and where, upon a triall the truth may be ascertained upon the Oath of 12 men or more, half English and half Portugeze, according to the laws of this Kingdome, and where the Judges do endeavour to act with all fairness, and encouragment to the Inhabitants, so as may consist but with the safety and welfair of the Island.

Award's answer to the above was as follows:

By the Answer that the Honorable Company of the West Indies made to Alvaro Pires de Tavoras Petition. (1) his Right and property in the dependancies of the lands that he claimeth are put in Question. (2) it is alleadged that he was contented with the small part of them that was left him by the Generall Agreement made in November 1672. (3) They lay upon him a Crime of Desertion, pretending thereby to confiscate all his Estate.

Public Record Office, C. O. 77, Vol. II, folio 209. [*sic*]

Upon the first point the Petitioner presents two Patents in the most Authenticall form, whereby the Kings of Portugall granted to his Ancestors 120 years ago, the Lands dependancies and Revenues in Question, with the same Right and in the same manner as they were possessed by the said Kings themselves, and belonged to them, and this with such distinction and clearness, that yet the least reservation are therein expressed, which Revenues and dependancies his Ancestors possessed and enjoyed without any trouble and Molestation, by the said King's Ministers, as he proveth by the Deposition of twenty Witnesses that he brings. And moreover by two sentences whereby (his said Right being put in Question) it was judged in the Court at Lisbon that the said Revenues and dependancies belonged to them, and so they remained in peaceable possession of them till such time as the Island was delivered to His Majesties Commissioners. And all that was so evident that thereupon Sir Humphry Cook, first Governor for His Majesty of Bombaim, gave an Order under his hand in September 1665 whereby he bids all the money of the Coles Fishers to be delivered to the Petitioner's Father, and to be the said Fishers Obedients to him as to their Lord, and to pay all what was used to be paid to his prede cessors in the former times. And though the Honble. Company upon consideration of them Reasons, was pleased to send Orders for the Petitioners Restitution (which were not executed) Nevertheless, the Petitioner humbly prayes that all the papers above mentioned may be viewed and examined.

As for the 2nd that the Petitioner was very well contented with what was left him by the agreement of November 1672, what could in that occasion a poor oppressed Gentleman doe, or what reason could he find at so many thousand leagues off distance from His Majesty and His Honble Privy. Councill, against the absolute power of a Governor who was able (had the Petitioner refused that consent) to deprive him of all the rest of his Estate, having nothing in the World but that to live upon, But to make Remonstrances and petitions to serve in manner of Protestations before the Ministers of the Councill there ? By which Petition (that he presents) it appears clearly that the Petitioner was forced to do soe to save something of his Estate, keeping for another time the prosecution of his Right.

And for what is alleadged that the Petitioner desired to have the Command of the Militia of Mazagaon it is to be considered that this Militia consisted only of the Petitioners Fishers, Tennants, Servants, and labouring-men, living in his lands and Villages, and so it was not much that he was made their Commander. But in the truth, when the Petitioner desired that, it was only out of the Zeal of a good and loyall Subject to his Majesty, because upon the news of coming of the Dutch fleet the Governor, applying with all possible care the Inhabitants to work at the Fortifications of the Island, and sending severall Orders to the Petitioner to have his fishers and labourers (who are the only Inhabitants of the Petitioners Lands) to work there as the others, the Petitioner was obliged (because severall of His men were out of the way) to desire to be more authorized by that Quality, and keep them so much better in obedience, in respect to the work. All them reasons and proofs the Petitioner humbly prayeth, That his Majesty would be pleased to cause to be examined with all exactness.

But for the 3rd point, wherein they wrong the Petitioner in his Honor and Reputation, which are far dearer to him then either life or Estate, he imploreth His Majesties Justice with all possible instance,

And beseecheth that His Majestie would consider that upon the News of the coming of the Dutch fleet, severall English men went out of the Island with their Goods, amongst which some of the Councill, as Mr. Jacob Adams, and Mr. John Chell. And whereas there was a Proclamation made that no person should go out of the Island, And the Petitioner desiring to secure his Goods as others did, the Governor gave him under his hand a Licence to go out of the Island with them (notwithstanding the Proclamation) without any limitation of time, which Licence dated the first of March, the Petitioner presents.

The same day in the Evening the Petitioner came again, having been out three hours in all, and hearing of the great passion that the Governor was incensed with against him, for having carried his goods, whereby his Estate should be forfeited and his person arrested, he went from his house to avoid the effects of his threatnings, with design neverth'less to make his innocency and Submission known, as he did by the letter that he writ him immediately, praying that hee would secure him of his anger, and suffer him to come to the Fort. To which letter the Governor would neither answer nor receive it, as it is seen by the answer of Luis Cazado de Lima Adjudant de Procurador General of the Honble. Company.

Seing then the Petitioner that by that way he could not be neither heard nor admitted, he went immediatly, the second of March, to Mr. Baron, Director of the French fleet, who in that occasion was in the Port, desiring his intercession for the same intent, as it appeareth by his Certificate. He went presently after to the Captain of Bacaim, whose Certificate he brings too, and seing all that would do nothing, and knowing not how to move the Governor's Clemency he went to the Vice Roy of Goa, and coming with a Letter from him for the same effect, he found a Placart on his house doors in Mazagaon, whereby he was cited to appeare and answer upon the accusation brought against him. But daring not appear in person he sent his Brother with a Petition to the Councill, because he knew that the Government had sent a Company of Musquettears to take him at Mazagaon which Petition was rejected as false and scandelous. Of all that the Petitioner brings authenticall Certificats, and proofs, which he humbly desires to be seen.

After all, That the Petitioner finding no way to be admitted, and the Governor giving no Answer to all his instances, and so considerable intercessions, but threatnings, he made his protestation, that he was ready to put himself in the Fort, desiring the Governor to secure the liberty of his person, and to* restitue him in his credit, reputation and Estate. And when he could do no more there, away he went, and came to this Court to implore His Majesties Justice, and give him a true account of all his proceedings.

Wherein it is to Remarke that the Petitioner in that short time that there was fear of an attempt of the Dutch, he pressed and solicited, not only with great instance, but with all the diligence imaginable, not loosing a moment of time, to be suffered to doe his duty in the Fort, whilst he was so highly threatned by the Governor.

And if the Governor saith that he hath not taken the Petitioners Estate, but left his Mother in possession of it, it is to be considered that his Mother does not administrate it but by way of depost, and yet an unconsiderable part of it, and she liveth upon some others that she hath ; which do not depend of Mazagaon in any manner.

All that considered His Majesty will be graciously pleased, to protect the Petitioner and not to suffer him by that unjust vexation, and upon a false accusation, to be deprived of his Estate, which (according to the 11th Article of the Treaty) he must enjoy plainly, and with the same advantages that His Fathers and Predecessors had under the dominion of Portugall.

Just now the Petitioner received Letters from the East Indies dated at Bacaim 5th of December 1675 from Joane Mendes de Menezes Sõr de Band[r]. Vistal his Brother in-Law and his Attorney, which advise him that the Petitioner's Estate hath been taken from his Mothers hands, whereupon the said Joan Mendes made a Protestation which the Petitioner humbly prays to be considered. And that His Majesty would be pleased to appoint some of his Honble Privy. Councill to examine all the proofs that the Petitioner doth produce.

ALVARO PIRES DE TAVERA.

These lengthy replies, and tedious rejoinders ended, at last, in a compromise, and the following Despatch of the Directors announces the settlement of this quarrel. Pirez received, a pardon and, what was of much more importance to him, his estate. The references to the jurisdiction of the "Court of Judicature" at Bombay are important.

* [*sic.*] Public Record Office, C. O. 77, Vol. XLIX, folio 240. (Letter to the Governor and Council Bombay for restauration of A. P. de Tavora's Estate.)

OUR GOVERNOR AND COUNCILL AT BOMBAY,

After our hearty commendations unto you, this letter serves to informe you particularly in the matter of Alvaro Pires de Tavora how hee hath proceeded with his complaints, how hee hath since made his submission, and lastly the favour wee have extended towards him. Hee did sometime in Autumne 1676 present a Petition to His Majestie complaining of many hardships received from you in Bombaim, as the sequestration of his Estate etc., a Copy of which Petition was sent unto Us with Order to returne Our Answer, as wee did thereunto, and of Our Answer a Copy was given to the said Pirez to which hee made a reply with much repitition of what hee had said before, and this being presented to His Majestie in Councill on the 17th January last, the whole matter was refered to the examination of a Committee of the Lords of the Boord appointed for the business of Trade and Plantations.

Wee had from their Lordships a Summons on the 3rd of June last, and all parties were by their Councill to be heard, which accordingly happned on the 12th June last, and the result was, That their Lordships thought it just and did accordingly Report to His Majesties Councill, That the Courts of Judicature constituted by His Majesties Royall Charter in Bombaim were proper for the decision of such like cases and made conformable to the Laws of England herein, That the Petitioner had never formally submitted himself unto or demanded any tryall of Justice there, That if his Majestie should give any sentence here in a cause originaly appertaining to those Courts, others would take examples to decline the Jurisdiction of the place, which would be very prejudiciall to that Soveraignty which it's fitt His Majestie should preserve and support. Wherefore Upon consideration hereof His Majestie was pleas'd on the 15th June 1677 to command that the Complaint should be dismist and that the Petitioner should apply himself to the Courts of Bombaim for relief.

On the 3rd of June Wee received a New Letter from the Lords of the Same Committee, enclosing the Copy of a Memoriall, which had for some time layn before His Majestie from the Embassador extraordinary of Portugall, and as wee suppose was given in together with the first Petition of the said Pirez, because one part of it is a demand of Justice in his behalfe, setting forth also much hardships used by you to the Inhabitants in generall, whereupon upon the 4th of September present their Lordships with such a vindication of your deportment towards the Inhabitants in generall and of the just motives you had for sequestring the said Pirez, that their Lordships declared an intire satisfaction therein and have ordered that a Copy of Our paper be given to the said Ambassador if he move any farther in those points.

But in the meantime Alvaro Pirez de Tavora, growing sensible of his own miscarriages, and seeing the necessity of abiding a tryall before you, he came and in most humble manner confessed his fault before Us and Implored Our favour, presenting and signing a Petition in Portugez, as also another in English (being the translation thereof) in the words following

> To the Right Worshipfull the Governor Deputy and Committees of the Honorable East India Company.
> The humble Petition of Alvaro Pirez de Tavora Subject to the King of Great Brittaine in the Island of Bombaim.

SHEWETH

That whereas Your Petitioner did, contrary to his duty, withdraw himself from the Island of Bombaim without leave from the Governor, and did also refuse to obey the Proclamation for his returne, by which hee incurred the penalty of the Law in the Sequestration of his Estate at Bombaim, and whereas hee did thereupon make severall Addresses, some to the French Admirall, some to the Vice Roy of Goa, and others since by his Petition to the Prince of Portugall for his releif, although hee is convinced that none of them either then had or now have any Jurisdiction in that Island, And whereas hee did also make his complaint to His Majestie of Great Britaine touching the injustice and injury done him by the Governor and Councill of Bombaim, and was thereupon heard before the Lords of the Committee of the Councill for Trade and Plantations. But on their Lordships Report to His Majestie in Councill was by His Royall Order remitted back to be tryed at Bombaim, Your Petitioner is at length made sensible of all his misdoings, not only in the first withdrawing himself from the Island aforesaid, but in wrongfully complaining against the said Governor and Councill of Bombaim, and in seeking redress where hee ought not. And therefore doth with great sorrow of mind most humbly begg pardon from this Honble. Company for all his said misdemeanors submitting himselfe intirely unto them, and beseeching them out of their great bounty and clemency, that they would be pleased to consider his distressed condition, together with the ruin of his family; praying most humbly for his own comfort to be in the first place restored to your Honours' favours, and next for the releife of them unto the Estate which he then there possessed. And hee doth hereby promise that at his arrivall at Bombaim, hee will make the like acknowledgment with this to the Governor there of his unfortunate miscarriages, and will for the future behave himselfe not only as a true and faithfull Subject to His Majestie of great Brittain, but submitt himselfe and be intirely obedient to this Honble. Company, and the Governors that shall by their authority be establisht there, And hee shall ever own that he enjoys his Estate by the favour of this Company, and shall pray for their lasting prosperity.

ALVARO PIREZ DE TAVORA.

17th October 1677.

The Demonstration of sorrow and submission did beget in the Court a sence of tenderness and compashion towards the Gentleman, so that being willing (according to the example of Our Gracious Master) to exercise favour where ever the matter will bear it, and to give testimony that wee seek not the undoing of any man, but meerly the support, honour and security of our Government in that Island, Wee did thereupon make the following Order. That the Governor and Councill at Bombay be directed, That upon Alvaro Pirez de Tavora, his appearing before them, and making the same acknowledgment there as hee hath before Us here, They forthwith Issue out a pardon unto him under Our Seale of Bombay of all his said delinquences, and thereby to restore him to the possession of all such land and Estate as did then rightfully belong unto him, and were sequestred into the hands of his Mother.

And wee do hereby Order and require you to see the said Order effectually executed, and that a pardon be Issued to him under Our Seale of Bombay of all his said delinquencies, that hee be restored to the Estate you did then Sequester, and that those into whose hands you did Sequester the same may be Ordered to Accompt and to pay to him the profitts thereof, first reimbursing you what charges you have been att in this affair, and so not doubting of your punctuall conformity with this Order, Wee bid you heartily farewell. From the East India house in London this 14th day of December 1677.

Your very loving friends,

WM. THOMPSON Governor

and 13 of the Court of Committees.

Parry, the English Ambassador at Lisbon, could obtain no satisfaction; the following mournful despatch narrates a miserable account of diplomatic finesse and royal duplicity.

LISBONE
April 30/*May* 10 1678.

SIR

Public Record Office, C. O. 77, Vol. XIV, folio 1.

I did not think it necessary or convenient to trouble you with a relation of my proceedings in the busines of Bombaim, till I could give you some account of the effect of them. I have frequently layd before the Prince the necessity of his sending orders to the Governors of Goa and Bacaim, to command the forbearance of all acts of hostility or forcible impositions on his Majesties Subjects of Bombaim, because of the inconveniences that must needs arise from resisting such force by force; which those his Majesties Subjects as well by the permission of his Majestie as by the law of Nature, for their own defence could not forbear to doe: And I press'd his Highnes to send powers to D Franco de Mello, his Ambassador in England, to settle this whole affayr, according to the true intent and meaning of the Articles in that behalf. The busines has been these 3 months before the Councel of foreign plantations: time enough, one would think, for it, to give a very full and particular Report, and his Highnes thereupon a satisfactory answer. But in lieu thereof the Secretary of State wrote me a letter on the 29th of April this stile, to this purpose, That his Highnes hoped that his Majesty will take a final resolution in what his Ambassador hath represented to him concerning Bombaim, and in order thereunto his Highnes commands that D. Franco de Mello be charged to represent the same to his Majesty and that answer should be given to his Majesties letter in this very form.

You see here is not a word of writing to the East Indies to suspend the tributes and impositions exacted by the Portuguese till the matter is decided, nor a word of impowering the Portuguese Ambassador to decide it, but an expectation of some concessions from his Majesty, as the delivery of Mahim, (which the Secretary in my first discourse with him in this affair, told me his Majesty was unjustly possess'd of) and the like, and a farther order to the Ambassador to demand the same; which is the scope of the answer sent to his Majestie's letter. So that instead of giving his Majesty satisfaction for the injuries done to his Subjects in Bombaim, they seem to expect satisfaction of injuries done to them. How this great difference will be avoided I can't tell. I have done all that is in my power, and have my final answer. But if it were true, that Mahim were of right belonging to the Portuguese, one would wonder they should contest it with his Majesty, considering how much He has done for them beyond the obligations of the Treaty of Matrimony. What charges they put him to before they gave him possession of Bombaim, and of how little profit Mahim would be to them, Goa itself, and all the places they possess in the East Indies being so many charges to the Crown: and you will doe it a kindness to take Carinjah and Salcote* into your possession, which certainly belong to you as well as Mahim, as appurtence to the Port of Bombaim.

I shall trouble you no farther, but with the hearty offer of my service to you being

Sir Your most faithfull
and most humble servant
FFRAN. PARRY.

Sir Wm. Thomson.

[*Endorsed.*]

A COURT OF COMMITTEES HOLDEN THE 26TH MAY 1682.

Court Book XXXIII, page 11. On consideration this day had, of the state of the Compas. affairs at Bombay; It is ordered that the same be referred to Sir John Banks Sir James Edwards and Mr Edwin, to peruse the transactions that have passed touching the obstructions that have been given by the Portuguez in the Compas. trade at Tannah and Carinjah, and to represent the same unto his Matie. in such manner as they shall think fitt.

A COURT OF COMMITTEES HOLDEN THE 31ST MAY 1682.

Court Book XXXIII, page 12. It is ordered, that it be referred to the Committees for the affayrs of Bombay to move his Matie. not onely for a free passage by the Forts of Tannah and Carinjah but that demand may be made of satisfaction for the damages and Losses the Compa. have susteyned by obstructions given them in their trade.

A COURT OF COMMITTEES HOLDEN 27TH APRIL 1683.

Court Book XXXIII, page 137. The Court desired the Governor to present unto his Maty. in Council, the petition that was formerly drawn up of the Compas. grievances touching Tannah and Carinjah.

The following document carries the history of this Conburery down to 1692.

Court Book 77, Vol. XVI. "An answer of the East India Company to the Portugese King's Memoriall concerning Bombay. All the inhabitants of Bombay subject to the Portugese king became subjects to His Majesty King Charles II. The Company have spent £400,000 in fortifying and maintaining the garrison there and in defending it. Again, all the inhabitants paid to the Portugese king ¼ part of the fruits of their land, besides their services in Arms; but the Company in the time of Aungier agreed to accept 20,000 xeraphins per annum for the surceasing of all duties into their hands. The Portugese have been listed and served in the militia. In the last Dutch War the inhabitants appeared in arms to the number of 7 or 8 thousand of all Nations, and such as did not, were confiscated according to the ancient law of the island, even during the government of Aungier. All persons in Bombay are bound to serve; but many of Portugese not only neglected to do it, but many did desert the island." The Company then defends its officers whom the Portuguese king charged with injustice, etc. Dated March 18, 1692.

The following extracts from the pamphlets in the British Museum, dealing, directly or indirectly, with Bombay, throw further light on the early history of Bombay. I have left out the account of Bombay by early travellers, as they are well known to students of Indian History and have already been published. I have cited a few pamphlets, in the first number of the *Journal of Indian History*, in my article on the "Company's War with Aurangzebe."

The translations and transcripts from the Portuguese archives at Lisbon which Mr. Danvers procured for the Record Department, India Office, have not yielded much. Copies or originals of all the documents on the early history of Bombay are preserved in the Public Record Office, and I have not come across any important authority for the history of the City. The MSS. Letter Books are, of course, on a different footing, and the Despatches of the Directors throw considerable light on this quarrel. Limitation of space is my chief excuse for omitting to reproduce some of these characteristic expressions of their policy. The first *Number* of this *Journal* contained extracts dealing only with the war with Aurangzebe. I may, later on, fill up this gap and reprint extracts from some of these Despatches.

Both the Bodleian and the British Museum Library are extremely rich in pamphlet literature, and Bombay figured prominently in the merciless literary warfare which the reckless adventurers, convinced whigs, and shrewd woollen merchants, launched on the devoted heads of the Company. I have selected only sixteen that deal directly or indirectly with Bombay. The list is limited to the Company's war with Aurangzebe, and its early history must be studied in books and pamphlets published during the years 1660—88.

(1) *Supplement to Former Treatise.* By Sir Josiah Childe. B. M.

(2) *The Great Oppressions and Injuries which the Company have acted.* Bodleian Library.

(3) *The Present State of the East India Company's Affairs.* Bodleian, Q. 658.

(4) *Reasons Against Making the East India Company, etc.*, B. M.

(5) *News from the East Indies.* * B. M.

(6) *An Account of the East India Company's War with the Great Moghul.* B. M.

(7) *Proposals for Settling the East India Trade.* B. M.

[* B. M. stands for the British Museum.]

(8) *Some Remarks on the East India Company's Accompt and Propositions.* B. M.*

(9) *The East India Company's Reply to the Petition of Charles Price.* B. M. Read also *Charles Price's Petition.*

(10) *An Account of the Trade to the East Indies.* By George White. * B. M. and Public Record Office.

(11) *A Letter to Mr. Nathaniel Fench in Answer to a Paper by Him.* By George White.

(12) *Answer of the East India Company to Certain Heads of Complaint Exhibited Against them by the Petitions Against the Said Company.* Duplicate in P. R. O.

(13) *The Company's Answer to White.* B. M.*

(14) *Some Considerations on the Nature and Importance of the Trade.* B. M.*

(15) *A New Account of the East Indies.* By Alexander Hamilton. This is a well-known book.

(16) *A Letter to a Friend Concerning the East India Company.* India Office Tracts, India Office Library.

(17) *A Letter from a Lawyer of the Inner Temple.* India Office Tracts, India Office Library.

(18) *A Letter to a Member of Parliament.* India Office Tracts, India Office Library.

(19) *Treatise on the Coins of England.*

(20) *Reasons Against E. I. C.* Bodleian.

All of these pamphlets deal mainly with the Company's war with the Moghul. This list is not exhaustive, and I have selected only the typical productions of the period. Some of these pamphlets are mere fly-sheets; others, however, are very important, and to the student of the early history of Bombay they are of essential use.

An interesting pamphlet, entitled, "*Reasons humbly offered against establishing the East India Company by Act of Parliament,*" (*Bodleian Library,* Rawlinson *MSS., Q.* 658, *N* 2) shows clearly enough the effect of the policy inaugurated by Childe. The *farman* is, as usual, the object of their dislike, and the Interlopers, who now adopted the high-sounding name of Free Traders, and

[* B. M. stands for the British Museum.]

whose views the author championed, show the absurdity of maintaining forts in India. "The Government and natives in India had always treated the Free Traders with singular kindness; they protect in their parts, as they did the ship *Success* last year, from the French. They have offered Fhirmaunds to particular Free Traders, inviting them to Traffic with most endeavouring motives. These, with the Humanity of the Indians, are great security to us in our Trade with them, and are sufficient. But Forts and Castles are none at all, in case the Great Mogul at any time offend us. If they meet at sea, our Forts and Castles cannot defend us. So that Forts in India are at best no better to us in point of security or defence against the enemies than castles in the air, but may do us much hurt, for they are likely to create jealousy in Moghul, and other princes of India."

Some, however, went even further. The Company, asserted the fanatics, had wrought havoc in Bombay; it had dishonoured the English name in Surat, and it had made the English nation contemptible in the eyes of the Great Mogul. Would it not be better to dissolve the old Company? Only by this means could England recover her reputation. This view found expression in a pamphlet, entitled "*Reasons humbly offered against grafting upon or confirming the present East India Company.*" (*Bodleian Library.*)

Apart altogether from the fear that "the mingling of a fresh honest estate with the unhallowed Remains of the old Leaves may subject it to miscarriage and a curse," the Government could not ignore the solid advantages that would be secured by the "disbanding the present Company and the establishing a new Company," as it "would be looked upon with a good eye in the Court of the Mogul, as a just answer inflicted on the said Company." This would, moreover, "be notable expedient to secure the Honour of the Kingdom that our King be sufficiently qualified with Honour and Justice, and will prove a proper method to recommend the English nation, and to extend our Commerce."

These complaints were followed by others. The Company's forts, its expenditure on their maintenance, and the system of its administration, were subjected to violent criticism, and people noted with surprise the extent of the losses sustained by it during the last ten years of the nineteenth century. The following extract from a pamphlet in the British Museum, 816 m 11, shows the length to which that peculiar species of criticism was carried in those days. The author, acting on the conviction that the "plain, honest way of making the Enquiry is by comparing what they have lost and relinquished since the former stock made a general transfer of all their rights and titles to them," found only the following additions to the Old East India Company's Stock, 1657.

"(1) Bombay, the uselessness of which is demonstrated in a letter only received from their General in 1690."

(2) For St. David's, which they purchased of an Indian Prince for £ 12,000.

(3) Bencoolen, where they have a very inconsiderable Fort.

(4) Tonquin, being built only with canes called Bamboos."

These were the additions. He then shows the losses. Of course, they were enormous. The Company lost, during the same period,

(1) Macasser, on the island of Celebes.

(2) Acheen and Jambee.

(3) Two factories in the Kingdom of Pegu.

(4) Bantam, Japarra, Cherrypoone, and Jabia, considerable settlements on the Java.

(5) Ahmedabad, Agra, Lucknow, and Scinde, four factories, from which they have since been driven out.

(6) Some places on the Island of Borneo.

(7) Their factories in Bengal are now in ruin."

To these charges, and to various others which poured forth in quick succession, Sir Josiah Childe made a bold reply. It is couched in strong terms, and is a mixture of mendacious statements, high-flown eulogies, and coarse satire.

"The Company," declared Sir Josiah, "do not desire to boast of the success God Almighty has given to their just arms, nor of their present condition. The case of the Company is that these are the very men that by an unparalleled Instance of Presumption, by diverse ships made such a combination in India as occasioned the loss of Bantam, the Rebellions of Bombay and St. Hellena, the subduction of all the English privileges by the native kings of India; and consequently great wars and bloodshed to recover those rights to the English Nation. Should they, *now*, hope to be received as the Assertors of the Rights of the People of England, as if our own Liberty should be converted into Licentiousness, and the Ruin of our Common Country by a Toleration to Join with Heathens and Papits in actual hostility against this Kingdom, to destroy the English interest in India?"

"The Company hope all Gentlemen know that the Governments of those Eastern parts of the world are merely despotical, and that the admired and beloved common laws of this Kingdom are plants too precious to be understood, or grow, so far Eastward, or on any other soil then that-of our blessed Nation.''

Childe then pays his tribute to his namesake in the following terms. The eulogy is exaggerated enough ; but so is the criticism directed against his beloved general by George Heathcote and his coterie.

"The Company's General of India, Sir John Child, who hath lived about 35 years in that country without ever seeing his own, is a person of known sobriety, wisdom, Truth, and Courage, esteemed and beloved by people of all Nations in India, that have so much ingenuity as to acknowledge virtue in an enemy, Something whereof will occur to every man's observation that knows he managed that hazardous war against the Mogul with such success and moderation as that he took almost all the ships of the Moguls' and his subjects' ships, sailing in and out of Suratt, without spilling a drop of their blood, and dismissed the prisoners with clothes and money in their pockets which gained such reputation to our nation even amongst the Moors themselves, that they became universally Advocates and solicitous to the Mogul for the pacification upon which, unconstrained, he delivered back all the Moors' ships, except Abdul Gophar's, who was a great incendiary towards the war."

It would hardly be fair to compare this eulogy of Sir John Child with Alexander Hamilton's pamphlet, entitled "*A New Account of the East Indies,*" 1727.

Childe's "*Supplement*"* to his treatise, *A New Discourse of Trade,* gives us further information on Bombay.

"Again, within the same time the Company have Built, Fortified, and Garrisoned three Forts in several parts of India, and coming from thence the 15 ships consigned to Bombay, and to the coast of India, their cargoes amounting to £356,000 (pp. 5-6). ......The Company have built new forts in and strengthened their Island of Bombay, and have ordered a dry dock to be built there. They

* Supplement, 1689, the Printed, 1681. British Museum.

have also reduced the principal part of their Trade of Surat to their own Island of Bombay. The Island has cost the Company in fortifying and garrisoning at times above £500,000, and never produced any return to the Company, *though it be one of the best ports in the Eastern world.* The former Committee could not make such a move (transferring the Surat trade to Bombay) for fear of (*a*) charges, (*b*) of the Mogul, whose people gained exceedingly by our ships riding in their ports."

"The Moghuls, therefore, durst injure and affront the English, while they had the President and all the chiefs of the Nation as a pawn continually in their hands, to secure their patient offerings of contempts whatsoever.

But the case is now altered by the conduct, cost, and courage of the late Committee, and the Moors must be and will be civil hereafter."

Childe then summarises the results of the "glorious" war with Aurangzebe in his usual way. The firman is flaunted before an ignorant public, and a great parade is made of the vindication of the honour of the English nation. Here, however, he over-reached himself, as some of his reckless opponents translated the *firmans* contemptuously granted by Aurangzebe, and exposed the devious crooked devices invented by this resourceful brain.

The Rawlinson MSS. 257 A, in the Bodleian Library, contains very useful copies of Grantham's Commission and Instruction; their importance lies, however, in Childe's letters (Nos. 69, 79, 81) to Charles II. He informed Charles of the Cost of Bombay to the Company, and asserted that "Keigwins rebellion was premeditated, its main cause being the "suggestion" of Interlopers to the conspirators, and their correspondence with John Pettit, and George Bowcher, "our late servants that have made themselves chiefs of all Interlopers in the Northern part of India."

He reminds the king that five mutinies had taken place within a comparatively short time, and concludes by suggesting that one Thorburn, "a scotch Taylor that went out a common soldier, and was, by his obedience, will, and parts advanced to be an Ensign in Bombay, was the principal Engineer, and contriver of the late Rebellion at Bombay," while Captain Keigwin, Captain Adderton, and Lt. Fletcher (stood) next to him in guilt."

Sir Josiah Childe's remedies are characteristic of the man. He proposed that "the litigation that has long depended may have a determination, that your Majesty's subjects may know their duty."

(2) " The Company's ships should be specially despatched to Bombay, Your Majesty being pleased to give such Commissions under Your Majesty's broad seal and such papers under Your Majesty's Privy seal, and signet (as may be necessary) "

(3) Your Majesty will be gracwously pleased by Proclamation or Privy Seal to command home such of the Principal Agents for Intertopers on such manner as may be highly penal to them, if they do not give due obedience to it.

(Signed) JOSIAH CHILDE.

" The *Memoranda of the Times and Seasons in sailing from Port to Port in several parts of India,*" Rawlinson MSS., 344 Bodleian Library, contains an interesting reference to Bombay. The author says :—

" Bombay is the seat of General or Principal offices of the English East India Company. It produces salt in abundance, and coaconut. It is a place of small trade, though it has conveniency for a very good road, and a good entrance to it, and having no danger in the way but a Sunkers (!) Rock, and a bank called the Modde Ground, which last is not in the way."

This account of the early history of Bombay may be fitly concluded by the following letters, one from the Viceroy of Goa, and the other from the King of Portugal.

The Viceroy declared, in his letter dated December 19, 1695 " These English, directly they become aware we intend cutting off their supplies, suggest to the enemies that they make some demonstration against our territories, and this they generally do, at a season before the crops are fit for gathering, when the inhabitants and Vassals of Bacaim, frightened at the idea of war, and fearing they may lose their crops, send them to Bombay for safer custody and a better sale. Thus the British secure larger supplies than they require, and sell the surplus for high prices. This is not all the English do ; they supply the enemy with arms and ammunition, to the great danger of the state, which could scarcely defend itself against its Asiatic enemies."

The King's reply is characteristic. " Having noted what you write to me as regards the English in Bombay having sent the Arabs of Muscat powder, shot, and all other necessaries for the equipment of their ships, thus interfering with the peace negotiations which they contemplated entering into, in consequence of the losses inflicted on them by our foregates in 1693, and that they, the Arabs, had carried the British flag and employed English Captains in order to avoid seizure and to be enabled to carry contraband goods; in reply to your question as to what action you are to take in such cases, I would say that at any time that any of the enemy's ships are encountered under the command of English Captains they should be seized. I would, however, recommend you to be cautious in these matters, and bear in mind the state of the weather and the forces at your disposal."

Such was the end of the happy alliance of poor Charles II. One of the shrewdest of men, he found himself tricked at every turn of the diplomatic wheel by the subtle Portuguese.

INDEX.